THE MAN FROM GOD KNOWS WHERE

Denis Carroll

The Man from God knows where

THOMAS RUSSELL 1767-1803

ᵹᴀʀᴄᴀɴ

First published in 1995 by
Ᵹᴀʀᴄᴀɴ
An imprint of The Columba Press
93 The Rise, Mount Merrion, Blackrock, Co Dublin, Ireland

Cover by Bill Bolger
Origination by The Columba Press
Printed in Ireland by Colour Books, Ltd, Dublin

ISBN 1 85607 130 8

Contents

Foreword

Florence Wilson's poem, *The Man From God knows where*, sounds but does not fathom the Russell enigma. The poem evokes the mystery with which popular memory has suffused the work done by Thomas Russell for the United Irishmen during the years 1795 and 1796. Likewise, it hints at Russell's vision for an Ireland which had long been exploited by a corrupt ascendancy at home and by a politics of expediency in London, the colonial epicentre. Moving to 1803 and the tragic rising headed by Robert Emmet, the narration accurately presents that mixture of ethical conviction and political enthusiasm which characterises the strangely admirable figure of Russell.

When Florence Wilson's County Down farmer refers to his 'strange up country talk' he probably describes an Anglo-Irish accent. For Thomas Russell was from an ascendancy background. He was born into a British army family. He twice held an officer's rank and, for a while, served as magistrate in Tyrone. He was a practising member of the Anglican Church.

There are many enigmatic features to Russell's persona which this book will endeavour to examine – religious, political and personal.

As to religion, Thomas Russell was a devout, biblically-inclined Christian. Yet he accepted the Jacobin model of the French revolution. Although he criticised what he saw as the irreligion of Paine and Godwin, he shared their radical contestation of monarchy and property. He engaged in scrupulous self-examination; nonetheless he had casual relations with many women and drank late into many a night.

Politically, he developed in a dramatic way. From being partial to Whig politics even in 1790 he had become a radical republican by 1796. His faith in the rank and file of the Irish people, Protestant and Catholic, was empirically grounded when compared to Tone's somewhat patrician ideology. Russell took the step of actually living among poor people. More than Tone and others of the United Irish leadership, he understood the poor and sympathised with them. Unfortunately, his long imprisonment from 1796 subtracted him from the events of 1798. As a result, he strangely underestimated the changes in Ireland after that year. Although a trained officer, he fatally bungled the attempted northern campaign of the Emmet insurrection.

There is also a personal enigma – Russell's unrequited and seemingly unrealistic love for Elizabeth Goddard; his apparent ignorance of Mary Ann McCracken's love for him; his driven sense of duty to his sister, Margaret; his persistence in helping parasites like Thomas Attwood Digges. Alongside the attractive characteristics which make him a hero ready made for Irish historiography, there is also a millenarian or messianic streak. It has been observed, most recently by Nancy Curtin, that northern radicalism at the time was liberally shot through with a belief that a 'new age' of political virtue was about to replace the 'old age' of corruption and venality. Certainly, Russell saw politics as a struggle between good and evil, a stage on which God would finally intervene on the side of justice and right. Because of this, he may well have misread events on the European continent. He interpreted the democratic stirrings in France and, indeed, in Ireland, as harbingers of the inevitable triumph of good. How otherwise could he have expected the men of the north to rise out with only pitchforks and pikes as weapons?

For whatever reason, Russell has remained another instance of the 'triumph of failure' being remembered so faithfully in oral tradition and popular culture. At our transitional stage in Irish politics, he provides a fascinating example of how some members of the Anglo-Irish 'nation' endeavoured to come to terms with their own 'Irishness', albeit at great cost to themselves. His long-standing association with Belfast radicalism shows that the aspiration to social justice, the rejection of corruption and the critique of aristocracy were shared by Protestants and Catholics. In this bicentennial decade of the United Irish endeavour, our people stand in need of a generosity and courage analogous to that shown by Russell and his colleagues.

This research has been facilitated by many strands. I express my indebtedness to Brother Séamus Mac Giolla Easbaig's biography in the Irish language. It is the finest extended study of Russell since R. R. Madden's outstanding work on the United Irishmen. Students of Thomas Russell are beholden to C. J. Woods for his unselfish work in so skilfully editing our subject's nigh-illegible journal. I have endeavoured to maintain a cautious interplay between the written accounts of Russell's work and the popular traditions about him expressed in Florence Wilson's ballad. Behind them all is the scholarly work, ancient and recent, devoted to this seminal period of Irish history.

Thanks are due to Stuart Ó Seanóir of Trinity College, Dublin. With his staff, he has been of signal help in regard to the Russell papers retained at the College. The staffs of the National Archives (particularly Greg O'Connor) and the National Library have been unfailingly helpful. John Gray of the Linen Hall Library, Belfast, and J. J. Kavanagh of Drumahane, Co Cork, have been generous in their assistance.

My especial thanks to Orla, my beloved wife, who invaluably helped me at all points of this book's preparation. I salute my father (who died while the work was in process), my late mother and my family. As well, I thank my friends of many decades.

CHAPTER ONE

From Cork to Dublin Via India

I was brave an' near to the edge of the throng,
yet I know'd the face again,
an' I know'd the set, an' I know'd the walk
an' the sound of his strange upcountry talk,
for he spoke out right an' plain.
Then he bow'd his head to the swinging rope,
whiles I said 'please God' to his dying hope
and 'amen' to his dying prayer
that the wrong would cease and the right prevail,
for the man that they hanged at Downpatrick gaol
was the man from God knows where. (Florence Wilson)

Downpatrick jail, for long a symbol of colonial oppression, is now a museum and heritage centre. The terrors of its gibbet and cells are no more, except in the vicarious sense of museum exhibition. Now, activity is relaxed and humane. Children learn to paint. Adults hear about the north-east of Ireland, its long history and many-stranded culture. Yet, the earlier purpose of the jail is not overlooked. A courteous staff will tell the visitor of prisoners who went through the gates to execution or transportation. Perhaps the most famous of all was Thomas Russell, hanged outside the jail in October 1803. An intrepid visitor to the graveyard nearby will see a headstone, impressive in its stark austerity. It is marked 'The Grave of Russell'. Mary Ann McCracken, sister of Henry Joy McCracken, commissioned the stone's erection. Russell was 'The Man from God knows where', whose legend remains alive, not only in Antrim and Down but wherever Florence Wilson's splendid ballad is recited. The enigma of the ballad raises further questions: Who was Thomas Russell? Whence did he come? What motivated his devotion to the cause of an Ireland wherein oppression of every kind would be contested?

Early Years

Near Mallow, County Cork, is the small village of Drumahane. Situated on the river Blackwater, it is surrounded by the prosperous farms and substantial houses which are a feature of Ireland's agricultural Golden Vale. For some years in the 1760s John and Margaret Russell lived here at Betsboro House with their children Ambrose, John and Margaret. Nearby was the equally impressive home of landlords named Foote (or Foott). From that family came the commander of the North Cork militia which earned infamy during the 1798 rising in Wexford. John Russell was an officer, junior in rank although not in years, of the regular British army. For some time he had been stationed with the Eighty Third (Infantry) Regiment, at Mallow. In the closing months of 1767 the Russells awaited the birth of another child. On 21 November the baby was born. Shortly thereafter, he was named Thomas Paliser in honour of a friend of John Russell. The baptism took place in the Anglican church at Newberry. The child, Thomas Paliser Russell, would become one of the most fascinating personages in the historiography of Irish republican separatism.[1]

John Russell was a native of Kilkenny city. Although forty seven years of age when Thomas was born, he was still a lieutenant. Having earlier studied for the Anglican ministry at Kilkenny College, he remained until the day of his death (1792) a gentle, likeable, tolerant man. Shortly before he died, he expressed very liberal opinions on the necessity for reform in Irish politics and fair treatment of the Catholic majority. Perhaps this dimension of his character – idealism and an inclination to piety – did little to advance him in rank. John Russell had served at the battle of Dettingen and, later, at Fontenoy. (It is an irony that many of his compatriots served, on the opposing side, with the Irish brigade at that battle in 1745.) After Fontenoy, Lieutenant Russell was detailed to the Duke of Cumberland's army in Scotland. Although present at Culloden, he had no part in the savage massacre in Culloden Moor since his regiment did not arrive on the field until the battle was over.[2]

Through his mother – an O'Kennedy from Tipperary – Thomas Russell would likely have had some contact with the Catholic tradition. Certain it is that she made a deep impression on him, although she died when he was only nineteen years old and, probably, in army service on the Malabar coast. It is of interest that his paternal grandmother came from a dispossessed Catholic family, the O'Cleeres of Kilkenny. Thus, two strands of the Irish religious context – the Anglican and the Catholic – ran through Russell's earliest years. As an adult, he would encounter the third strand which played so honourable a part in the history of the 1790s, viz. Presbyterianism. He later observed that his O'Cleere ancestors had become Protestants by accident, and were sent into life 'Protestants and beggars'. Thus, one student of Russell's life can argue that he was never fully at ease about his position within the Anglican ascendancy.[3]

As an adult, Thomas Russell had a broad command of English literature and an ability to write in learned style. It has been remarked that his calligraphy bordered at times on the illegible while his uncertain spelling-patterns caused at least one historian to suggest dyslexia. According to R. R. Madden, Russell's extraordinarily broad education was imparted by his father. Despite non-attendance at school or university, he became literate in a range of subjects: chemistry, botany, mineralogy, economics, history, poetry and several languages. His knowledge of the Christian bible was so exact that he could argue with professional theologians on biblical interpretation from both Greek and Hebrew. In regard to his early years, there are many signs of a family marked by kindness, respect and affection. Thomas himself retained memories of deeply loving parents who were much loved in return. With the exception of William (the youngest son and somewhat a ne'er-do-well), the Russells would retain close personal bonds throughout financial distress and political difference. Margaret, the only daughter of the family, retained a continuing link with her brothers. Despite the poverty and dependency which afflicted her after her father's death, she was an effective point of reference in the family circle. From such a home background Thomas Russell brought habits of chivalry, honour and a deep religious sense.[4]

At Drumahane, Thomas Russell may well have acquired that sympathy for the Irish language which marked his later life. Irish was widely spoken throughout north Munster in the eighteenth century. Here may have originated the openness to Gaelic culture which motivated Russell's collaboration with Edward Bunting (on Irish music) and Whitley Stokes (on a Gaelic trans-

lation of the Bible). It is an irony that the North Cork militia, almost entirely Irish-speaking, committed many of the atrocities
which marked the tragic summer of 1798 in Wexford and
Wicklow. Perhaps it is a further irony that Colonel Foote, the
commander of the North Corks, is buried in the graveyard of the
church at Newberry, where Russell had earlier been baptised.
This small but very beautiful church is now a craft centre while
the graveyard remains, at time of writing, neglected and un-
tended.[5]

To Durrow and, then, Dublin

The few indications about Thomas Russell's growing years suggest that the family moved to Durrow, County Laois, in the early
1770s. Doubtless, this was due to John Russell's army commit-
ments, perhaps at Maryborough (now Portlaoise). In a journal,
commenced in the 1790s, Thomas Russell would narrate how, in
their Durrow home, Ambrose 'thought he saw someone going
to strike his father and in spight (sic) of my mother and all in the
house, he rushed out like a lion and pulled him to the ground'.
During the early 1780s the family moved again – this time to
Dublin. The new chapter opened sufficiently late for Thomas to
remember walking through fields, most likely in the Phoenix
Park, from an academy where his brother was a student. John
Russell had been appointed a 'captain of invalids' at the Royal
Hospital, Kilmainham, adjacent to the Phoenix Park. Here, a
military hospital served 'such aged and maimed of our ... army,
as shall not be thought fit to be any longer continued in our service'. By no means luxurious, the hospital was chartered as a
place 'to prepare for eternity'. The inhabitants were exhorted
that their 'moderation be known unto all'. And, if they were
likely to forget the fact, they were reminded 'The Lord is close at
hand'.[6]

John Russell had now a comfortable appointment. Alongside
the master and deputy, the chaplain, the physician and surgeon,
the bursar and inspector of work, was another group of major
officials known as 'captains of invalids'. John Russell (now
given a courtesy title of Captain, although still gazetted a
Lieutenant) was one of these. Good residential quarters would
have been enjoyed by him, his wife and their growing family. To
their enormous sorrow, Mrs Russell died in 1786 and was buried
in the grounds of the Royal Hospital. In subsequent years

Thomas wrote often of his mother's gentle influence. Even William Russell, younger than Thomas and emotionally shallower than the rest of the family, retained 'unforgettable memories of love at the Royal Hospital'. For Thomas, his father's posting meant that, through the 1780s and early 1790s, a home was available to him at the Royal Hospital. Here he was unfailingly welcomed by his father and sister. Vicinity to the fashionable world of Dublin society ensured that he had ample opportunity to meet rising young intellectuals such as Peter Burrowes and, later, Theobald Wolfe Tone. A thorough, albeit informal, education and an intellectual curiosity enabled him to move easily in the 'society' of his day.[7]

Through the early 1780s Thomas Russell's path seemed to lie in one or other of two directions: the church or the army. A proficiency in biblical studies and an interest in religious practice evinced suitability to church ordination. And yet, when he embarked on a career it was in the army where John and Ambrose Russell were serving honourably although without major distinction. Early in 1783, Thomas Russell, future republican and separatist, entered an army career in the 52nd Regiment of Foot. This regiment had already served in America where it incurred severe losses. During that campaign Ambrose Russell had been wounded, although by 1783 he was ready once again to serve with his regiment.

On 13 February 1783, the 52nd Regiment was ordered to prepare for service on the Malabar coast of India. Here, it was to protect the commercial interests of the British East India Company. Already, the 68th Regiment of Foot and the Athol Highlanders had refused the assignment, even to the point of mutiny. When the 52nd Regiment was ordered to India, it received soldiers from other regiments and young volunteers, of whom Thomas Russell was one, eager to gain appointment as ensigns. Russell was little more than fifteen when he embarked for India in March 1783. A new life seemed to open for him although there is little reason to believe that he would receive much cossetting. Doubtless, it helped to have the company and, perhaps, the encouragement of a brother who was extremely popular in the regiment. On the trip to join the army at Liverpool, the young volunteer was relieved of five pounds by one Jonathan Tone, an uncle of Russell's future collaborator, Theobald Wolfe Tone. It is not known if the boy – as a volunteer, in receipt of no pay – was ever reimbursed. Jonathan Tone wrote to Peter Tone (Theobald's father) for the five pounds: Peter sent the money but was careful to disclaim future responsibility.[8]

On 9 July 1783 an ensign was gazetted, not to the 52nd Foot, but to the 100th Foot. The new ensign was Thomas Russell, still only fifteen. Promotion was not due to bravery or special ability since Russell had had no opportunity for trial as a military officer. Yet he was now in receipt of pay and was on the ladder of further advancement. Doubtless, the esteem in which his father and brother were held redounded to the credit of the untried ensign. Russell's appointment gained him access to army circles and, in many instances, the friendship of officers destined for senior rank. Even warrants for his arrest in 1796 and, again, in 1803 accorded him not simply a military rank but one considerably higher than he had ever attained. At that later stage, both in Dublin Castle and among law agents of the crown, he would be referred to as Captain Russell or Russel.

Thomas Russell in India

Madras, Bombay, the Malabar coast, Mangalore, Tillicherry, Cannanore : these are the places which figure in the experience of Ensign Russell. General Jones, Colonels McLeod and Barry, Captain Ambrose Russell, Ensign Jack Crofton, these are the officers, senior and junior, who are mentioned in what survives of his writing during this period. Kaider Ali, Tipu Sahib, an unnamed local queen whose territory surrounded Cannanore, are the people detailed in a lengthy epistle to his family, written in his difficult, almost illegible, hand. It is possible that Russell kept a diary or journal while on army service in India. In 1822, when advanced in age, Margaret Russell appealed to the viceroy, Lord Wellesley, for the return of her brother's papers then impounded by the authorities. She referred to 'a Manuscript Journal which Mr Russell kept while in India, and a Religious Tract, with some others not connected with political matters'. It may be, however, that Margaret was in error as to the particular journal and confused it with the diary hereafter spoken of as Russell's journal.[9]

When the 52nd Regiment landed at Madras it came under the command of Colonel Norman McLeod. The regiment was sent

to the relief of a British garrison at Mangalore, beseiged by
Kaider Ali. Discovering that Kaider Ali would allow the garrison to be provisioned, Colonel McLeod felt bound by instructions to fall back on Tillicherry. Soon thereafter, according to
Russell's letter home, the regiment was ordered to march against
Cannanore, a town about fourteen miles from Tillicherry. The
local queen had detained English soldiers and had sent their officers as prisoners to Tipu Sahib. Somewhat coolly for his years,
Russell described how Cananore was taken in three days and
how 'the next day the Queen surrendered and is bound as tribu-
tary to the Company'. In this battle at Cannanore, Colonel
Henry Barry was wounded and taken from the field, some say,
by Thomas Russell. Later – in the 1790s – Wolfe Tone could approach Barry to have Russell placed in congenial employment.
After Cannanore, a promotion of the regimental quartermaster
occasioned Thomas Russell's elevation to acting-quartermaster.
Referring to his sister-in-law (Nancy Russell, wife of Ambrose),
Thomas writes of an invitation from the local queen who
'showed a great curiosity to see an English lady and … asked her
(Nancy) a great many questions'. As a parting gesture the queen
'presented Mrs Russell with a gold chain of very lovely work-
manship'.[10]

Years later, Thomas Russell alluded to experiences of his service
in India. In late September 1793, as he journeyed along the
shoreline of Lough Neagh, he recalled walking from 'the camp
at Cannanore down to Tillicherry, 15 miles in that burning climate and for what? To get a wench!' Here is, perhaps, an unin-
tended notice that his short army career had introduced Russell
to habits of which his parents would have disapproved. John
Gray's somewhat abrupt comment that in India he 'learned the
rough ways of the garrison and whore-house' can be placed in
this context. Yet, it should also be noted that Russell made periodic, sometimes very severe, examinations of conscience and
that at the time of which he wrote he could not have been more
than nineteen. After Ambrose died in 1793, Thomas in his grief
imagined the farewell of an army regiment to an officer deeply
loved: 'I see the ramparts of the town where we had often been
happy together, the pomp of the funeral, the troops marching to
his house, his own grenadiers receiving the dead body of their
captain who had so often led them out and always led them to
honour and whom they loved as well as served. I saw him cov-

ered with the colours under which he so often fought and his
sword on which he used to rely and the sash which had been his
father's, and which on that account he so valued, placed on his
remains. They move slowly to the ground where his friend
Cliffe remains. I heard the solemn music vibrate along the tow-
ers of the fort, the echoes from the firing over his grave'.[11]

When an accord was signed with Tipu Sahib (Kaider's son), the
52nd Regiment remained in India, based near Madras. However, its young ensign did not keep his appointment. In 1786 or
1787 he returned on half-pay to Ireland. When placed on half-
pay, Thomas Russell was still less than twenty and had prose-
cuted a remarkably brief military career. Many reasons have
been advanced for this early severance, none of them more than
conjectural. Given his later stances it is tempting to explain his
exit from the British army by idealism or some form of protest.
Thus, R. R. Madden speaks of the ill-treatment of two local
women as a factor which turned him from Indian service. In
similar fashion, James Morgan alludes to the young officer's disgust at the ill-usage of an Indian woman and her family as a reason for his premature return. B. M. Dunlop cites the corruption
of the East India Company as the cause of this departure from
the 52nd Regiment. Yet, there is no evidence that Russell ever
conceived a dislike either of military service or of army personnel. Many times in later years he spoke favourably of his former
colleagues. And when an opportunity came of returning to active duty he appears to have lost no time in availing of it. Hence,
the less 'heroic'suggestion of Seamus Mac Giolla Easbaig may
be the more likely – reduction in public spending ensured that
regiments such as the 52nd and 100th were pared back and that
Thomas Russell, despite any other ambitions he might have
formed, was constrained to go on half-pay.[12] There are other hy-
pothetical considerations about this period of Russell's life. Did
he come to the notice of Lord Cornwallis when the latter was
governor-general and army commander in India? Did he carry
Colonel Barry from the field at Cannanore and thus attract
favourable attention for bravery? As to any connection between
Russell and Cornwallis, it should be noted that the dates of their
respective service in India do not coincide. Nor do the surviving
documents of either man suggest that they knew each other personally. Barry and Russell were certainly acquainted but Russell's
own letters give no hint of personal military glory at Cannanore.

In Dublin on Half Pay (1787-1790)

With an ensign's salary and on half-pay, Russell's income was small indeed – no more than £28 per annum. Nevertheless, it is reasonable to assume that he had free quarters with his family at the Royal Hospital. How he spent his time, if not his wealth, is yet another question without definite answer. In subsequent years the extremely wide scope of his reading was more than evident. His literary and scientific culture became unusually broad and ran through more than one specialist topic. These years of leisure may well have been the time when the basis of his scientific, philosophical and political education was consolidated. It has been suggested, although without documentary foundation, that at this period of intermission he studied for the Anglican ministry and, even, travelled to the Isle of Man for ordination.[13]

For a young, personable officer, an entrée to rich and powerful circles in Dublin would not have been difficult. Later, in Belfast, Russell was a welcome guest in the most fashionable homes. Women of all backgrounds found him irresistibly attractive. In male company he was esteemed and respected. Hence, it is not excessive to conjecture that he spent the years immediately after his return in the society of Dublin's rich and powerful. Many of those who would later be his political enemies were personally known to him. Like Tone, Russell on more than one occasion had opportunity to discuss social questions with prominent Whigs such as Henry Grattan. As to politics, Madden has argued that at this stage he had not advanced beyond the view that 'the end of government was the happiness of the great body of the people'. This was coherent with monarchism allied to liberal, even democratic, institutions. Such opinions, however worthy, did not go beyond incipient Whig liberalism or, for that matter, the views of Henry Grattan.

A Fateful Meeting

On a July day in 1790, the paths of two men who would influence Irish history for generations crossed in the visitors' gallery at the House of Commons on College Green. Thomas Russell and Theobald Wolfe Tone had been attending a debate on the threatened war with Spain. In conversation it emerged that Russell's estimation of the Whig party was somewhat higher

than Tone's. Although he had already issued a pro-Whig pamphlet – *A Review of the Conduct of Administration* – Tone would
nonetheless remark somewhat wryly that he had more experience of 'these gentlemen' than had Russell. Undeterred by this
minor divergence, the two men agreed to dine together on the
following day. Thus arose a kinship between people different in
character yet indissolubly linked in Irish history. They were different in age (Tone – four years older); in notoriety (not only had
Tone published his *Review of the Conduct of Administration* but he
had also brought out *Spanish War!* while Russell was an un-
known twenty three year old); in experience of Irish politics (despite his relative youth, Tone had moved in Whig circles at
Trinity College, at the law courts, and through his friendship
with Richard Martin, a prominent Whig member of parliament).

The friendship of Russell and Tone would transcend political
cooperation to become a congenial fellowship, a mutual support
through imprisonment and exile. Tone's biographer, Marianne
Elliott, places the exact date of their meeting as 24 July. Elliott's
further observation is exact: this friendship affected the ideas
and the personality of both Tone and Russell. Each was a foil for
the other and they influenced each other more deeply than they
perhaps knew. Theobald and Matilda Tone came to occupy a
primacy in Russell's affections (alongside Margaret Russell and
Elizabeth Goddard), which lasted until the end of his life. On the
other hand, Russell exercised a fascination over Tone through
his charming manners, his social graces, and – strangely in view
of Tone's subsequent development – through the allure of his
foreign military service. To cite Marianne Elliott: '(Russell) was
everything Tone was not. An officer on half-pay, he had recently
seen active service in India and had a commanding military
presence, his huge dark eyes and thick black hair offset by fine,
almost aristocratic features. His good looks and "stately " bearing commanded attention from both men and women alike'.[14]

For whatever reason, the friendship developed with extraordinary rapidity. Russell and Tone, ever appreciative of fine wines
and convivial in the fashion of the day, dined together, not once
but several times. They met frequently at Irishtown where Tone
had rented a summer lodge. Irishtown was not the hub of fashion
yet it was a pleasant seaside resort with unpretentious houses for
rent. The summer weeks there would remain etched on Tone's

memory. In his autobiography he eulogises 'the happy days we
spent during that period ... the delicious dinners, in the preparation of which my wife, Russell and myself, were all engaged, the
afternoon walks, the discussions we have had, as we lay
stretched on the grass ... These were delicious days'. Russell
visited Irishtown frequently during July-August 1790, more
than once accompanied by his father. His personal charm
deeply impressed the normally realistic, sometimes acerbic,
Matilda Tone. When Matilda later complained of her husband's
periodic neglect, she emphasised that if all men were like
Thomas Russell then life would be much more pleasant for
women. As for Tone himself, he regarded his friendship with
Russell as one of the most fortunate circumstances in his life:
'There cannot be imagined a more perfect harmony, I may say
identity of sentiment, than exists between us; our regard for
each other has never suffered a moment's relaxation from the
hour of our first acquaintance ... I think the better of myself for
being the object of the esteem of such a man as Russell ...'.[15]

Tone and Russell discussed many things. On political matters
they found exact agreement. As Tone put it: '... we extended
our views and fortified each other in the opinions, to the propa-
gation and establishment of which we have ever since been devoted'. The two friends hit upon the idea of forming a political
club for the following winter. Subsequently, Russell prepared a
lecture for the club on removing the disabilities still placed on
Catholics and Presbyterians. Less seriously, Russell, Tone and
William Tone composed ballads, poems and political squibs by
way of divertissement. A small book of elegies and songs survives among Tone's papers. Attributed to 'William Tone and
Others', the document provides a hint of Russell's later ability to
write political satire.[16]

At this stage a political neophyte, Russell was drawn into a
scheme already devised by Tone at London's Middle Temple.
The plan had its context in the British-Spanish dispute over trading rights off the north-west coast of America. Somewhat para-
doxically, Tone was proposing development of the Sandwich
Islands (Hawaii) and, in particular of the island of Oaha, as a diversionary move. The scheme was sent to London where it was
politely rejected, first by the Duke of Richmond and then by the
foreign secretary, Lord Grenville. The interest of Russell and

Tone in the project suggests that they were seeking involvement in the political and administrative affairs of the day. Their discussions give a clue to their political enthusiasms at this early point in their development. Their thought was broad even to imprecision. Yet, as their concerns became more sharply focused in the following months, neither Tone nor Russell lost interest in the Sandwich Islands project. Tone retained his papers on the scheme while Russell took further advice which he later commmunicated to Tone.[17]

The free ranging nature of these discussions is instructive. It suggests that in summer 1790 Tone could still envisage service within the British ambit. Nor was Russell averse to such employment, if it eventuated. It appears that he developed Tone's ideas in the direction of a war of liberation in the Spanish colonies of South America. Both men would have opposed the government at College Green, founded on Protestant ascendancy and arrogantly exploitative of the great mass of the people. In their conversations at Irishtown, Tone and Russell discussed parliamentary reform and the removal of religious disqualifications from the law of the land. Yet the concepts of separation from England, collaboration with French revolutionaries or the institution of an Irish republic had not matured in their consciousness. It is well to note Nancy Curtin's reminder that even before the foundation of the United Irishmen '... a political vocabulary already existed in the lexicon of the civic humanist or commonwealth tradition, with its emphasis on public virtue, the subordination of self-interest, and the rights ... and responsibilities of citizens to secure ... the *res publica*.' This may accurately describe the stances of Tone and Russell in summer 1790.[18]

CHAPTER TWO

Belfast: 'The Athens of the North'

'All clinquant, all in gold' – thus appeared Thomas Russell at the
Tones' summer house in September 1790. What Tone described
as his 'very fine suit of laced regimentals' availed him little. The
uniformed officer was set to work in the kitchen of the Irishtown
villa. One must presume that the finery was jocosely presented
and was so taken by Theobald and Matilda Tone. They would
already have known of Russell's new appointment as an ensign
of the 64th Regiment of Foot, stationed in Belfast. According to
R. R. Madden, Russell had met Sir John Irwin in Fermanagh and
was presented by the latter for nomination as a full-time officer.
There is a possibility that Russell had relatives in Fermanagh
and so he may have had some knowledge of the north before his
nomination to the 64th Regiment. His appointment would date
from 31 August 1790 with seniority backdated to 9 July 1783, the
date of his first commission. This move became as significant in
Russell's life as his meeting with Tone earlier in July. His friendship with Tone and his activities in Belfast came to shape his
career in a way he could little have expected.[1]

When Thomas Russell arrived in Belfast it was a thriving mercantile community. There were problems besetting the town –
'In 1791, it was congested and dirty, with dunghills a constant
nuisance in the streets and pigs wandering at will'. Despite this,
an ever-improving harbour linked Belfast's commercial fleet
with the European mainland and North America. In 1782, eight
years before Russell's appointment, the town had a population
of 13,105. By 1791, the figure had grown to 18,320. Thus, when
Russell came to live there, Belfast was a developing, although at
first sight somewhat austere, town. The Anglican church at
Donegall Street, the Linen Halls (White and Brown), the Market
house and the Poorhouse, were among the most prominent
buildings. There were five Presbyterian meeting-houses, three

23

of them in Rosemary Lane. The first Methodist chapel had been opened at Fountain Street in 1787. Three years earlier, in 1784, a Roman Catholic chapel had been opened with every sign of goodwill from the Protestant inhabitants.[2]

In her 'Belfast Panorama' Mary McNeill observes that 'Behind a rather sober exterior, the town provided a great deal of gaiety and sociability'. There were dances and card games in the Assembly Rooms at the 'Four Corners' where Rosemary Lane, North Street, Waring Street and Bridge Street abutted. Similar activities took place at the Donegall Arms. Belfast may well have been unpretentious place – 'a practical little town with few embellishments'. Nevertheless, drinking, gaming and dancing were available in clubs for the wealthy landowners, the prosperous merchants and the officers at the garrison of which Thomas Russell was now a serving member. Despite its calvinist simplicity, Belfast had an aristocracy of sorts. The Chicesters (Lord and Lady Donegall) formed the apex of a social élite devoted to amateur theatricals, hunting and cards. Lord Donegall, the Earl of Moira, Robert Stewart the future Lord Castlereagh, Sir John O'Neill, belonged to an extremely rich ascendancy class. Self-defining and self-promoting, they retained easy, almost automatic, access to the great offices of the land. With power of tax and patronage, this group resembled the corrupt aristocracy of pre-revolutionary France.

There was another group, economically and culturally developed, yet relegated to the margins of political influence. Somewhat like the Third Estate in France, this group comprised families whose fortunes had been made, or were in the process of being made, through far-reaching commercial and professional activities. The skilful deployment of new technology ensured that by 1790 Belfast had surpassed Dublin in the export of Irish linen. Due to its commercial fleet, Belfast enjoyed not only prosperity but also self-sufficiency. At the time of Russell's appointment, many prosperous merchants traded in linen, textiles, drapery, tannery, weaving and milling. Alongside these was a myriad of small businesses: carpentry, ropemaking, ships' chandlers, etc. Among these burghers there was close interaction. Professionals, businessmen (and women such as Mary Ann McCracken), clergymen, met at each other's houses for social and recreational pursuits. The McCrackens, the Simms, the

Templetons , the McCabes, the Crawfords, the Sinclairs and – in less affluent circumstances, yet still part of the circle – the McTiers of Cabin Hill, made up a cohesive, generously welcoming community. They represented 'a tightly knit, often intermarried business world, its centre within yards of High Street, the main thoroughfare'. Finally, there was Dr James McDonnell of Donegall Place, physician and philosopher, who remains enigmatic in the narrative of Russell's life.[3]

The political temper of these families was distinctly radical. Of them it has been claimed that 'They disliked prelacy, aristocracy, privilege and the entire hierarchical system central to eighteenth century government and society'. Despite their economic prosperity, they were by definition excluded from the polity. It is not surprising that the revolution in France should have impacted on a group enjoying extensive trading contacts with that country. Events such as the fall of the Bastille, the deliberations of the Constituent Assembly, the move towards a secular republic, were spoken of in Belfast almost as if such happenings occurred in Ireland. Free trade, increased participation by the middle classes in the affairs of state, were viewed with favour by northern merchants. Close trading links with the continent (and later the foundation of the radical *Northern Star*) ensured that events in France became known in Belfast with accuracy and rapidity. It was, after all, kinsmen and women of Belfast Presbyterians who had figured prominently in the American revolution. The concepts of democracy and republicanism, the ideals of fraternity, liberty and equality, were highly valued in Belfast, sometimes called the Athens of the north. As was the case in France and America, radical ideas were prevalent chiefly in middle-class circles. In France, the *sans culottes* had yet to emerge as a political force. In America, there was a careful neglect of the rights of black people. It took some years and the consistency of a James Hope, a Henry Joy McCracken, a Thomas Russell or a Mary Ann McCracken to apply the new radical ideas in favour of the labouring classes, the domestic servants and the Catholic tenantry. However, re-echoes of volunteering days in the 1780s ensured that in Belfast the ideas of religious toleration and basic rights for all remained alive. A declaration from Belfast Whigs in October 1790 carries an overtone of such radicalism. Part of their resolutions ran: '... the Protestant Dissenters, fully convinced of the constitutional principles of their brethren the Roman

Catholics, and of their zeal to support and defend the Liberty of their country, will on all occasions support their just claim to the enjoyment of the rights and privileges of free born citizens, entitled to fill every office, and serve in whatever station their country may think proper to call them to.'[4]

Thomas Russell in Belfast

The arrival of a personable officer in a small garrison town has provided material for many a literary creation. Russell's immense popularity in Belfast is all the more remarkable in that the army was not universally popular there. Much depended on the political context, on personalities and, indeed, on the attitude of the regional commander. Russell's impact on the local community and, in turn, its effect on him, cannot be explained in any romantic fashion. The argument of Brendan Clifford that he was 'the aristocrat that Belfast lacked, an exotic bird of paradise among the solid bourgeoisie' remains unsatisfactory. Certainly his personal traits were extraordinary. His graciousness of manner, his genuinely enquiring mind, his sensitivity to the well-being of others, perhaps even his aura of foreignness as an army man with service in India, would have marked him out in any Irish town. For Russell, the democratic spirit of Belfast, with its notable rejection of aristocratic exclusiveness, was congenial. Here, perhaps for the first time in his life, he found the warmth of a community unavailable either in Dublin or in India. Nonetheless, one has to look for yet other factors which marked him out from his colleagues of the garrison and brought him into contact with politically advanced groups at Belfast.[5]

Within a short time Russell was a welcome friend in many Belfast families. Amongst them he would have noted the cultivation which made the region of Belfast not only the most literate in Ireland but also an area of wide vernacular culture. This popular culture produced among Presbyterians 'a Sunday school movement, local academies, circulating libraries, book clubs and reading societies' where the most advanced views of the day were current. Belfast captivated him and, all due proportion guarded, he captivated Belfast. Martha McTier, a kindly yet caustic assessor of people, later referred to him as 'the most admired, the most loved among the gay, the witty and the fair ... '. During his years in Belfast Russell would be admired by many women. Mary Simms, sister of Robert and William Simms, became his affectionate friend. Isabella Tomb considered him 'the first of men'. When he was later imprisoned, Isabella set herself to learn his favourite tune, 'Away with you kiltie', to play when he would be released. The most impressive of them all, Mary Ann McCracken, detailed her near reverence for Russell when, much later, she described his impression on her as a young woman of twenty. She assessed him thus:

> A model of manly beauty ... one of those favoured individuals whom one cannot pass in the street without being guilty of the rudeness of staring in the face while passing, and turning round to look at the receding figure. Though more than six feet in height, his majestic stature was scarcely observed owing to the exquisite symmetry of his form. Martial in his gait and demeanour, his appearance was not altogether that of a soldier. His dark and steady eye, compressed lip, and somewhat haughty bearing, were occasionally strongly indicative of the camp; but in general, the classic contour of his finely formed head ... and the benevolence that beamed in his fine countenance, seemed to mark him out as one who was destined to be the ornament, grace and blessing of private life ... His manners were those of the finished gentleman, combined with that native grace, which nothing but superiority of intellect can give. There was a reserved, and somewhat haughty stateliness in his mien ... and those who knew him, loved him the more for his reserve, and thought they saw something attractive in the very repulsiveness of his manner.'[6]

Russell's journal for this period tells us little about his army life. Most probably, he would have lived at the Artillery Barracks a small distance south east of Smithfield. The few references are to 'offices of the day' and being 'at church with the men' (Sunday, 24 April 1791). He alludes to dining at the army mess – probably in March 1791. Again, he writes of drinking with colleagues, Captains Hall and Tomkins as well as Lieutenant James Mercer. Nor did army duties keep him from the Belfast Coterie, a club which met at the Assembly Rooms. Journal entries for April 1791, seven months into Russell's Belfast army service, detail bouts of inebriation and more than one casual sexual encounter. While consistently attached to the doctrines of Christianity, he oscillated between self-reproach and self-indulgence in moral

behaviour. John Gray's words are stern but true: 'In the world of
the garrison debauch, he could triumph all too easily, and that
brought with it its burden of guilt.' Granted that he was except-
ionally strict in self-analysis, yet an element of dissoluteness is
clear from his journal: 'Dine with the two Gordons. We all get
drunk. Go in a body to the club. On our way there, I fall on my
knees to some women and we follow some others. At the club
get myself proposed as a member. We sit till near 3, then ramble
through the town as the night before.' The journal entry for the
previous night ends; 'Sit till 2, then go to all the whores in town.'
Again, for 25 April Russell enters: 'Dined at the mess. In the
evening Hall and I walk in search of game. Meet a girl at Coates
the hairdresser. She introduces me into the house of her master.
Stay till near eleven. Near being detected. In my return to the
barracks fall over a heap of dirt. Find a party after supper. Sup
with them till late.' A note of self-disapproval, even of guilt, can
be discerned here, as if Russell was tormented by a conflict between high ideals and failure to achieve them.[7]

There is, however, another dimension to Russell's interests
which may account for his rapid acceptance among reforming
circles in Belfast. People such as Samuel Neilson, the Simms
brothers and William Sinclair, were exploring new paths in economics, science, politics and religion. Thomas Russell shared these
interests. His journal opened soon after his arrival at Belfast
refers to these very matters. He had visited Dublin for a lecture
to the political club mooted by himself and Tone during their
weeks at Irishtown. The lecture centred on oak bark for use in
the tanning industry at Dublin and Belfast. Some weeks later, he
put the material in order for publication – the more polished
form is found in an extended journal entry for March 1791. The
proposals for obtaining oak bark cheaply and plentifully do not
need expansion here. Yet Russell's views on the practical implications of patriotism bear directly on an understanding of his
concerns at this time: 'As the pro(s)perity of my native country
has always been the great object of my wishes I (as I think every
honest Irishman ought) have endeavour(ed) to procure information on such subjects as may improve its trade and manufactures
and to find the cause of the decay of some branches of them and
the reasons why others for which this kingdom seems eminently
qualify(d) are either not attempted or remain in a state of sickly
infancy.'

One reason for economic underdevelopment was that protection of English interests worked to Ireland's disadvantage. This protection had become a matter of policy and worked in two ways, viz. import duty on Irish leather up to seventy per cent and prevention of export to Ireland of oak bark. Russell had discussed the tanning industry with Henry Grattan, in particular the importation from America of oak bark for use in the industry. According to Russell, the Whig leader was 'fully possessed of the advantages of it'. However, Grattan had been informed by Sir John Parnell (chancellor of the exchequer and great-grandfather of Charles Stewart Parnell) that any bounty to help Irish tanners 'would offend the people of England and therefore it would not be done'. In a vein of irony, Russell comments: 'There is a good government and a precious rascal for chancellor of the exchequer.'[8]

Although such ideas were robust, they were not exceptional. They reflect the unease of Belfast merchants – the McCrackens, the Simms, the McCabes and others – at the subservience of Ireland's political and economic interests to those of England. In Dublin the same positions were adopted by James Napper Tandy and Archibald Hamilton Rowan. In Russell's case, the significance of his ideas lies in their potential for a radical critique of the Dublin administration and separatism in regard to English rule. Meanwhile, his circle of acquaintances in Belfast grew wider. He was admitted to the Northern Whig Club under the sponsorship of William Sinclair. At the McCrackens' he met Edward (Atty) Bunting, the collector of Irish lyrics and airs. There, too, he came to know John and Eliza Templeton. The Templetons, brother and sister, proved good friends in later adversity. Templeton's proficiency in botany and Russell's expertise in mineralogy issued in joint field trips throughout Ulster. Russell's journal for these early months in Belfast discloses not simply the range of his own reading but also the breadth of scientific and political culture in the town.

Allusion has already been made to Russell's friendship with Thomas McCabe. Originally a partner in a cotton warehouse at Rosemary Lane, McCabe had shown remarkable spirit in opposition to slavery in the colonies. Later, he engaged in jewellery and watchmaking at North Street. In the same year as Russell's appointment to Belfast, McCabe had welcomed another outsider, William Pearce of Manchester. Pearce had already invented refined spinning and weaving machinery in his native city but was robbed of the credit by one Arkwright. In Belfast McCabe and Pearce joined in a new venture: 'machinery, looms etc. for the manufacture of linen, cotton, calico, checks, thicksets, corduroys etc, and for the getting pattents (*sic*) or premiums for their invention'. In February 1791 Pearce and McCabe asked the Irish parliament for a premium on an improved linen and cotton loom. Their petition was treated with cynical disregard by the parliamentary clique even though a committee of enquiry was set up to consider the application. Russell was preoccupied by the mistreatment: 'What a country to slight such a man', he wrote in March 1791. He noted Pearce's disillusion as well as the uncharitableness of neighbours: 'The people of this town, except a few, glad of McCabe's disappointment. Selfish.' The journal for 10 April 1791 mentions Pearce's distress: 'his never having been so vexed in his life; his memory impair'd, his hand shakes, oweing (*sic*) to vexations … If he had been encouragd (he) would have brought his own loom to the greatest perfection…'[9]

Separation from England and Catholic Emancipaton

Through March 1791, Russell considered issues which would figure dramatically later in the decade. In his journal he raised the question of separation from England. Was it practicable? Was it feasible? His interlocutor was Thomas Attwood Digges, an American transient in Belfast who would play an enigmatic role in his life. On 1 March Digges discussed with Russell 'the practicability of seperation(*sic*)'. Digges believed separation was useful but not immediately feasible. People of property were unwilling to take chances. Hence, a readiness for risks could not be presumed. The most promising avenue of change was parliamentary reform. Or, as Russell himself put it, 'Parliamentary reform the best way of beginning.'[10]

Another question, linked yet vastly different, was repeal of the penal laws against Catholics. Even at this early stage, Russell was unequivocally partisan of Catholic emancipation. His journal details the opinions of those favourable to such reform yet aware of its difficulties. Russell cites the view of an acquaintance named Sinclair (not William Sinclair) that 'all those who do think in this part of Ireland would apprehend no danger from the repeal…'. Whatever the difficulty, it lay in mutual fear of

Catholics and Protestants. Likewise, people were lulled by government propaganda about the prosperity of the country. And
so, there was 'a strange revolution since the times of volunteering'. In lines somewhat unusual for an officer of the King's army
Russell put it: if England were 'engaged in war and obliged to
withdraw their troops, the people would be then obliged to arm
as before and then be led on to the necessary steps'. It should be
noted that his partisanship of Catholic emancipation was not
about instituting a new politico-religious establishment. Rather,
it had to do with the freedom of all citizens from disqualification
because of their religious persuasion. A significant entry to the
journal, probably towards the end of March 1791, shows awareness of the need for compromise on all sides: 'The Catholicks
(*sic*) would have no objection to diminish the now power of the
pope if the Protestants thought it necessary, viz. would take
from him the appointing of bishops, etc, etc.' Needless to say, in
Russell's view what applied to Catholic emancipation applied
also to the full enfranchisement of Presbyterian Dissenters.
They, too, smarted under exclusion from citizenship according
to the prevalent notion of Protestant ascendancy. In September
1792 a declaration by Dublin Corporation defined that ascendancy as the hegemony of Anglicanism: 'A Protestant
(Anglican) King of Ireland. A Protestant Parliament. A
Protestant Hierarchy. Protestant electors and government, the
benches of justice, the army and the revenue through all branches and details Protestant and this system supported by a connection with the Protestant realm of England.'[11]

Despite his somewhat advanced sentiments, Russell carried on
his military duties. The journal gives little clue as to his attitude
to that dimension of his life. Instead, it expresses his views on
the structure of government and related social questions. On
government, his radicalism had still to develop considerably. In
March 1791 he noted his own doubts about Tom Paine's stances
in the *Rights of Man*. Russell still believed that in England the
'whole power of the King, lords and commons would be
ineffectual to crush an individual however obscure'. Without expansion he added: 'Experience justifies this'. Perhaps naïvely,
Russell was confident that the nation at large would take up the
oppressed individual's case. Further, in England 'absolute power
resides neither in the nation nor the three estates'. In terms of a
much later time, Russell would appear to have reached the posi-

tion of an advanced social democrat. It is not surprising that at this stage he might have had some difficulty with the notion that 'absolute power is supposed in the nation', a position which he understood to apply in France. As one concerned with the idea of liberty he asks about the security of the individual who runs foul of state power : 'Does it much matter, if a despotism does exist, by whom it is exercised?' Again he asks: 'Is reformation or revolution more like to promote the happiness of a society? In a violent revolution, thousands are reduced to poverty while it is not clear whether the many are relieved from poverty.'

Russell was unhappy with Paine's argument that the present generation were the only people to be considered in radical social change. He asked – in the event of that position being fully adopted – 'why then not leave posterity to take care of themselves and enjoy as much of life as we can?' There is an echo here, surely, of the traditional Christian view that each person is unique and that no person – much less a whole generation – may be sacrificed for another. One may conclude that in early 1791 Russell was critically examining the most forward ideas of the day. His thought was evolving rapidly. Yet, it had not gone beyond constitutional monarchy ruling through institutions answerable to the people. In a sense, constitutional monarchy and republicanism (with religious and political toleration) were vying with each other in the mind of this extraordinary young officer of the King's army.[12]

Related Social Questions

The brief mention of Christian teaching on the sanctity of the individual is also a reminder of Russell's lasting attachment to moral principle. It connects with other entries to the journal through the early months of 1791. Influenced by the recently published work of a Jesuit, Pierre-François-Xavier de Charlevoix, Russell considered the system of government in Paraguay. There a regime had been instituted by the Jesuit fathers with results startlingly beneficial when compared with colonial rule in Latin America. At a time when the Jesuit order was in disfavour, Russell adjudged the Paraguayan system of government as 'beyond compare the best, the happiest, that ever has been instituted'. To the canard that Christianity was intrinsically favourable to tyranny, Russell answers: 'When tyrants and hypocrites saw Christianity making a progress they affected to embrace it and endeavoured and succeeded in securing themselves through its means.' As he saw it, tyranny endeavoured to support itself 'by perverting Christianity from its purposes and debasing its purity.'[13]

Nearer home were other problems besides the restrictions placed on the mercantile classes of Ireland. There was mismanagement at the 'foundling' hospital in Dublin and the so-called house of correction in the city. The journal notes these as well as the abuse of women convicted of small offences and the arbitrary committal of the poor to 'houses of correction'. Russell's laconic comment discloses his own view that 'the laws do not afford their protection to the lower orders'. He is clearly aware of injustice all about him. A grant by the exchequer of five thousand pounds damages against a servant for criminal conversation with his mistress was, he wrote, 'repugnant to every principle of law, equity and justice'.[14]

There can be little doubt that 1790-1791 was of seminal importance in Russell's life. During that year he had encountered most of those who would figure largely in his personal and political history. As the summer of 1791 approached, he had become a man of liberal and progressive views, imbued with a deep sense of justice, aware of abuses in Ireland and abroad. His own instincts were generous and altruistic. Thus, on a parliamentary reform where the bulk of the people, and not merely a rapacious aristocracy, would have a voice in the affairs of the country, he was an avowed democrat. Already he had considered the issue of Catholic emancipation. In a lengthy paper committed to the journal during the months from February to July 1791 he detailed the objections to emancipation rebutting each one. A generous measure would, he felt, have the positive effect of wresting from 'the zealots of intolerance, civil and religious, every shadow of argument ... from the hands of this profligate government their strongest weapon – the distrust that these two religions have of each other.' It is worthy of note that at this time Tone was preparing in Dublin his *Argument on Behalf of the Catholics* which bears the publication date of August 1st 1791.[15]

It would be a mistake to view the Thomas Russell of 1791 as what he later came to represent. Armed rebellion, much less French help, had not yet arisen as an option either for him or for Tone. Russell's separatism had not yet taken definitive shape.

Nor does his strong opposition to ecclesiastical tithing, that unjust tax in the name of established religion, find expression in his
journal for this period. Yet, it is undeniable that he – a member
of the ascendancy class through his family, an officer of the
army, a Protestant of the Anglican tradition – was moving towards radical politics on many issues. As a member of the
Belfast garrison he was displaying an unusual familiarity with
local people who were growing ever more disaffected politically
and ideologically from the Dublin government. With his friends,
Russell had embarked on a course of reflection, study and analysis which would eventually make him one of the marked 'sub-
versives' in the eyes of Dublin Castle administration.

In April 1791 Russell first met Eliza Goddard, the woman who
fascinated him through the rest of his life. Eliza Goddard was
from Newry where her father, John Goddard, was a high official
of customs and excise. She was a frequent visitor to Belfast
where she accompanied Martha McTier to many of the social
functions which Russell attended. Yet, Russell's first sight of her
was accidental. On 21 April he saw her at a window as he
walked from the Mall. Immediately he was infatuated: 'I was
struck prodigiously with the beauty and expression of her countenance and expressed my admiration of it in the warmest terms
though I did not myself then observe how much I was taken.'
Some days later, 26 April, they met at the Coterie in the
Exchange Rooms. Martha McTier introduced Russell, at his request, to 'the finest girl in the room'. They danced, exchanged
pleasantries and parted. When Dr McDonnell quipped at
Russell's taking Eliza from her partner, he answered: 'Who
would not be a robber in such a case?' The journal details
Russell's anguish at being seated far from Eliza at supper and
how he 'damned' McDonnell for 'sitting by such girls'. From
this period, Eliza Goddard's name appears in the casual jottings
of the journal. Already one gets the impression of a *folie d'amour*
which, however, Russell seemed incapable of bringing to effect.
Thereafter, in good times and bad, Eliza Goddard exercised an
obsessional sway in Russell's mind. The unsettled dimension of
his character focused on the chimera of happiness with Eliza to
the exclusion of other, perhaps more realistic, attachments.[16]

Russell leaves the Army

Another outsider welcomed to Belfast was Thomas Attwood

Digges from Warburton in Maryland. A man of some accomplishment, he had been an intermediary between the American and British governments in regard to war prisoners. His liberal, even radical, views gained him access to the circles frequented by Thomas Russell. Through Russell he later met and favourably impressed Wolfe Tone. Fully twenty five years older than Russell, his name frequently appears in the latter's journal. There he is presented as a figure of political astuteness and a sharp observer of character. He cautioned Russell against overestimating how far men of property could be relied upon, even when they professed radical views. Again, he noted the satisfaction of some colleagues when McCabe and Pearce were refused their business premium. Russell commented: 'Digges desires me to mark the trait and think what can be expected from it.'[17]

Nonetheless, Digges ran into some difficulties at Belfast. There was the matter of silver spurs belonging to Samuel Neilson which Digges did not return. According to R. R. Madden, a bond of two hundred pounds was required to rescue Digges from serious embarrassment. With an habitual generosity, although advised not to do so, Russell entered the bond and, on the American's default, was required to furnish the two hundred pounds. On 30 June 1791 he relinquished his commission, perhaps to meet the vicariously incurred debt. As in the case of his sudden homecoming from India, the historian can offer no more than a conjectural explanation. Both R. R. Madden and James Morgan agree that Russell had to sell his commission as a result of Digges's bond. This, however, is by no means certain: one notices that neither Russell nor Tone showed any subsequent diminution of regard for the American.[18]

From 30 June 1791, Thomas Russell was out of the army. Among other notices, the Viceroy, Lord Westmorland, informed the King that 'Ensign Thomas Russell who purchased his commission prays leave to dispose of the same at the regulated price'. For whatever reason, Russell had surrendered his niche within the Irish establishment. In mid-July, a James O'Grady was nominated to Russell's place in the 64th Regiment. As to Digges, he was later found to be a petty thief and disappeared from the Belfast scene. There remains a suspicion that the enigmatic American was in touch, at least once, with the Dublin administration to the detriment of Tone and, indirectly, of Russell.[19]

Bastille Day in Belfast

On re-entry to civilian life Thomas Russell did not immediately quit Belfast. Instead, he remained for some weeks in the town, probably at the house of Dr James McDonnell. Certainly he was in Belfast for a convention of the Whig club to mark Bastille Day in July 1791. William Drennan, perhaps the most advanced among radical thinkers of the time, drafted an address for the convention. Drennan had already spoken of a brotherhood, a benevolent conspiracy, which would 'go further than speculation or debate and come to grips with the practicalities of achieving reform'. Already, too, he had mentioned separation from England and privately had envisaged collaboration with a more assertive Catholic Committee for political and social reform. Many of his ideas had been discussed with Samuel McTier, his brother-in-law, and through McTier were known to others in Belfast.[20]

William Drennan's address, composed for the 14 July convention, welcomed the French revolution, spoke of the 'brotherhood of interest' which was uniting the human race, and warned of the limits to civil obedience. The declaration proved too radical for the northern Whig club which demurred from Drennan's call for an end to religious intolerance. Despite indications to the contrary, the liberal shift among northern Whigs did not extend to relinquishing an endemic suspicion of Catholicism. The Whig club withdrew its proposal for a joint meeting with the Belfast Volunteers, an association which had remained in existence since the institution of Grattan's volunteers in the early 1780s. Nevertheless, the first Belfast Volunteers company, in the main composed of dissenting Protestants, was willing to adopt a further pro-Catholic amendment composed by Drennan. Drennan's patience was tested by a request for additions to his troubled declaration. He pleaded lack of time. Instead, he recommended Tone, mentioning the latter's 'ready and excellent pen'. Tone did have a ready pen: although he was asked for the resolutions only on 7 July, yet an 'elegantly written document' was in transit to Belfast by 9 July.[21]

A comparison of these resolutions with Russell's journal for Spring 1791 gives some insight into the parallel development of both men since their meetings at Irishtown the previous summer. On political reform, on the 'Catholic question' and, even, on separation from England their views show a notable similarity. What, then, did Tone's resolutions propose? The first resolution sternly criticised the constitutional state of Ireland: parliamentary representatives were totally unanswerable to the people and were in the pocket of a tiny clique of aristocrats. Hence, the resolution urged a thorough-going reform of voting rights, 'a more general extension of the electoral franchise is indispensably necessary'. The second resolution adverted to the excessive influence of English administrators on government in Ireland. It proposed that all Irish people should unite in 'a cordial union' to safeguard their freedom and ensure the development of Irish trade, commerce and industry. The third resolution is interesting as much for its implicit content as for its explicit claim. Explicitly, the resolution urged that the well-being of Ireland depended on full unity among Irish men and women – 'a complete internal union of all Irish people'. Tone now proposed the primary objective of ending distinctions among Irishmen, a disunity which hitherto had brought only 'mischief and misery and disgrace' to the country. The resolutions were explicit on parliamentary and economic reform. Another concern, shared by Russell, is implicit, viz. the civil and political disqualification of Catholics and dissenting Protestants. Although the resolutions nowhere mention Catholics by name, yet Tone calls for measures 'tending to the abolition of distinctions'. Without doubt, he refers here to that great majority of the people disenfranchised by the penal laws. On the iniquity of these laws, and the necessity for their repeal, both Russell and Tone were at one.[22]

Tone's own views went further than his resolutions for the Belfast convention. Forwarding the text, he signalled as much to Russell. Any dissimulation was, said Tone, a matter of tactics – 'Truth itself must sometimes temporise'. For himself (and, it would appear, for Russell) it was impossible to envisage political reform without relief for Catholics. Even more, English influence on an all-too-venal Irish government was at the heart of the trouble. While the connection of the two countries perdured, the destruction of Irish prosperity would continue. Tone informed Russell that he had deliberately avoided any word of separation. Yet, he wrote to Russell : 'I give it to you and your friends as my most decided opinion that such an event would be a regeneration for this country.' Perhaps in a reprise of their earlier differences about Whig intentions, Tone informed Russell that the

Whigs were not sincere friends of the popular cause. In Tone's opinion, they dreaded the people as much as did the Dublin administration. Tone concluded by telling Russell : 'My Lord Charlemont and, I am pretty sure, Mr Grattan would hesitate very much at the resolutions I send.'[23]

The fluidity of Irish politics in the 1790s is demonstrated by Tone's uncertainty of how far Belfast Protestants were prepared to go on 'the Catholic question'. Russell had already discussed Catholic emancipation with Sinclair and Digges. There is some evidence that he had corresponded with the Catholic scholar, Charles O'Con(n)or of Ballingar, Roscommon, on the same issue. William Drennan and Samuel Neilson remained unsure of how far the Catholics were trustworthy on broader issues of social change. Drennan feared the innate conservatism of the Catholic leadership who, he thought, were interested only in the repeal of their own disabilities. Neilson later spoke of Catholic leanings to tyranny on the divine right of kings and the hegemony of the Pope. Drennan's view finds some corroboration in the attitudes of Catholic aristocrats such as Lord Kenmare and the pragmatic conservatism of the Catholic bishops. On the other hand, the Catholic Committee was less dominated by aristocrats and prelates than hithertofore. A new, middle-class leadership had more edge for political and social reform than Lord Kenmare or, for that matter, Archbishop Troy of Dublin. In this new more radical group, Russell saw promise for the resolution of a festering problem.

Although the northern Whigs found nothing exceptionable in the anti-English sentiments of Tone's resolutions, they baulked at his third resolution as evidence of 'an alarming Catholic paper'. To avoid a split between the northern Whig club and the first company of the Belfast Volunteers, Tone's 'pro-Catholic' resolution was held back. The volunteer societies, having assembled at the Exchange, paraded through the streets on 14 July with banners and scrolls. Instead of proposing the union of Protestants, Catholics and Dissenters, they pledged the health of Lord Charlemont, George Washington and Benjamin Franklin. Amid 'sentiments of patriotism, liberty and benevolence', they evoked the somewhat undisturbing memory of John Locke, Viscomte Mirabeau and John Jebb.[24] Doubtless, it was a disappointment to Russell with his strong convictions about the necessity for union between all Irish people. According to Tone, Russell informed him of the Belfast proceedings by letter. Shortly thereafter, Russell set out for Dublin where he arrived on 17 July. Without delay he sought out Tone and perhaps was in time not only to help the latter 'think about the state of the country' but also to shape Tone's celebrated *Argument on Behalf of the Catholics of Ireland* which would be published within a matter of weeks.[25]

Argument for the Catholics

Tone's pamphlet was addressed to Protestants in general. Yet, as Marianne Elliott notes, 'it was aimed specifically at those Ulster Dissenters who, while radical in politics, were squeamish about the Catholics.'[26] The reasons for this 'squeamishness' ranged from suspicion of Catholicism as an inherently conservative force (Drennan and Neilson) to theological mistrust of 'Romanism', almost endemic to Presbyterian sensibility. Tone called for unity, collaboration and tolerance. Arguing from principle, he spoke of 'the natural rights of man' to urge the complete enfranchisement of Catholics. Arguing from consistency, he pointed out that if Protestants opposed Catholic relief they should 'cease to murmur at the oppression of the Government which grinds us'. Irish people should refuse to be pitted one against the other: if they continued to quarrel on religious grounds then government would '… play upon the terrors of the Protestants, the hopes of the Catholics, and balancing the one party by the other, plunder and laugh at and defeat both.'[27]

The pamphlet was a powerful argument for the enfranchisement of Catholics. In publishing terms it was a resounding success. Among Belfast's Dissenters it had major effect. Tone's argument may well have enabled northern Presbyterians in particular to recognise the importance of a common cause with all disenfranchised Irish men and women. Sectarian prejudices, it was clear, enabled governments in Dublin and London successfully to resist every proposal for reform. Tone's *Argument* in its structure resembles the case already made, albeit disjointedly, in Russell's journal through Spring 1791. This strengthens the likelihood that Russell and Tone had maintained contact through the year since they came to know each other. It also raises the possibility that Tone's writing was influenced by Russell after the latter's arrival in Dublin. Russell's knowledge of current political thinking at Belfast may well have informed the closing stages in the composition of Tone's new booklet. Within a short time, scepticism in Belfast on 'the Catholic question' had developed into a readiness for collaboration with Catholics in the work of political reform.

The laconic remark in Tone's *Life*, that Thomas Russell was now in Dublin 'on his private affairs', disposes one to argue that Russell spent early Autumn 1791 at Kilmainham's Royal Hospital. Entries in his journal are few – two, to be exact. One is a notice about the death in July of his 'intimate friend', Archdeacon Darby. The Reverend William Darby – most probably the person to whom Russell makes reference – had been chaplain at the Royal Hospital during Russell's boyhood. The other entry for July is short. It discloses Russell's preoccupation with 'the Catholic question'. In the main, it is a set of notes on Thomas Leland's *History of Ireland*, published in 1773. Russell's notes concentrate on the attempt by Richard Boyle and Adam Loftus (Viscount Ely) to penalise Irish Catholics 'because they were inimical to the interests of England'. Russell details the passage of laws prejudicial to Catholics during Thomas Wentworth's vice-regency in Ireland. The conveyance of land to Catholics by long lease was prevented. The English king was given wardship of minors, thereby facilitating the diversion of Catholics to the established church. At this juncture, Russell displays his interest in the 'hidden Ireland' – 'Heard that the common people of Ireland often educate children who are not their own (but) who are forsaken by their parents or are their godchildren etc. The adopted child is if anything taken more care of than their own.'[28]

CHAPTER THREE

The United Irishmen

The foundation of the United Irishmen was neither fortuitous nor haphazard. Detailed preparations had already been made when a public meeting at Sugar House Entry, off Belfast's High Street, inaugurated the society. Through the summer of 1791 there had been active interchange between radicals in Dublin and Belfast. In Dublin, James Napper Tandy, Archibald Hamilton Rowan, Richard McCormick and John C(h)ambers maintained contact with William Sinclair, Samuel McTier and Thomas McCabe in Belfast. Doubtless, Russell's friendship with McTier, McCabe and Sinclair would have further expedited these contacts. Drennan's earlier talk of a 'brotherhood' seriously committed to reform had taken root. Even more, proposals for such a brotherhood and plans for the dissemination of Tone's *Argument* had been drawn up before Tone and Russell set out for Belfast in early October 1791. According to Marianne Elliott, 'The name of the society and its prospectus had already been decided. Tone's July resolutions were to be remodelled... printed and widely distributed, and a special United Irish Society edition of his *Argument* was already being printed.'[1]

Russell and Tone in Belfast

Thus, an invitation to Russell and Tone from their Belfast contacts had a specific purpose. The two friends embarked on a journey which Tone would remember with something akin to nostalgia. At Belfast, Russell gave a report of his dealings with the Catholic Committee, including correspondence with the noted scholar O'Con(n)or of Ballingar. Russell and Tone now encountered a mood of openness to political reform and collaboration with Catholics. Whereas in July Tone's resolutions for the Bastille Day celebrations had been found 'too hazardous', now they were regarded by some as rather tame.[2]

A committee was formed on 14 October with the task of preparing a more public meeting for the 18th. The committee numbered William Sinclair, Samuel McTier, Samuel Neilson, William McCleery, Thomas McCabe, Robert and William Simms, Henry Haslett, John Campbell, Gilbert McIlveen and William Tennent. The inaugural meeting of the United Irishmen took place on 18 October. Twenty eight people approved a declaration of the society's objectives. This declaration identified the central grievance that Ireland had no national government: '... we are ruled by Englishmen, and the servants of Englishmen, whose object is the interest of another country, whose instrument is corruption, and whose strength is the weakness of Ireland ...'. The measure essential for the prosperity and freedom of Ireland was 'an equal representation of all the people in Parliament'. Three central positions were adopted in the declaration: (i) to seek out 'a cordial union among All The People Of Ireland, to maintain that balance which is essential to the preservation of our liberties, and the extension of our commerce'; (ii) 'That the sole constitutional mode by which this (English) influence can be opposed, is by a complete and radical reform of the representation of the people in Parliament'; (iii) 'That no reform is practicable, efficacious, or just, which shall not include Irishmen of every religious persuasion.' The meeting also resolved to send the declaration to James Napper Tandy and Richard McCormick in Dublin, as well as to distribute it elsewhere in Ireland. It is noticeable that Tandy and McCormick could ensure that the new organisation was introduced to both Protestants and Catholics.[3]

The declaration, then, urged constitutional reform, union among Irish people and the removal of all religious disqualifications. It was remarkably similar to the resolutions drawn up by Tone for the Belfast convention in July. Nonetheless, it was more sharply focused than the material for the Bastille Day celebrations. Its call for political reform and religious toleration is definitive. Rejection of divisions fostered by government and omission of favourable reference to Whigs, reflect the advance of Belfast radicalism on which those who framed the declaration could now rely. As to symbols, the badge of the society was to be a harp over the words: 'It is re-strung and shall be heard'.

During the visit of Russell and Tone, the question of separation from England was canvassed. William Sinclair predicted that although there would be a temporary interruption of trade yet an independent Ireland could ultimately outdo England in commerce, manufacture and the arts. Russell expressed the view that the English army would be decisively beaten should a revolution occur. Yet despite these statements, armed revolt was not seriously considered at this time. To cite Marianne Elliott: 'Even Tone was not an active separatist until 1795, whatever his views of the viability of an independent Ireland.' Although the new society carried a more radical promise than even the most reform-minded Whigs, its emphasis was on a programme of union and constitutional reform.

There were signs that the new radicalism had yet some ground to cover. At the Whig club, where Russell and Tone were generously entertained, there occurred what Tone called 'a furious battle' on Catholic relief. Again, at a dinner given by Samuel and Martha McTier, the Reverend William Bruce argued against Catholic emancipation on grounds noted in Russell's journal some months earlier. Bruce felt that Catholics would establish an inquisition if they got the chance, would repossess the lands of which they had been deprived and would form a government 'incapable of enjoying or extending liberty'. Tone observed that most of the Whig club supported Bruce with the exception of Thomas Russell, Robert Getty and himself. The club members protested their goodwill towards Catholics and support for emancipation in principle, but held to the pretext that the time was not right. Tone remarked on the members' 'sad nonsense' about scavengers becoming members of Parliament and their hostility to the doctrine of the Rights of Man. Though Russell disagreed with Paine on religious grounds, this did not prevent him opposing Bruce. Tone would later write: 'Almost all the company of Bruce's opinion, except P.P. (Russell), who made desperate battle, McTier, Getty and me.' The dinner ended with people feeling ill-disposed towards each other and Tone 'more convinced of the absurdity of arguing over wine'.[4]

The contretemps at McTier's table did not impede the progress of the Belfast United Irish society. On the very evening of the dispute with William Bruce, a meeting of the society ballotted five new members, including the Robert Getty who had earlier supported Russell. Nor did Belfast hospitality diminish in the slightest. On Sunday 23 October the Dublin visitors dined 'with a parcel of squires of County Down'. To the disgust of Tone – and, doubtless, of Russell – talk was about 'Fox-hunting, hare-hunting, buck-hunting', as well as about the superiority of northern pota- toes. At the theatre in Rosemary Lane Russell and Tone desultorily watched a performance of *Carmelite* while spending the rest of the time searching the audience 'for a pretty face'.[5] On the same day, at religious service Tone barely endured a sermon against smug- gling while, scrupulous as ever, Russell took the tirade deeply to heart. Afterwards, they walked on the Mall; when Tone com- mented that all the women were flirting with Russell, the latter was attacked by feelings of religious guilt. Tone's journal for these weeks gives an impression that he and Russell did much smoking and drinking late into the night. Tone refers to his friend's tendency to self-doubt: Russell was, he wrote, 'in the blue devils, thinks he is losing his faculties'. Again Tone put it: 'P. P. (Russell) at home in the horrors, thinks himself sick generally'. Only four years senior to Russell, Tone presumed to advise his younger, in some ways more experienced, friend on personal conduct. After the launch of the United Irish Society Tone entered his journal: 'I have been lecturing P. P. on the state of his nerves, and the necessity of early hours; to which he agreed, and as the first fruits of my ad- vice, and his reformation, sat up with Digges until three o'clock in the morning, being four hours after I had gone to bed.'[6]

Thomas Russell and Wolfe Tone left for Dublin on 27 October with many reasons for satisfaction. They had set up a political club, the future of which they could scarcely have foretold. Russell informed an unnamed corrrespondent: 'I confess I am quite proud of this club. It is the first ever instituted in this king- dom for the removal of religious and political prejudices. I think it as an event in the history of the country and, if properly man- aged, as the dawning of liberty.' Tone had come to respect the Belfast radicals and they showed every sign of reciprocation. For Russell, Belfast showed more than respect: it was a liking com- pounded of personal affection, trust and admiration. The three weeks in the town had been enjoyable as well as productive and Tone would remember them as 'perhaps the pleasantest in my life'. The Belfast members of the new society had enjoined on their departing guests 'to cultivate (in Dublin) the leaders in the popular interest ... and, if possible, to form in the capital a club of United Irishmen'.[7]

The Society in Dublin

The next moves were made through James Napper Tandy. Tandy convened what was in effect the inaugural meeting of the Dublin society at the Eagle Tavern, in Eustace Street. Here, on 9 November, a constitution for the Dublin society was agreed. Under the chairmanship of Simon Butler and the secretaryship of Napper Tandy, it was decided to invite other prominent figures, such as the barrister Peter Burrowes and the Trinity academic Whitley Stokes, to join the society. Although they had instigated the inaugural meeting, neither Russell nor Tone attended. At the next meeting, also in November, William Drennan proposed a test or promise to be taken by all members. The test committed each member 'To promote a union of friendship between Irishmen of every religious persuasion and to forward a full, fair and adequate representation of all the people in Parliament.' It also detailed the means for accomplishing 'the chief good of Ireland', i.e. 'a brotherhood of affection, an identity of interests, a communion of rights, and an union of power among Irishmen of all religious persuasions'.

Surprisingly, both Russell and Tone opposed the oath. Tone described it as 'superfluous', 'commanding', and likely to deter new members. The opposition was not well received. Drennan reported that neither man was appointed to a 'corresponding committee' of twelve members. Tone himself did not take the test until much later. Burrowes and Whitley Stokes seem to have been deterred by the dispute since thereafter they ceased to attend. Drennan found Tone and Russell too reserved, although he thought them 'sincere, able and zealous'. He resented that they spoke as if they were official representatives of the Belfast society, intent on recruiting 'instruments rather than partners'. As well, there were rumours of a split in the Belfast club on the same matter of an obligatory test. In the event, Tone maintained a distance from the Dublin club and devoted himself to the affairs of the Catholic Committee. Marianne Elliott remarks: 'It was possibly Russell's influence which made him (Tone) so combative at the turn of the year, and he (Tone) only resumed his prominence in the Dublin Society after Russell's departure for Dungannon in January 1792.'[8]

The social composition of the Dublin society is of interest. While it included Protestants (Simon Butler, Archibald Hamilton Rowan,

William Todd Jones), and Catholics (William McNeven, Richard
McCormick and Theobald McKenna), it was nonetheless – at
this early stage – composed of a wealthy, albeit socially re-
formist, élite. At the outset, there were no poor men within its
ranks. Butler, Hamilton Rowan and Todd Jones were from exten-
sively land-owning families. Drennan, Emmet (Thomas Addis),
and McNeven were successful medical doctors. Tandy, Bond,
Sweetman and McCormick held substantial commercial interests. The distance from Whig circles was by no means as great as
it would later become. Yet, the new society displayed generosity
towards the excluded majority of Irish people and resentment at
the oppoition to reform by a venal legislature. In his *Memoirs*,
Valentine Lawless, the future Lord Cloncurry, links the foundation of the Dublin society to the dashing of hopes that political
reform could be attained in Parliament as it already stood.
Several years later, Thomas Addis Emmet, Arthur O'Connor
and William McNeven would claim that the United Irish Society
in Dublin aimed to further 'the idea of uniting both sects in pursuit of the same objects, a repeal of the penal laws, and a reform
including in itself an extension of the right of suffrage to
Catholics'. Although the context of their deposition has to be
kept in mind, it is nonetheless significant that they state: '… no
such object as separation from England was ever agitated by its
members, either in public debate or private conversation, nor
until the society had lasted a considerable time, were any traces
of republicanism to be met with there.'[9]

The Dublin United Irishmen met on alternate Fridays, normally
at the Music Hall, Fishamble Street, in the shadow of Christ
Church and only a few steps from Dublin Castle. Almost from
the start, at least one member was reporting to Castle officials on
the society's operation. Thomas Collins gave regular accounts of
meetings and drew attention to Thomas Russell's presence on 30
December 1791. Russell may have shared with Tone an unease
at quasi-aristocratic preponderance in the Dublin society. Tone's
eulogy, written some years later, of Belfast republicanism con-
tains implicit criticism of a different temper in Dublin. Of the
Belfast Dissenters he wrote: 'They have among them but few
great landed proprietors.' As well, according to Tone, 'they have
ever, in a degree, opposed the usurpations of England, whose
protection … they did not, like the Protestant aristocracy, feel
necessary for their existence.' Although there is no written evid-

ence of Russell's view on the Dublin society, from his subsequent attitudes it can be divined that any dilettante approach to political questions would enjoy neither his approval nor his support.

Initial Steps on the United Irish Programme

The necessity for co-operation between Protestants and Catholics to attain political reform and religious emancipation became ever clearer. Concessions to Catholics became a ploy on the part of the government to head off collaboration with Protestants in search of more radical political reform. At Belfast, William Sinclair expressed fear lest sectarian attacks on Catholics in Armagh should destroy all possibility of an alliance between Protestants and Catholics. For Russell, the desired union across the religious divide was inevitable if those who aspired to it worked 'tooth and nail'. Meanwhile, the administration viewed the emergence of co-operation between Protestants and Catholics with alarm. It was noted that 'Russell has certainly commenced a correspondence in Galway, Mayo and Roscommon, and, I think, Leitrim.' Yet, the full significance of the United Irish project had not become evident. The Lord Lieutenant of the day went on to note: 'as it is all Russell, Tone and Tandy, I hope (it is) nothing of consequence.'[10]

A strategy of the United Irish movement, quickly adopted and well executed, was dissemination of its ideals through handbills, travelling emissaries and, even, broadsheet newspapers. This work of publicity is an important arm of the movement's activity which has received all too little attention. Preparations were made in Dublin and Belfast for newspapers independent of government and committed to the programme of the United Irishmen. A prospectus for the Dublin paper, the *National Journal*, was issued in October 1791. The launch was set for January 1792 with Thomas Russell named as editor. According to the prospectus, the *National Journal* would seek 'to unite and emancipate All the People of Ireland'. Instead of support for government or parliamentary opposition, the new paper would serve 'the party of the people'. In accordance with the ideals of the new society, the publication would help to 'remove all distinctions between Irishmen'. The reform objective was clearly signalled – to 'secure the people their due weight, by purifying completely their representation in Parliament'. In parallel with

the *Journal* another publication, the *Northern Star,* was projected
for Belfast, with Samuel Neilson as editor. Whereas the *National
Journal* petered out after a few issues, the *Northern Star* would
prove a remarkable success in both commercial and political
terms.[11]

Thomas Russell, Magistrate

The *National Journal* was published without its first designated
editor. Before the paper appeared, Russell had been appointed
to a magistracy in Tyrone. His nomination to the bench of magistrates illustrates a paradox of Irish radical politics through the
1790s. As was the case with several figures in the United Irishmen, Russell belonged by birth, religious affiliation and social
position to that colonial élite in Ireland, the Protestant ascendancy.
In their small, numerically constricted group, Russell had opportunity to meet on terms of friendship many who controlled
patronage in a country marked by influence and favouritism. It
is true that he had not yet fully developed his ideas on political
reform, on Catholic emancipation, on breaking the connection
with England, on ecclesiastical disestablishment, etc. Yet, even
as he accepted a magistrate's commission, his views on liberty,
equality and the common bond between all people, were discon-
sonant with that Protestant ascendancy which government had
as its primary object to preserve.

The appointment as magistrate for Tyrone was, doubtless, medi-
ated with government by Thomas Knox (Viscount Northland) of
Dungannon. In India, Russell was a subaltern of the regiment in
which a son of Lord Northland's had also served. Nevertheless,
it is more likely that another son of Northland's, George Knox,
had made the necessary introductions. George Knox had been a
frequent visitor at the Royal Hospital and was referred to in
Thomas Russell's journal as 'my friend Knox'. It is an interesting
consideration that John Fitzgibbon, the chancellor of the Dublin
government, was in a position to know of Russell's association
with Tone, Tandy and other Dublin radicals. All the same, the
appointment to Tyrone was allowed to stand from 22 December
1791.[12]

Alongside the magistracy, although separate from it, came an
appointment as Seneschal to the Manor Court of Dungannon
with jurisdiction through some forty parishes. This, too, was in

the gift of Lord Northland. The dual appointment gave Russell a position similar to that of District Justice in contemporary juridical organisation. He would have competency over cases of damage and dispute up to the sum of twenty pounds. In addition, he had the task of administering oaths – for example, where people wished to join the army or militia. In her account, more than forty years later, Mary Ann McCracken gives the impression that Russell spoke rarely of this period in his life. However, he does appear to have expressed regret at having facilitated the enlistment of many young recruits to both army and militia.

At the time of Russell's appointment, the magistracy was almost universally reserved for friends of government – the loyal squirearchy and the parsons, eager to prove their dedication to the Protestant interest. Rarely trained in law, magistrates were notable for their political entrenchment rather than any commitment to equity. Displaying partiality and sectarian bias, they showed personal arrogance to a marked degree. At first blush, therefore, this was an unpromising assignment for one of Thomas Russell's courtesy, humaneness and dedication to justice. As his journal barely alludes to his stint at Dungannon, the historian is forced back on exiguous indications of how he viewed his new situation. One such indication is Mary Ann McCracken's impression to which allusion has already been made.

There were advantages to the Tyrone appointment. For the first time, Thomas Russell had the use of a house. Up to this, he had lived either in army quarters or with his family at the Royal Hospital. As one who appreciated the domestic side of life and the gentler arts of daily converse, he is likely to have found his nomadic existence somewhat difficult. At Dungannon, he could entertain his much-loved sister and his father – they visited him in November 1791. It is of some interest that a local inn-keeper, John Campbell, charged Russell for fifteen and three quarter gallons of whiskey to the sum of £5.12.9. This very considerable quantity of spirits was supplied in the period June to November 1792. A sympathetic biographer explains, albeit with some embarrassment, that Russell's duties as clerk of petty sessions obliged him to provide entertainment for visiting lawyers and judges. Yet, Madden's defensiveness of Russell should not hide the fact that, like Tone, he was accustomed to drinking either wine or spirits in the company of his friends and colleagues.

Several years later, Robert Simms would admonish him about his over-indulgence in drink.[13]

In Autumn 1792, Thomas Russell relinquished his appointments in Tyrone. The date given for the cessation of his magistracy is 15 October. The journal of the House of Commons, on the other hand, notes without further comment that Russell's commission ended from 15 February 1793. Since his papers give no reasons for this, his third departure from an apparently comfortable situation, Russell's motives in quitting Dungannon remain unclear. R. R. Madden's double clue may be apposite. Madden suggests that because Russell tried to protect weavers against linen merchants in Tyrone, he was regarded as 'a man with dangerous leanings towards the people, in fact a republican'. Again, perhaps drawing on his conversations with Mary Ann McCracken, Madden argues that Russell 'could not reconcile it to his conscience to sit as a magistrate on a bench where the practice prevailed of inquiring what a man's religion was before inquiring into the crime with which a person was accused'. This argument has the note of verisimilitude, given Russell's detestation of partisan laws and his awareness that much of what was termed 'outrage' was linked to earlier dispossession. With such views he would have found the presuppositions of the bench difficult to maintain. The later comment of William Drennan that Russell had given up a comfortable living on a matter of principle is coherent with Madden's suggestion.[14]

A letter from William Jones Armstrong, written some weeks after Russell had left Dungannon, gives some insight into the style of his work during the months as magistrate. The main thrust of the letter bears on the disposal of his furniture. One reference mirrors the respect for him entertained by Armstrong – 'as to the bed you are so anxious about I have it safe till you choose to send for it and have a kind of reverence for it, whenever I think of the man whose companion it was'. Armstrong, who may have succeeded Russell, mentioned a treatise on the Linen Laws and requested: 'If you recollect any remarkable cases that are likely to occur in the office of magistrate I'd thank you to communicate them, as I know you had a deal of experience for your time.' In a valedictory question which perhaps reflects the nuances of Irish politics in the early 1790s, Armstrong enquires of Russell if he had heard lately from Tone. Another letter from

Armstrong avows its author's continuing debt to Russell in regard to the magistracy: 'I am going on as Gustass tolerably well and find no little assistance from being so often with you when cases came before your Worship.'[15]

There are but two entries to Russell's journal for this period of his life, pocket book entries for June 1792. The first concerns dreams – a topic which fascinated his supple mind. In particular, Russell speaks of the belief that his mother appeared in dreams whenever a catastrophe was about to visit the family. Thus, Ambrose Russell, before engaging in battle at Fort Montgomery dreamed of his mother. He entered battle fully convinced of impending death – in the event, he was severely wounded. Again, Thomas Russell notes that during an illness of his father from 16 September 1791 he (Thomas) had dreamed of his mother on 22 September. One notes the precision in regard to the dates both of the dream and of John Russell's illness. Nonetheless. there is a rational self-examination in the closing comment: 'I make this memorandum to cure or confirm myself of regard to dreams etc, etc. My father, thank God, recovered. If he had died, I should probably be recollecting dreams during my life.' The other, very brief, reference is to Sabbath observance. Russell saw this as a divine ordinance. Since it conferred no material advantage either in war or commerce on those who observed it, the Sabbath could not be traced in its institution to human self-interest.[16]

Thus ended Russell's somewhat tentative association with the organs of state. In both army and magistracy he would have had time to acquaint himself with their forms and, perhaps, to understand their mode of operation. It is all too tempting to overplay the significance of his term as magistrate and of his resignation. Neither his Belfast colleagues nor Wolfe Tone allowed it to bulk large in their considerations. He himself did not make much of the episode. On the other hand, Russell's army experience and, now, his close contact with the lives of tenant farmers, weavers and farm labourers, would feed into the evolution of his thought. Certainly, at Dungannon and its environs he would have observed a somewhat larger diversity of opinion in regard to reform than among his Belfast colleagues. And he would have had a closer view of social injustice as it pressed upon powerless men and women.

Anti-Slavery: Letters and Actions

An impressive feature of Thomas Russell's stance on freedom is
its universal sweep. Along with his friend, Thomas McCabe,
Russell made clear his anti-slavery views on more than one occasion. While at Dungannon he drew impassioned attention to
the abuse in the *Northern Star*, on 17 March 1792. An editorial
comment took the less generous view – agreeing with Russell
but pointing out the immediate necessity to liberate three mil-
lion slaves in Ireland. Russell did not make that distinction. As a
veteran anti-slavery campaigner, Mary Ann McCracken remembered that as a young officer in Belfast Russell '... abstained
from the use of slave-labour produce until slavery in the West
Indies was abolished, and at the dinner parties to which he was
so often invited and when confectionery was so much used he
would not taste anything with sugar in it ...'. It is argued by
Seamus Mac Giolla Easbaig that Russell authored a letter,
signed 'G', published by the *Belfast Newsletter* on 2 December
1791. With graphic detail, the letter outlined the abuse of human
rights involved in slavery. Analysing the interests subserved by
the practice, 'G' reminded the readership that slavery existed for
the sole purpose 'of contributing to the luxury and avarice of
Europeans'. 'G' then cited with approval another writer – 'On
every lump of sugar I see a drop of human blood.' With that
strain of religious feeling notably Russell's, 'G' put it: 'the blood
of the Africans cries to God for the vengeance of these wrongs'.
It was, wrote 'G', the slave traders who had 'introduced the
vices of Europe, fraud, subtility and ingratitude among them
(the victim countries) ... war and desolation over-run their once
happy countries'.[17]

CHAPTER FOUR

From Belfast to Dublin and Back

Returning from Dungannon in November 1792, Russell would have noticed an ambivalence in the political climate of Belfast. With perceptions sharpened by his experience in Tyrone he would have noted that friends like Sinclair, Neilson and the McCrackens still maintained their commitment to political reform and religious emancipation. Yet, in the larger scale the picture was not quite so clear. Already, in July 1792, Tone had encountered residual anti-Catholic feeling during his second visit to the town. Bastille Day celebrations for 1792 were arranged for the Falls district and were planned to highlight the demand for reform and emancipation. The convention was attended by John Keogh, a leader of the Catholic Committee, based in Dublin. From Dublin also came William Drennan and Theobald Wolfe Tone, the latter now regarded as an agent for the Catholic cause.

During the night of the 13th, Samuel Neilson awakened Tone to inform him of attempts to incite anti-Catholic feeling among Volunteer corps from the countryside. Whereas Tone had previously overestimated how far the United Irish ideal had penetrated the north, he now was faced by anti-popery among volunteer bodies from Co Down and around Belfast itself. Tone was later to write of some of these as 'no better than Peep-of-Day boys'. Samuel McTier's bleak remark of months earlier was verified: '(Tone) mistakes the situation of this town and country round, they are still full of prejudice, which only time can remove.' Nevertheless, the Bastille Day celebrations ended well – much better than Tone or Neilson could have hoped when the day commenced. By evening, Tone's pro-Catholic resolutions – couched in implicit terms, as a matter of tactics – had been accepted by the convention. Several Presbyterian clergymen, among them Sinclair Kelbourne, had endorsed Tone's resolutions with enthusiasm. On the other hand, a number of the country corps withdrew before the end of the proceedings. Was this because of their disagreement with Tone's address? Or was it due to their long journey home? Marianne Elliott comments: 'Whichever way, there can be no doubt that opposition to the address would have been greater had the County Down volunteers remained.'[1]

It was this somewhat ambiguous context that Russell entered on his return to Belfast. His stay in the town would be short. From now on, he would be so frequently on the move that people remarked on the difficulty of finding him at home. An air of mystery seems to descend on his movements which may partly have inspired the soubriquet, 'The Man from God knows where'. In the opening days of December Russell left for Dublin to present resolutions from the Belfast United Irishmen at the Catholic Convention scheduled to meet on 3 December.

Death of John Russell

On Monday, 3 December, Russell arrived in Dublin on the Belfast coach. En route to the Royal Hospital from the terminus at Capel Street, he was intercepted by a servant, M'Kenzie, who informed him that John Russell was grievously ill and 'extreamly (sic) anxious' to see his son. Russell's journal intimates a suspicion that John was unwell, but the urgency of M'Kenzie's tale alarmed him: 'I was not surprised, as his health had been declining fast, but I had not apprehensions of any immediate danger.' On arrival at the Royal Hospital, Russell 'instantly saw that he was dying and that he knew it himself'. The ensuing conversation, even though recorded in journal fashion, evinces the nobility of character in both men. Neither wished to alarm the other. Both had extreme regard for Margaret's feelings. Thomas endeavoured to shield his sister not only from exhaustion through sleepless nights but also from being overwhelmed by their father's death, 'which I saw was inevitable and which she flattered herself was not – to let her see this by degrees was necessary'. The journal entry for these days gives valuable insight to Russell's immediate family. It seems to have been as closely knit as in the early days at Mallow or Durrow. Amity between father and children, friendship among the siblings, are amply documented. So, too, is the unremitting dedication of Margaret Russell, her attention to the smallest comfort of her father being carefully minuted by her brother. Russell felt increasing anxiety about her future. As for the present, he ensured she got a modicum of sleep and watched her with an attention almost equal to that he showed their father.[2]

William Russell, 'a wild man with little sense yet with good nature' now made a brief re-appearance in the family's life. Margaret and Thomas had been informed of his return to Dublin; as a result, they arranged a meeting in the city for Tuesday, 4 December. Realising 'poor William's love for him (their father) and how unhappy he would be if his father died without his seeing him', they endeavoured to re-introduce him without upsetting the sick man. Thomas prepared his father for the visit – 'broke it to him by degrees, first telling him that he (William) was in Dublin and marry'd'. A full reconciliation did take place, much to the comfort of John Russell and, indeed, of Thomas, who wrote: 'My feelings quite got the better of me. I cried violently and the effort I made to suppress it only increased it. My sister and Will were equally affected. We loved each other much and to see him who had been away so long now returning only to see his father expire ... all together the emotion was too great.'[3]

Through the week, Thomas, Margaret, and sometimes William, attended the sick bed. Religious devotions were repeatedly undertaken by them as well as by Mr Lehey, a clergyman friend of the house. As to Thomas Russell's profoundest sentiments there are some clues. Somewhat typically, guilt alternated with exaltation. A feeling of guilt arose from his fear 'that I was in some measure the cause by my being so unsettled as to my prospects in life'. On the other hand, there was exaltation in feeling 'so assured of his (John Russell's) eternal felicity as it is possible to be assured on such (a) subject'. Thus, grief, anxiety and uncertainty vied with each other. The grief at his father's impending death was compounded by anxiety for Margaret, soon to be without a home. Yet another emotion, frequently a cause of difficulty for Russell's many-sided personality, was a sense of duty unfulfilled. He was aware that he had availed of some opportunities to bring joy into his father's life. Yet there is an overtone of self-reprobation in his remark: 'When I look back now, how few, how very few, do they appear to be to what they ought to have been.' As to his own future, this was deeply uncertain. On arrival at the Royal Hospital, he had mentioned a plan to em-

igrate to France, 'as my income did not answer and I had an enthusiasm for the cause of liberty'. Here was another source of
tension which caused divergent feelings. The desire to avoid
grieving his father by emigration produced such confusion 'that
I doubt if I wish'd his recovery which I considered as bringing
(him) back to a world of misery … yet I dreaded the event (of his
death)'.[4]

Concern was not limited to Margaret, although she ever would
remain Russell's primary concern. There were also Ambrose
(still in India) and John (now in London). And so, Russell mentioned them to his father, especially Ambrose. An extraordinary
considerateness made him anxious that his father should make
explicit mention of Ambrose, 'as I knew the fervent love
Ambrose had for him and that the only consolation he would
feel when he heard of his death would be that he was kindly
mentioned, remember'd and bless'd by his father in his last moments'. There was no cause for worry. In keeping with his generous disposition, John Russell 'fervently pray'd for and bless'd
him and all his children'.

John Russell died on the evening of 6 December 1792, aged a little
over seventy. The journal account is striking for its vivid detail
of his life's closing days. The concluding paragraph displays
Thomas Russell's attachment and the vehemence of his grief:

> As soon as this happen'd I scarcely recollect anything for a
> time but remaining on my knees in the posture I was in …
> weeping most violently and talking to my father as if alive,
> asking his forgiveness for all my faults which I had most
> earnestly desired to do while he was living but had not from
> the fear of affecting him to(o) much, and not being able to
> contain my grief, my brother and the servants urged me to
> go, but I did not mind them. My heart required a vent at last.
> Whatever it proceeded from I thought my father stirr'd in the
> bed. Terrify'd and amazed at this, fearing that the noise of
> my sorrow had disturb'd him, which I had been so careful to
> suppress, I fell back on the floor. My brother and poor
> McKinzee (sic) dragged me out of the room. Mrs Tone then
> came to take me away, but I would not go till, in spight of
> their intreatys, I had look(ed) into the room. I then went to
> my sister. Poor Will was as distracted as I was. Afterward for
> my part, I was now calm. I went to Tone's with my sister.'[5]

The funeral was in the Royal Hospital, early on 8 December. John Russell, once an ordinand of the Church of Ireland, once an officer at Fontenoy, was interred with his wife in the south-west corner of the grounds. Strangely, it was Wolfe Tone who wept. Russell did not weep. Instead, as his journal attests: 'I looked into the grave, heard with pleasure the fine service read and remained in the sure hope of (my) father's having a blessed resurrection.'[6]

Catholic Convention at Tailors' Hall

During his father's illness, Russell left the Royal Hospital at least twice. On Tuesday, 4 December, he met William, the ne'er-do-well member of the family, who had arrived in Dublin with his wife. Out of that meeting emerged the reconciliation of William and John Russell. On Monday, 3 December, Thomas Russell went to Tailors' Hall in Back Lane, near Christ Church. Here, the Catholic Convention had opened on the same day, attended by delegates from throughout the country. Tone as secretary to the Catholic Committee had executed the huge task of organising the Convention. This visit to the Convention was one of Russell's objectives in coming to Dublin. Margaret's letter summoning him to his father's bedside had not reached him. The Belfast United Irishmen, particularly Samuel Neilson and Robert Simms, were fearful the Catholic Convention might be deflected from full demands for political reform and religious emancipation. The influence of gentry representation (Lord Kenmare etc) and 'moderate' bishops (Archbishop Troy and Bishop Moylan) gave ample reason for such a fear. Talk about 'deals' and 'half-measures' exacerbated the old suspicion that Catholic unrest could be assuaged by minor confessional reforms. In this unsettling context, Russell carried declarations of support from the United Irish at Belfast for thoroughgoing demands to government by the Convention.[7]

At the Tailors' Hall, the Convention overlapped with a meeting of the Dublin United Irish society. Tension existed between both groups as the Convention sought to attain consensus and, above all, avoid a split. The Catholic aristocrats and the pragmatically conservative bishops were already in conflict with a more assertive group led by John Keogh, William McNeven, Richard McCormick and other middle-class spokespeople. Perhaps for this reason, a delegation of United Irishmen was not admitted to

the Convention floor. Nor did Tone keep Neilson informed of
the business of the Convention, much to the latter's annoyance.
Although not a delegate, Russell felt his commission/message
from Belfast necessitated leaving his father's bedside. To leave
the Royal Hospital on the night of his arrival caused him deep
worry : 'I don't know that I was ever more uneasy or undecided
whether to go or stay. I knew he would be uneasy at my absence
but thinking it more necessary I went as he seem'd quieter.'[8]

The 'Catholic Question', being far from answered in 1792 or
1793, would recur for many a day. Through 1793, negotiations
with the chief secretary for Ireland, Robert Hobart, stirred the
murky water of politics at College Green and Whitehall. Bright
hopes in 1793 were raised only to be dashed subsequently on the
hard face of expediency. As to the Catholic leaders, some – for
example Lord Kenmare – were so attached to a society of defer-
ence that they remained utterly inimical to the United Irish project. The Catholic hierarchy, at once answerable to the reactionary politics of Rome and preoccupied by institutional concerns in Ireland, could do no more than profess loyalty to the
crown and excoriate those who entertained republican ideals. In
his *Duties of Christian Citizens*, the Archbishop of Dublin endeavoured to show that royalism and the faith were not disconson-
ant. However, new Catholic leaders were emerging – amongst
them Keogh, McNeven, Sweetman and the Teelings – who were
ready to travel far along the road of Russell and the United
Irishmen.[9] Thomas Russell's journal does not inform us of his reception at Tailors' Hall. It is, however, worth noting that he was
at the forefront of attempts to cross the sectarian divide in the
service of political transformation and religious freedom.

Aftermath of Bereavement. Unsettled Months

Through December 1792, Thomas and Margaret Russell had to
contend with private grief and uncertainty of prospect. The journal captures the depth of their bereavement in Russell's moving
account of their father's last days. As to their home of many
years, the Royal Hospital would no longer be open to them.
Thomas (and, through him, Margaret) was an ever-welcome
guest at Chateau Boeue, the Tone's jocularly-named little house
in Bodenstown, Co Kildare. Yet, Russell was already several
weeks without employment and Margaret was without a permanent home. Although Tone had loyally sought references

from Archibald Hamilton Rowan, Richard Kirwan and Thomas Wogan Browne, Russell's plan for emigration to France had receded. This may well have been due to his sense of obligation to Margaret. Also, the outbreak of war between England and France in early 1793 and the incipient terror in Paris would have been disincentives to his scheme for emigration.

The informer, Thomas Collins, still assiduously forwarding accounts to Dublin Castle, reported that Thomas Russell attended a meeting of the United Irishmen at Tailors' Hall on 14 December 1792. Collins referred to him as 'courier extraordinaire' with an address 'near Belfast'. Was this an ironic allusion to Russell's intermediacy between the Belfast United Irishmen and the Catholic Convention earlier in the month? One remains cautious about Helen Landreth's claim that Collins had in mind Russell's journeys 'through the country preaching the doctrines of the Society and urging turbulent Catholics who had become defenders to align themselves with the United Irishmen'. That would come, but not until later. It is certain that Russell attended two meetings of the Catholic Committee (not to be confused with the Catholic Convention) early in 1793. With John Sweetman he shared Tone's fear that 'the sneaking spirit of compromise (on the part of the committee) would enable the government to deal with the radical reformers in the north'. The fear was not ill-founded. Through 1793, Catholics were kept waiting and, therefore, pliant. Promised reforms were delayed while a Militia Act and several other measures laid groundwork for repression of all dissidence in the north of Ireland. In April 1793 Russell lamented the success of government dissimulation. While Catholics remained 'with their hands tied up ... (the government) had time to attack the spirited Protestants and that head of liberty – Belfast – and show their weakness to pull down the freedom of the press etc.' In 1796 Russell would lament that unity of purpose had not been maintained to ensure 'the great *desideratum* of Ireland', viz, reform. As he saw it, Catholic emancipation was a step which was useless without broader reform. Then was the suitable time to persist in the deeper 'union and spirit of the people'. In his 1796 *Letter to the Irish People* Russell would expand on the causes and effects of that failure.[10]

Organising The Dublin United Irishmen

Through the early weeks of January 1793 Russell made himself available to the United Irish Society in Dublin. In fact, it had many troubles. A penchant for theatrical posturing by more prominent members had caused needless difficulty. In far retrospect, the elitist membership of the society in Dublin – gentry, lawyers and merchants comprised the great majority – gives the impression of verbal rather than effective radicalism. Attendance at meetings was uneven. Among some early members the outbreak of war and Jacobin excesses in Paris may have induced disillusionment with radical politics. Russell was among the twenty one men deputed on 11 January 1793 to construct a plan of reform for the Dublin society. The chairman of the society, Simon Butler, its secretary, James Napper Tandy, William Drennan, Theobald Wolfe Tone, Oliver Bond and Archibald Hamilton Rowan were other members of the committee. The group commenced work immediately.

By 3 April the principal recommendations for reform had been agreed. Yet, for whatever reason, these conclusions did not become generally available until 1794. Even then, the document was hardly extreme. The new programme called for universal suffrage, yearly parliaments and payment of members of parliament. Yet, it was hesitant about the abolition of property qualification for electoral franchise. Only a tiny majority (two) of the committee was favourable to the abolition of such qualification. In Marianne Elliott's judgement: 'There was no desire to undermine the existing monarchical constitution, and nervousness about charges of republicanism deterred publication when the plan was finally completed in April 1793.' Such tenderness for monarchy or mistrust of non-propertied people did not represent Russell's own view. When, by royal proclamation, a general fast was called on 19 April 1793 to mourn the execution of Louis XVI, Russell entered his journal: 'The day of the fast, whenever the King was prayed for, stand up. Drink the fate of Louis to all crowned heads, George the last etc, etc.'[11]

As to his concern for people of little property, some indication of Russell's priorities can be gleaned from his behaviour in late March 1793. A summons had come from John Fitzgibbon to attend a secret committee of the House of Lords set up 'to enquire into the causes of the disorders which prevail in several parts of this Kingdom'. Finding that his attendance at the Omagh assizes was required by the family of two young men accused there, Russell sent back the *sub poena* to Fitzgibbon. It was better, he judged, 'to risque their anger than to risque two lives'. An ominous backdrop to the summons fom the House of Lords was an examination of Whitley Stokes about a letter to Russell in July 1791 in which Tone recommended separation from England. What was, at most, subversive in 1791 could be viewed, in the circumstances of the England-France war in 1793, as treasonable. In the journal, Russell recollects that he had given Tone's letter for copying to Digges and with remarkable charity asks, 'Surely he (Digges) could not be such a villain?' The ever-realistic William Drennan was less tentative about Digges being, in reality, the informer.[12]

Return to the North: Omagh and Enniskillen

And so to the north. Here Russell's task was a dual one. In Omagh he proposed to speak for the two prisoners who had asked his help. Before that, however, he would visit Enniskillen where his friend, the Reverend John Stack, had been appointed rector at Derryvullen. It is likely he also had in mind to find a home for Margaret and for his nieces, Mary Ann and Julia Ann. Mary Ann and Julia Russell were the daughters of John Russell, a chronically impecunious man who, in the throes of marital difficulties, emigrated to London at the end of 1792. His daughters had been left in Ireland and, with Margaret, became utterly dependent on Thomas Russell. Between Margaret and Thomas there was now more than affection; Margaret's dependency on her brother had become almost pathological. As for Thomas, his sense of duty kept before him the promise to his father that Margaret 'would never want a protector so long as God spared me my life, that I would consider it the first duty to take care of her.' Meanwhile, Margaret was complaining of cold, expense and 'of buying my own wine and making Julia take a glass every day.'[13]

Arriving in Omagh on 22 March, Russell found the assizes town 'horribly expensive and disaggreable (*sic*)'. With four or five days in hand, he could observe the political temper of the region he had known as a magistrate . On 23 March, he dined with the grand jury of the assizes finding them 'High Aristocrats' – in Russell's parlance, a term of strong disapproval. He noted their trumpeting 'God save the King' and the despicable arrogance of a juryman who threw a glass at a blind fiddler for playing 'The White Cockade', a Jacobite air. Nevertheless, the Tories were not uncontested. Russell found that a document signed by him as acting secretary of the Dublin society 'had been much liked'. This presumably, referred to a *Declaration to the Irish People* of the Dublin Society of United Irishmen which had appeared on 3 March. On the 24th Russell dined with members of the bar. The encounter reminded him of his army experiences, being at once pleasant and frivolous. In the journal he briefly mentions similarities between the bar dinner and an army mess. He noted the lawyers' prejudices: in their politics they were Tories; in their talk they were full of rumours of insurrection. Reflecting on this he wrote: 'Wonderful what improbable lies … the gover(n)ment have gull'd a number of people with'. Russell dryly added: 'The opposition, as they call themselves, aid the government.'[14]

Until the trial on 27 March, Russell met diverse people. Linen buyers had come to market at the town. Their politics were different from those of the lawyers and gentry. From the linen buyers, Russell gleaned that the 'great mass of the people' shared an anti-government view. Even in 1793, he could foresee conflict. Much would depend 'on France, the war we are engaged in, and the conduct of the Catholics'. During these days, Russell was entertained by John James Hamilton, Lord Abercorn, in Baron's Court, near Newtownstewart – 'dinner edifient', noted the journal. Here is a hint of the wide social ambit of his observation – from the Duke of Abercorn's table to pedestrians on the roads of Fermanagh, a week later.

At the assizes, Russell's appearance for the accused men proved effective. Laconically, he noted that 'The father of the two boys (was) very greatful (*sic*) for my trouble'. From Omagh, he journeyed on foot to Enniskillen, once more to visit Stack at Derryvullen. On the road near Derryvullen he fell in with a Methodist who claimed to know the political feelings of the people in Cavan, Fermanagh and Leitrim. Russell noted that they favoured the French and the abolition of tithes. Even 'the middle orders' hated the government, although they were fond of the King. Desire for reform, opposition to the war with France, hatred of the government, these are the factors detailed by Russell as representative of what a much later time would term 'the hidden Ireland'. He learned from his Methodist interlocutor that

Hamilton Rowan's proposal for a reforming convention similar to the Catholic Convention of December 1792 had been well received. The realities of life, however, were more distressing. In the same counties there were mutual fears of Protestants and Catholics. Russell summated it thus : 'The Protestants think the XX (Catholics) are to murder them on the 15th of February and stand in arms all night. The XX equally frighten'd and fly to the mountains with their goods.'[15]

Interval in Dublin

The return on foot from Enniskillen took three days. In Dublin there were unpleasant political realities to face, along with the burden of private grief. The French had been defeated at Neerwinden on 21 March and their commander, Dumouriez, had defected. In Ireland, 'strong government' was in the ascendant. Drennan commented: 'a perfect Inquisition reigns'. The entry of aliens was being controlled, militias were being raised, the army was in process of augmentation, the volunteers were set for disbandment by the Lord Lieutenant. On the Catholic question, Russell's friends anticipated that the Catholic leadership would settle with government short of political reform. There was fear that the leaders of the Catholics would leave the United Irish cause in the lurch. 'All despond', commented Russell. He forecast that if the Catholic alliance broke down, then 'The north will emigrate in astonishing numbers'. This overtone of depression is continued in his journal entry that Neilson, McCormick, Tone and himself 'dined together and – *tempora mutantur* – could scarce keep each other awake.'[16]

It is difficult to estimate how Dublin Castle and the powerful Fitzgibbon viewed Russell. His resignation of the Tyrone magistracy was certainly known to them. So, too, was his close association with Tone, now the object of Fitzgibbon's ire. Russell's membership of the United Irishmen was a matter of public knowledge. The administration had moved rapidly against Simon Butler and Oliver Bond when, as president and secretary of the Dublin society, they had signed a critique of the House of Lords. After Beauchamp Bagenal Harvey and Thomas Russell replaced the arrested men, the Castle would have been informed by Collins. In any case, that matter was not secret since Harvey and Russell had signed the United Irish *Declaration to the Irish People* of 3 March 1793. Drennan believed the administration would not move further than Butler's and Bond's arrest. Nor is there any hint of perceived danger in the journal entries for this time beyond the awareness of risking Fitzgibbon's displeasure when he (Russell) sent back a *sub poena* to testify before the select committee.[17]

For Russell, Tone, Sweetman, McCormick and Neilson the question was of whether the Catholic Convention would hold out for political reform. In Russell's own view 'If that is carried all will go well. If not, America ho!' The Catholic Convention did stand firm on its demands, at least for the moment. It displayed some mettle by refusing to vote chief secretary Hobart a proposed service of plate. It sanctioned gifts of £1,500 for Tone (with a gold medal), £1000 for Todd Jones, £500 for Simon Butler and a service of plate for Samuel Neilson. There is no hint of envy in Russell's notice of the largesse. Only William Drennan pointed out the irony: Russell was not even mentioned by that group for whom he had so long spoken and so generously acted, even to the point of resigning a comfortable post as a matter of principle.[18]

Enniskillen again

Russell set out once again for Enniskillen on Wednesday, 24 April. His journal reports the tenor of conversation on the coach. A 'mixed company' reflected government's success in propaganda. They believed that the House of Lords had saved the country, that Major General White had properly dispersed 500 Belfastmen under threat of burning the town, that Grattan believed the United Irishmen had prevented the Whig opposition from 'going the lengths they otherwise would have done'. As to Grattan's disapproval, Russell was pleased: 'If the club has done that, it has served the country by exposing that vile, ped(d)ling, pitiful faction.' Russell now understood the Whigs better than in July 1790![19]

The purpose of this second visit to Enniskillen was to find a home for Margaret and her nieces. After arrival, Russell noted: 'Settle the women.' He had secured for Margaret a small house outside the town, at Drumsluice. Thereafter, he prepared to travel for Belfast or, as he and Tone termed it, 'Belfescu'. Nevertheless, before he set out he was handed a summons by the postmaster of Enniskillen from the Lords' committee, over the signature of Lord Farnham. Farnham had instructed the postmaster to deliver the summons to Russell's hand. It is not surprising that Russell wondered: 'How the devil did they trace me?' Now it was 'Dublin ho!', not quite 'America ho!' Meanwhile, he had heard from Tone that the Catholic Convention had stiffened its back by declaring for reform. Yet, pessimistically, Russell wrote: 'The spirit of the people is broken at present.' He believed that the government had cleverly prised apart the more radical Catholics and Protestants, by promising yet deferring Catholic emancipation. The ploy had established 'the tyranny of government' and, he asked, ' who will dare begin to resist it?' Somewhat enigmatically he remarked: 'We had our day and let it pass. Will it ever return in our time?' With a hint of dispiritment, Russell asserted: 'I see nothing but the continuance of the present ruinous war.' A few days later, he would record his opinion that 'this war (will be) long, bloody, general and almost the last with which Europe will be infested and then it (will) end in republicanism very generally.'[20]

Lords' Select Committee

By 9 May 1793, Russell was back in Dublin. He now prepared, albeit unwillingly, to testify before the select committee of the House of Lords. Already, James Reynolds had been imprisoned for non-compliance with a summons from the committee. Russell's friends had convinced him that it would be futile to risk imprisonment also. Margaret Russell, ever prone to anxiety, wrote on 11 May that she would be very uneasy 'till I hear from you on account of the unpleasant business that took you to town'. In Dublin, there was hardship: manufacturers were in difficulty, business failures had occurred, shops had been broken open by people searching for food. Russell himself had no fixed abode. On his return from Enniskillen, he may have received lodging in Werburg Street, beside St Patrick's Cathedral, from John Ball, a draper and a delegate to the Catholic Convention. Untypically, he mentions being at 'John Ball's old house. Frightn'd in the night by will (o' the wisp), etc, etc, etc.'[21]

On 10 May, Russell found the peers 'evidently rascals, stupid, unfair and either ill-informed or pretending to be so'. They asked him his opinion on the French, on volunteering and other matters. Tone's letter to him, on which they had examined Whitley Stokes, was not mentioned. Russell felt he had outwitted them through remaining non-committal and answering in such fashion 'as could not be pleasing to them'. Yet, the Lords had their revenge by refusing him expenses. 'Sad dogs', remarked Russell. That evening, both Tone and Russell went to a meeting of the United Irishmen at Tailors' Hall where, Russell noted, there were not above forty people.[22]

For lack of money, Russell's journey from Enniskillen to Dublin had been on foot. There were compensations, even in the deprivation. Crossing the Sperrin mountains, he felt so tranquil as almost to 'doubt whether man was formed for society'. Even then, he thought of emigration – 'I think the woods of America with a family would afford me the most pleasure.' Near Tempo, he delayed by a river, charmed by its sounds: 'No sound but the gentle noise of the water – calm, serene and dark.' Furze was in bloom and, some distance away, there was an angler. The history of Catholic dispossession entered Russell's mind – he alluded briefly to Hugh Maguire, whose Catholic ancestors had been chieftains of Fermanagh and who was now a Protestant in order to save his lands.[23]

After his joust with the select committee Russell went to Bodenstown. Both he and Tone spoke vaguely of emigration. There is a hint that Tone was considering a journey to France *en mission* for the United Irishmen. Whatever the scheme, Russell agreed to it, as did Richard McCormick when consulted in Dublin. It is possible that at this time Russell went from Bodenstown to Portarlington to distribute political literature. Margaret Russell expressed anxiety at rumours about her brother: 'I hear that you have been seen driving through the streets of Portarlington in a phaeton distributing seditious handbills among the inhabitants – who were very much enraged – you know whether we have been misinformed.' Margaret cautioned him 'for fear of the Chancellor's bill'. By now, it was evident that Russell felt more at home in Belfast than in Dublin. With the summons to the House of Lords discharged, he could resume his journey to Belfast so unexpectedly interrupted by Lord Farnham's letter. A note of insouciance marks the end of his stay in Dublin. With funds desperately low, he comments on his departure for Belfast: 'P. P. (Russell) sets off having raised the wind by virtue of Mr Hutton's (Tone) time piece.'[24]

CHAPTER FIVE

Political writings
and travels in the North

Almost three years after his introduction to Belfast as an infantry officer, Thomas Russell returned there on 20 May 1793, unemployed and without income. Yet, his friends were loyal as ever and from this period William Sampson would refer to him as 'the incomparable Russell'. As an ensign of the 64th Foot, Russell would have had quarters at the army barracks. Now, he had to find his own accomodation. For some months, Dr McDonnell gave him lodgings at his house in Donegall Place and provided minor commissions in quasi-scientific research. On arrival in the town, Russell sought out his United Irish colleagues to assess the political situation there. From Neilson he learned that 'the spirit of the north (was) as high and perhaps higher ... than at any other period'. Antrim, Down, Tyrone, Derry and parts of Armagh were firmly against the government. This widespread opposition was fuelled by indiscipline of the army, the demands of the Militia Act, and economic hardship caused by the English-French war. Indeed, the assiduous operation of United Irish agents in book clubs and through the columns of the *Northern Star* would have helped to raise consciousness of popular grievance. From the perspective of the United Irishmen such dissatisfaction gave added strength to the demand for radical social change. Parish meetings, area conventions, masonic lodges and resolutions published in the *Star* were all part of this context.[1]

Nevertheless, in regard to other objectives of the United Irishmen, viz. 'to forward a brotherhood of affection, an identity of interest, a communion of rights and an union of power among Irishmen of all religious persuasion', there remained a difficulty. Many of the more radical Protestants felt rebuffed after 'having held out their hands to the nation (i.e. the Catholics) to join them in the reform'. As a result, the northern reformers felt isolated:

'At a time they were making the greatest exertions the southern papers were abusing them.' Emigration was spoken of; many Belfast people would go to America if they could dispose of their property. There was, wrote Russell, a slender hope that 'The spirited people will be keep'd for a while and things may come round'. As to himself, Russell merely comments: 'P. P. has ruined himself in the pursuit of the good of his country.' Has this to do, one asks, with his resignation of the Dungannon magistracy? Russell's journal does not tell us more than that one enigmatic reference. Meanwhile, Martha McTier was complaining to William Drennan about lassitude in Belfast – 'Not a public place, a pretty girl nor a smart fellow. Streets dirty beyond enduring … no politics any day and a general gloom or a forced gaiety on every face …'. Mrs McTier's plaint found corroboration when citizens of the town, including several members of the United Irish Society, wrote to the Sovereign of Belfast, the Reverend William Bristow. The memorial criticised 'the disagreeable, dangerous and reproachful situation of the Streets of the Town, owing to the very bad state of the pavement, and the still more uncomfortable and hazardous situation of so large and populous a Town, passing the long and dreary nights, without the advantage of lamp lights'.[2]

The tensions of Summer 1793 are re-echoed by Russell's allusion to riots in Belfast and Castlereagh. He notes the difficulty in getting a true account of 'the conduct of the officers in the town'. In fact, two 'riots' had occurred in Belfast (one on 9-10 March, the other in April) when arrogance of the military was the primary cause of the trouble. On 28 June, there was 'a serious scuffle' between the residents of Castlereagh and a detachment of dragoons, after the hearing of objections to service in the army. Several people died in the disturbance.[3]

Prosecution of The Northern Star

Then there was the harassment of the *Northern Star*. Under Samuel Neilson's editorship, this paper had achieved widespread readership and by the mid 1790s had a circulation of 5,000. It had quickly become the main organ of publicity for the Belfast United Irishmen. From 1792 until 1795, while the main thrust of the society's activities lay along communication and discussion of the printed word, the paper's influence throughout the north was considerable. The *Northern Star* was eagerly read at parish meetings and book clubs, even in the most remote areas. For those who could not read, its contents were made available in discussion, both formal and informal. Thus, its influence far outstripped its estimated circulation. The *Star* comprehensively reported events in France almost as they occurred and printed vigorously anti-government editorials. A kind of 'multiplier effect' was produced as parish meetings adopted the positions of the *Star* on the war with France or in regard to the government in College Green. Russell contributed articles and supported the paper with his advice and what little money he could afford.[4]

In January 1793, the proprietors of the *Star* and its printer, John Rabb, had been charged with sedition. A game of cat-and-mouse then followed with government repeatedly deferring trial, in order to intimidate the proprietors and printer. Russell feared lest an unspoken compromise had taken place – 'No prosecution, No politicks'. Aware of the need to save the paper, he seemed nonetheless disheartened by the thought of any compromise by the radical *Star*. In regard to government he asked: 'Can we drive these men from their ground?' Even at this stage, neither he nor his United Irish colleagues appear to have considered armed resistance. Reflecting the current policy of the society to argue its case and, hopefully, to convince interlocutors, Russell veered to the double weapon of writing and disseminating political criticism. Thus, he resolved to use his time in writing: 'Must try (to write) ... Determine to write a book.' From this period comes his long poem 'The Fatal Battle of Aughrim' modelled on Smollett's lament for Culloden, 'The Tears of Scotland'. Russell's feeling for the old Gaelic order becomes evident in his opening lines:

> Mourn, lost Hibernia! ever mourn
> Thy freedom lost, thy laurels torn,
> Thy warriors sunk on Aughrim's plains,
> And Britain loading them with chains.[5]

Observation. Reflection. Political Analysis

Such writing would be of limited value if crafted only in an armchair. In these months of unemployment, Russell did not remain in seclusion at Dr McDonnell's. He visited – indeed, he lodged in – the homes of people like the mill-worker who had invited him to his cabin to drink whiskey. He was sufficiently heartened by his host's political awareness to annotate the man's words: 'I think liberty worth risqueing life for. In a cause of that sort I think I should have courage enough from reflection to face death.' Impressed, Russell asked: 'When would a man of fortune reason thus?' The contrast was evident: 'Our senators and great think of nothing but their own sordid interests.' Even more, they despise people such as the mill-worker, thinking them incapable of self-government. This tendency to dismiss the 'mob' annoyed Russell, especially when it came from self-styled reformers: 'Nor is the language (dismissive of the poor) only of the corrupt and interested. Wise and good men have led into it, and I obser(v)e of late (within these seven months) many even in my own small circle.' At this point, the journal reflects a decidedly anti-aristo-cratic feeling that wealth corrupts as well as hardens the heart. Russell's opinion is clear: evil in society comes from 'the rich making the laws'. As things stood, property was placed before life. Hence, political transformation was necessary even as a matter of basic morality. Not for the first time, a religious strain appears in the journal: 'He who knew the recesses of the heart loved not the rich.'[6]

Given the preponderance of wealthy merchants, professionals and gentry in the Dublin Society of United Irishmen, one won-ders if these remarks do not imply a critique of Russell's Dublin colleagues. As well, since he anticipates a query from Dr McDonnell – 'Where does the good or evil of the government af-fect him (the mill-worker)?' – there may be a criticism of social élitism among Belfast *soi-disant* radicals. This is not the sole in-stance of Russell's sensitivity to the potential of a hitherto ex-cluded majority. He notes with evident approval the existence of a reading group, probably an artisans' club at Doagh, outside Belfast. He remarks on its provision of books for women as well as men. Mary Ann McCracken's stern disapproval of the exclus-ion of women from equal partnership, even in the United Irish Society, would probably have found sympathy from Thomas Russell!

By now, he accepts Thomas McCabe's view that 'The lower or-ders alone ... will produce a revolution.' A presage of United Irish strategy is given in his further note: 'When the majority feel themselves slaves they will resist.' And he adds: 'Information

being diffused will produce this.' After a convivial evening with
Samuel Thompson (a supporter of the *Northern Star*), an otherwise unidentified Mr Dicky, and Alexander McManus (a prominent Whig), Russell made his own comment on McManus's references to 'mob' government: 'All gentlemen of property aristo-
crates (*sic*) in Ireland.' It appears, too, that Russell was publicly
abused in an anti-Catholic tirade by one Jones of Moneyglass.
The same journal entry carries his assessment that the men of
property throughout Ireland 'whether landed or commercial,
are decidedly against a struggle which might risk that (property) and will do nothing'. As the poorer people understood their
own oppression, they would themselves undertake the struggle
and then 'adieu to property'. To which Russell simply adds:
'Tant mieux'.[7]

These, then, are weeks in mid-1793 when Russell's social radicalism was developing faster than even that of Tone. As distinct
from many of his colleagues, he was closely observing the realities not only of religious discrimination but also of social/politi-
cal exclusion. The immediate agents of such injustice were the
people of wealth and power. Behind them was the government
at College Green, an instrument of Whitehall's colonial programme and the guarantor of a radically flawed society.
Adverting to this side of Russell's political analysis, one recog-
nises the justice of James Hope's later remark that the condition
of the labouring class was the fundamental question in the
struggle between the rulers and the people during the 1790s.
And Hope's further remark is apposite: 'None of our leaders
seemed to me perfectly acquainted with the main cause of social
derangement, if I except Neilson, McCracken, Russell and
Emmett.'[8]

'E' letter to Northern Star

Through Spring and Summer 1793, the war with France had induced an hysteria of reaction in College Green. The Whig opposition (led by Henry Grattan) repeatedly facilitated government:
the Gunpowder Act, the Convention Act and the Militia Act
were nodded through parliament. On the suppression of the
Volunteers even Grattan proved malleable. Among the United
Irishmen there was some dismay as the French revolution
turned on its own creators. In Dublin, through 1793, the society
lost members who, disenchanted by their brush with radical

politics, reverted to loyalism of one kind or another. For some others, who included Russell, a different avenue was opening up – away from the deferential politics of the constitutional opposition, away too from dependence on the goodwill of hierarchical establishments of either the Anglican or Roman Catholic kind.[9]

As the summer of 1793 drew to a close, Thomas Russell appears to have dismissed all potential for reform in the Whig opposition. On 30 August, he published a thorough-going criticism of Henry Grattan in the *Northern Star*. This letter of considerable length, signed 'E', attacked Grattan with the combined force of irony, sarcasm and straightforward argument. In Russell's view, Grattan had tried to mount a rhetorical opposition during the previous session of parliament while carefully avoiding damage to government. When the government was in no danger, Grattan had fulminated against it. When, however, the same government could have been defeated, he had supported it. Earlier in the year, while there was a real possibility that the will of the people might prevail, Grattan had urged moderation on the Catholic leadership. With little need of such advice, the axis of Catholic aristocrats and conservative bishops had shown due moderation. On the war with France, argued Russell, Grattan had played a double game. He had made populist sounds but, once again, had sided with government: 'he pedled (*sic*) and he pranced, he reviled the government and the French – he reviled sedition and mobs – republicans and levellers – and all the etcetera peddled by knavery and corruption.' On all measures desired by government he had been pliant – the dispersion of the Volunteers, the Militia bill, the Gunpowder bill, arbitrary fines and imprisonment. The pattern of support for government, either tacit or explicit, showed that Grattan 'deemed a strong government so essential that, for its attainment, both the forms and the substance of Liberty were to be violated …'.

Russell went on to argue that 'the people should be told at least who are not their friends'. He alluded to Grattan's much earlier proposal to work for freedom 'till not one link of the chain of British Tyranny was left to clank at the heels of the meanest Irish peasant'. In the matter of abolishing the penal laws, Grattan had now disavowed his former protestations – 'his conduct during the session shows that whatever objections he might have to

English chains, he has none to load the Irish peasants with those of Irish manufacture'. Russell concluded his letter by deriding the opposition now mounted by Grattan: after having sacrificed the happiness of the country, 'we see him once more return to his insignificant opposition, and again declaiming and grinning and chattering at the abuses of that ministry, which but for him would not now exist'. A careful reading of this letter will show that Russell's opposition was every whit as much to the aristocratic clique in College Green as to the administration at Whitehall. A few days after publication, while on a scientific expedition to the Mourne mountains, he heard complimentary remarks on 'E' from the Reverend Edward Berwick, chaplain to the Earl of Moira. The identity of 'E' would not be known were it not for a journal entry of 27 September. Here Russell, with a touch of self-deprecation, discloses that the authorship of the letter was known to his Belfast colleagues: 'They knew the handwriting. It was a good joke to think of disguising my hand.' From Neilson he learned that the letter had been favourably received in Dublin. There was question of reprinting the text for circulation to a wider readership.[10] The 'E' letter is worth especial attention since it illustrates a significant development in Russell's own stance. Any previous confidence in Whig liberalism had disappeared. Instead, he had begun to see popular organisation as the best means of effecting both emancipation and reform. Such a course of action would be reprobated even by the most forward of the Whigs. From now on, Russell saw the excluded majority, Catholics and Dissenters, as the bearers of social change. Thus can be interpreted his allusions to weavers, artisans, mill workers and others, whose views were ignored even among the United Irishmen. His ability to contact people in modest circumstances anticipated later connections between the United Irishmen and the Defenders of south Ulster and north Leinster.

Other Personal Concerns of 1793

The journal for August–September discloses more private concerns. In this time of relative inactivity, Russell wrote a lengthy account of his father's death, nine months previously. As well, he noted with agitation that his feelings for Eliza Goddard had not changed. Hearing that Eliza had been sick but was now recovered, he felt relieved not for her good health but because she had remained unmarried during his absence from Belfast. This introspection is characteristic of him, as is the self-castigation with which he asked: 'Are all men as bad?' Further, the journal records drinking bouts with Neilson and, as a consequence, being led 'into other vices'. Once more, Russell's strong religious sentiment drives him to profess: 'I must amend, for which I beg the grace of God, my strength daily declining.' There is a suggestion that these were difficult times for him, when personal frustrations exacted their toll on his peace of mind.

A note on the Russell family history, a comment on a sonnet of John Milton, a longer memoir on the philosophy of Socrates, Antoninus and the Stoics, are other substantial entries to the journal of these weeks. Russell's wide reading continued, despite personal difficulties. During the summer of 1793 he read Bede's *Ecclesiastical History of Ancient England*. Somewhat by contrast, he also read William Godwin's *Enquiry Concerning Political Justice*. On its publication in February 1793, Godwin's work was regarded as a handbook of political radicalism in England. Russell did not criticise Godwin's politics but rather the views on marriage and immortality of this one-time clergyman. As Russell saw it, Godwin's idea of duty was to be found, backed up by 'weightier arguments' in the New Testament. That Russell had now sufficient time to write on these topics is clear from his proposal of writing to Priestly or Paine on the subject of Godwin's *Enquiry*.[11]

Field trips through the north

Despite the sketchiness of his formal education, Russell possessed a remarkably thorough foundation in natural science. A combination of reading, observation and an empirical cast of mind, gave him expertise in geology and mineralogy well beyond the skill of an interested layperson. In addition, he was interested in the application of science to Irish industry for the amelioration of the lives of small artisans. These inclinations would find ample scope with the newly constituted Belfast Society for Promoting Knowledge in which many of his friends were active members. It is probably under the aegis of this society and with the encouragement of Dr McDonnell that, in the Autumn of 1793, Russell undertook two lengthy field trips through Antrim, Down, Derry, Fermanagh and Armagh. It has been argued that these trips were undertaken for purposes of spreading the United Irish organisation throughout Ulster. While it is unlikely that Russell would make a sharp distinction between his political and other interests, nonetheless the journal focuses on the ecology of the locations visited. References of a political nature are made but they are incidental to the text. It is safer, then, to take the accounts of these trips at face value while remaining alert to the clues they may afford to other develop-ments in Russell's political activities.[12]

The first of these extended journeys was undertaken in the early days of September 1793 with John Templeton. Templeton was a close friend of Russell's, a United Irishman, and a botanist of international repute. A man of gentle disposition, he would re-main a loyal supporter of his friend through later imprisonment and exile. Russell and Templeton explored the county of Down from Ballynahinch, Castlewellan and Rathfriland to Rostrevor and Kilkeel. Russell concentrated on rock formations in the Mourne mountains, collecting samples and annotating them for later classification. As well, his journal offers minute descriptions of mountain wilderness, on the one hand, and of towns such as Ballynahinch and Castlewellan, on the other.

Russell did not overlook political indications. For example, he noted with approval a young girl carrying a copy of the *Northern Star*, near Ballynahinch. A hint that he was doing more than sci-entific observation is given in his cool remark: 'Here give them copies of the *Northern Star*, which they read with avidity.' He noted that a tenant farmer had to pay fourteen shillings an acre for poor land. For Russell, this kind of rackrent made it under-standable that people found it necessary to live by smuggling. He also noted that the inhabitants of Ballynahinch were favourable to the French: their only demur was at the recent exe-cution of Louis XVI. The beauteous scenes of early autumn evoked in Russell a longing for Eliza Goddard. Yet he could write: 'I should not repine ... for though I have had great an-guish, yet when our passion first commenced my pleasures were exquisite ... A flower that smelt so exquisitely sweet that the sense ach'd at it – I am now near her no more.'[13]

Repeatedly, the journal observes that the people were, in the main, favourable to the revolution in France. Near the Cooley peninsula – across Carlingford Lough – the boatmen 'all avow themselves smugglers'. It would seem that the interlocutors of the two travellers confided in them to a surprising extent. Doubtless, the accumulation of this sort of local knowledge would be useful when the time came for the United Irishmen to undertake strategic planning of a less relaxed kind. Russell's innate courtesy emerges in his toleration of an over-talkative guide: 'I would not hurt him by seeming inattentive'. One notes Russell's haste to recognise 'the remarkable number of beautiful women' in the area near Bryansford – he mentions that two of them were in his lodging as he wrote. He had already remarked on 'pretty women riding near Portadown to Newry' and would later speak of women bathing near Cooley 'which I once before observed in the mountains of Wicklow.'[14]

Returning through Ballynahinch, Russell and Templeton arrived in Belfast on 7 September. There, Russell learned of French advances and of General Custine's court martial. Hearing of Custine's breakdown before execution, Russell marvelled that a man so brave on the battlefield should be timid on the scaffold. He added: 'I am certainly more affected than by anything I have long heard … Let all men look only hereafter for their rewards and then the guillotine will have no terrors.' A meeting with two politically aware militia sergeants caused him to comment: 'the militia act will serve further to make people know each other in this kingdom, which is all that is wanted'. At a later time, he believed that some militia corps would align themselves with the people in the event of a popular insurrection.[15]

At the end of the month, Russell again set out on foot for Drumsluice. Here, 'P. P.'s women' were living in conditions of extreme frugality. The overt purpose of this trip was to settle arrangements for the marriage of one of 'P. P.'s women', i.e. Mary Ann Russell, to William Hamilton, then serving with the Enniskillen Yeomanry. Nevertheless, he also made time to collect rock fossils and, as in the case of the Mournes expedition, to index them as carefully as possible. Hence, the journal is interesting not only for personal details but also for its many observations on the countryside from Belfast to Enniskillen. The journey took Russell through Antrim Town, Randlestown (sic) and Toome. Thence he walked to Moneymore and on to Cookstown. Here was a locality where he was known as a magistrate – he remarks somewhat enigmatically: 'The fear of being known rendered me less accurate'. 'Accuracy' may well refer to the methodic annotation of rock specimens, yet the question arises as to whether Russell was also engaged in political scouting which he wished to keep secret.

At Pomeroy, Russell detailed the mineralogical features of the Sperrin mountains. Dissatisfied with his success in the task, he lists his fatigue and 'the apprehension of being known where all the weavers etc, etc. had been before me', as reasons for not examining the area more thoroughly. This reticence about recognition and lack of money, caused him to linger well into the night in an area where 'if solitude, silence and wildness could have produced a ghost, I certainly should have seen it'. There is a further poignancy in his comment on the day's expenses – 'two shillings and tuppence' – as excessive, and his remark 'My feet are not beaten'. From Pomeroy the journey led through Sixmilecross and Fintona. After a walk of 28 miles through 'rain and violent storm in my face the whole day', Russell arrived in Drumsluice.[16]

Having settled the details for Mary Ann's wedding, he spent a short while in the neighbourhood of Enniskillen, where he laid 'the foundations of a club'. In yet another enigmatic reference, he speaks of this club as of the deepest importance, and predicts that 'Hamilton may be a great man here'. The enigma is compounded as Russell adds: 'What a shame for him to be in the army.' With some days in hand, Russell wrote a paper for the new club which was, very likely, an extension of the United Irish Society. On Tuesday, 15 October, he set out on foot for Belfast where he arrived on the following Friday. Once returned, he met Samuel Neilson to finish and correct a defence of the *Northern Star* proprietors who were being brought to trial. The defense was probably intended for publication in the *Star*. However, John Rabb advised him not to publish the text. Despite an initial reserve about the advice, Russell later came to recognise its tactical expediency, particularly in view of the lack of support from the Catholic leadership, now bent on cooperation with government.[17]

Hostile encounter with the army

By late 1793, the army in all its branches had become thoroughly unpopular in Belfast. Gross indiscipline had been ignored by army leadership and compounded by arrogant insult to the inhabitants of the town. Writing to her brother, Martha McTier adverted to the violent distemper of government measures and, in a singularly prophetic vein, noticed that 'the people see that nothing but arms is left'. In the late hours of 13 November, Russell had a sinister entanglement with roistering militia officers in the streets of Belfast. The confrontation is a pointer to his own disenchantment with an arrogant establishment which had forfeited any right to govern a people they so evidently despised. Given Russell's familiarity with army service and his personal links with the military, his readiness to meet agression with agression may also show his identification with the people and, perhaps, his personal excitability at this time.[18]

A reception had been arranged for Archibald Hamilton Rowan and Simon Butler, who were en route from Scotland. As people dispersed at the conclusion of the dinner, there were several scuffles with drunken militia officers. One man who had called a cheer for the United Irishmen was nearly bayoneted by the militiamen. When it was taken that he was a 'gentleman', a duel was fixed. At the inn where the dinner had been held, it was reported that the United Irishmen had been insulted. Russell and McCabe encountered the officers, including an over-excited young aristocrat called John Willoughby Cole. According to Russell, he was himself wrong at the beginning of the affray while the militia were wrong later. Martha McTier describes the incident somewhat differently. In a letter to Drennan she describes how 'Russell went up close to them, did not speak one word, but surveyed them with such a countenance that, after McCabe had got past them, they pursued, and coming up with Russell, demanded the reason for that look of insolence.' Cole wanted to fight Russell but it was another officer who pressed a duel for the morrow. An amusing circumstance to an otherwise charged incident is that while Cole repeatedly proclaimed his rank as *Lord* Cole some bystanders responded: 'You are very fond of that title: take care, or it may not be long till you lose it.'

The duel was never fought. On the morrow, the officers 'sought out Russell and apologised to him in the fullest manner'. Although McCabe had stood by him during the altercation, he later deemed Russell at fault 'by a look, which even at moonlight was, it seems, worse than a sentence'. McCabe prevailed on him to write an apology but this was anticipated by the arrival of the officers to deliver theirs. The journal has a different emphasis to Martha McTier's account. It details Russell's misery on the day set for the duel. No mention is made of any apology suggested by McCabe. Russell simply alludes to 'mutual apologies next day'. He had steeled himself 'to put the duel on them and not fire in return'. In a remorseful self-examination he remarks on his lack of purpose to renounce duelling and notes: 'With a prostitute that very night when the next day I might be in the presence of God.'[19] The incident makes an interesting vignette of Belfast life in 1793. Compared with other incidents of confrontation between the citizens and the army, it is perhaps of no major import. Yet it raises questions of the toll on Russell's morale during these years of unstructured living. Was the flare-up with the militia officers and the fledgling Lord Cole the reaction of a man under severe internal pressure? Or was it the initiative of one who, despite his personal high regard for many army personnel, now felt deep resentment at the wrongs inflicted on his adopted town? One notices the fortunate occurrence of chivalry on both sides of the incident as well as the effect which even Russell's stare could have on this group of recalcitrant officers.

Martha McTier retained her affectionate, if maternal, interest in Russell. To Drennan, she further observed on his way of living in late 1793: 'His dress betrays poverty, and he associates with men every way below himself, on some of whom, I fear, he mostly lives.'[20] The reference by Mrs McTier may well connect with extension work undertaken by Russell for the United Irishmen. He was engaged in writing 'a paper for the County Down' and an introduction to what he termed 'the tradesmen's rules'. This is probably a reference to the inauguration of one of the artisans' clubs which commenced to proliferate in conjunction with the United Irishmen. There were clubs such as the Mudler's Club at Peggy Barclay's tavern on Sugar House Entry. Ostensibly, the club helped working men on their arrival in town. Yet, it was also a front for recruitment when the United Irishmen began to expand during 1794, despite the government's proscription. According to James Hope, the club's 'ostensible business was jovial amusement, its real one extending the connexion of the United Irishmen and it was visited by every man of known integrity who came to town.' Hope also remembered that Russell and Neilson put their time, energy and advice at the disposal of the Mudler's Club.[21]

To Dublin via Enniskillen

From May 1793, 'P. P.'s women' had settled at Drumsluice in a small cottage. Letters came regularly from Margaret, full of sisterly advice and with recurrent allusion to lack of money for her nieces, herself, and a mysterious young man called Stephen Hamilton. Thomas Russell endeavoured to meet these requests even after his incarceration at Newgate. On 15 November, he arrived at Drumsluice where he remained until the end of the month. During this intermission he visited Devenish Island and wrote a detailed account of the historic ruin. In the company of William Hamilton, he discussed the politics of the day with local men, re-echoing their criticism of the Catholic leadership for its acceptance of partial reform. In several journal entries Russell noted that he had drunk excessively while in company. On Saturday, 30 November, he set out with William Hamilton for Dublin, where they arrived the following day. In Dublin, Russell and Hamilton parted company. Before leaving the city for Bodenstown, Russell met Richard McCormick, a member of the Catholic Committee, and dined at the Thatch'd House in Castle Street.

Ever a welcome guest of the Tones, Russell stayed at Bodenstown (with brief intermissions for trips to Dublin) until 4 January. The first of these intermissions was on Tuesday, 3 December, when he returned to the city for a meeting with McCormick. From McCormick, he learned about the parlous state of the United Irish Society in the city. Russell judged that 'nothing in a political way is doing. All talking.' In fact, government legislation had already intimidated the less intrepid members, while others were disturbed by the turn of the French revolution. Even though a new programme had been launched by the Dublin society a month previously, it had failed to rally those members whose aspirations went little further than the Volunteers in 1782. For Russell, McCormick's report on the decline of the Dublin society would have been a matter of dismay.[22]

Nor were reports from the Catholic leadership any more cheering. Endemic squabbles persisted, fomented by uncertainty in face of government's strategy on reform. The Catholic hierarchy was bitterly opposed to the United Irish programme, opting rather for compliance with government's 'carrot and stick' approach. Under John Keogh's guidance, the lay Catholic leadership was still courting Whigs such as Lord Moira. Some months earlier, in August 1793, a dinner for Moira was given in Dublin by the Catholic leaders at Daly's New Rooms. Toasts were proposed to Moira and other Whigs but, to the chagrin of Samuel Neilson, the Belfast United Irishmen who had consistently supported Catholic demands were either forgotten or deliberately ignored. Now, at the end of 1793, Keogh, McCormick, Russell and Tone discussed the organisation of another dinner by way of redress. When some of the Catholic leaders proposed that the Whig opposition should again be invited, Tone was doubtful while Russell, perhaps mindful of Grattan's earlier collusion with government, was resolutely against the idea.[23]

A letter from Hamilton Rowan brought Tone and Russell again to Dublin in early January, 1794. Their business was to attempt the formation of a new club which would 'bring up the south to reform by writing and distribution'. The similarity to the *modus operandi* of the northern United Irishmen is clear. Names mentioned for the new club were Thomas Addis Emmet, John Sweetman, Archibald Hamilton Rowan, Theobald Wolfe Tone and Thomas Russell. Even here Catholic dissensions operated, since tension between Keogh and McCormick prevented their collaboration in the proposed departure.

Russell's journal for his days at Bodenstown affords an engaging glimpse of a milieu very different to Belfast, the Mournes and the poor cottages where he felt so well received. With Tone he visited Thomas Wogan Browne whose splendid residence at Castle Browne, near Clane, he minutely noticed for its gothic style, its elegant and well-chosen library. In Russell's view, Wogan Browne understood 'the art of living well the best of any man I have seen…'. It is an unusual compliment for Russell to pay and, perhaps, relates to his view of Wogan Browne's politics as 'very rational for a man of fortune'. The journal then carries a reflection on this form of enlightened selfishness and on its unpromising contradictory: 'If measures are not taken by the ruling people they (the majority) will take the matter into their own hands and then woe … to the rich. The example of France will be followed and perhaps exceeded … I wonder no people of fortune consider this, but on the contrary they wink hard to avoid seeing the gulph (*sic*) on the brink of which they tread and go on flattering themselves that France will be crush'd and its example not follow'd. Fatal Delusion.'[24]

Both Russell and Tone were now approaching a critical juncture in their personal lives. Russell was in his twenty-seventh year. He had made several attempts at a career, and had been virtually unemployed since he quit the Tyrone magistracy. His love for Eliza Goddard and, even more, his inability properly to declare his feelings for her, caused him recurrent anguish. His sister's condition, without either means or prospects, also preoccupied him. As for Tone, his secretaryship to the Catholic Convention had already ended. Only a small part of the monies voted him had been paid. Little wonder, then, that both men should have discussed their uncertain future during these weeks in Kildare.

CHAPTER SIX

The Belfast Library

On 17 January 1794, Russell was informed of his nomination to the librarianship of the Belfast Society for the Promotion of Knowledge. This society, which had been in existence some years, numbered among its members several United Irishmen. For three or four years it had been active in its stated aims: 'To conduct enquiries by experiment and investigation, to correspond with similar societies, to receive communications and read original papers at their subsequent meetings, upon the various branches of arts, science and Belles Lettres.' Although the society excluded from its remit matters relating to 'local politics, polemical divinity, and practical branches of law and medicine', it had taken a stand on national politics. In January 1792, it had resolved that 'Ireland can never deserve the name of a free State while a great majority of her inhabitants are totally governed by the will of others; in a word, while they are unjustly excluded from all share in the making and the administration of the laws under which they live.'[1]

The society's library had been located for some time in the house of Robert Cary, who also served as unpaid librarian. In December 1793, the *Northern Star* announced Cary's intention to emigrate. It also carried the society's advertisement for a paid librarian. The library contained a wide range of books in history, philosophy, natural science, theology and politics. Within a carefully managed budget and through some generous donations, its stock had increased steadily. There was an active committee which included John Templeton. Dr James McDonnell also maintained an energetic involvement in both the library and the society. It was McDonnell who nominated Russell for the librarianship, at a meeting at Drew's Tavern on 8 January. Russell's wide reading, his interest in the very subjects covered by the society and, perhaps, other reasons made him a suitable nominee. Despite the interest of Robert Telfair, who had offered the use of his house to the library, Russell's nomination was approved. The committee also resolved that 'the expense attending a house for the Library, Museum etc., and the Librarian's salary should not exceed £30 per annum.'[2] It was a congenial offer on the part of the library directors who, doubtless, wished Russell to remain in Belfast.

However, the journal intimates that Russell had misgivings. Perhaps the salary was too small, perhaps he feared the position would interfere with other interests. It took the persuasion of Tone and Whitley Stokes to put him 'out of conceit' with the offer. His further remark that Tone 'recommends matrimony' suggests that his friends were worried about his nomadic state. Tone had also rebuked him for quitting the Dungannon magistracy. On Saturday, 18 January, he left on foot for Enniskillen accompanied by Tone to the end of the Phoenix Park. There they parted with 'Mr Hutton (Tone) and P. P. (Russell) low enough'. A little over a month later, on 20 February, having taken advice from William Sinclair and Robert Simms, Russell officially accepted the Belfast librarianship. Both Sinclair and Simms believed the position would lead to something more substantial. As well, the salary had been increased to £50 per annum. The journal implies that the original invitation and the improved terms were due to the friendly regard of the library committee.[3]

The first task, to find a house for library and museum, was accomplished within a week. Russell negotiated terms for premises at Anne Street, near the White Linen Hall and opposite the Discount Office or Bank. On 27 February, the committee instructed him 'to prepare one of the rooms for the reception of the books at the expense of the Library'. On 9 March, Russell took up residence at Anne Street. For the first time in more than a year, he now possessed a home and also the services of a housekeeper, Judy Clarke. Thereafter, the duties were light: to open the library for three hours daily from Monday to Saturday; to oversee the lending of books; to correspond with donors; to prepare committee meetings. If he could not be present, he was authorised to depute another in his place. As C. J. Woods remarks: 'The position was a perfect 'cover' for a revolutionary: he was always accessible, with time on his hands, present at the coming and going of the more intellectual of the Belfast radicals.' Nor did the librarianship prevent him from travelling either from Belfast to Dublin or throughout the province of Ulster.[4]

Yet, the new librarian was far from inactive. During Russell's incumbency, the committee's interest in books written in Irish was maintained and expanded. A sum of £10 per annum was devoted to the purchase of such books. Russell himself took lessons from Patrick Lynch, of Loughinisland, a professor of Irish. In addition, through his early months at the library he acted as intermediary between Lynch and Whitley Stokes in their translation to Irish of the New Testament. The first Gaelic magazine – *Bolg an tSolair* –is said to have had Russell's collaboration. A brief introduction to an Irish dictionary would seem to have come from his pen.[5] Edward 'Atty' Bunting's proposal to issue a collection of Irish airs and melodies, garnered throughout Ulster and Connacht, was facilitated by Russell at the library. The new librarian steered the sponsorship of Bunting's publication through many sessions of the committee. Even in Newgate prison, Russell maintained interest in the work. To the end of the decade, he intermittently alluded to the 'Airs' and collected further items for inclusion in any later edition. Another project, mooted by Russell himself, was an institute of elementary and higher education to be situated at Belfast. The project only came to fruition some years after Russell's death when, in 1810, William Drennan formally opened the Belfast Academical Institution.[6]

Further Political Observations

Our narrative saw Russell and Tone part at the northern end of the Phoenix Park. Both men had ample material to consider in regard to politics. As well, their personal affairs were charged with uncertainty. Tone, perhaps in depression, ('low enough', declared Russell), believed that nothing was to be expected unless from the *sans culottes*. For all his radical leanings, Tone neither knew nor seemed to care for the people of no property. This suggestion is borne out in Russell's notice that Tone believed the *sans culottes* in Ireland 'too ignorant for any thinking man to wish to see in power'. There is much evidence that Russell himself thought otherwise. He esteemed the people who dwelt in small cabins, people of little or no means, whose opinions he consulted, and from whom he had received frequent hospitality. Less than two weeks after leaving Dublin he noted approvingly the Reverend John Stack's finding 'the lower orders very grateful and good and ... far, far better than the rich'. In a parenthesis, Russell added: 'this has been my opinion.'[7]

Now, in January 1794, as he left Dublin for Belfast via Enniskillen, Russell believed that nothing could hinder a revolution in Ireland. The question was only of time-scale: he thought, accurately, that the cataclysm would occur in four or five years. The journal entries for these weeks tell much about his estimation of the political state of the country through which he passed. People were disaffected from an oppressive government. To an extraordinary degree, they were aware of events in France and, on the whole, approved of the revolution. Near Dunshaughlin, Russell heard that in Monaghan the people strongly favoured the French. Also, the Defenders were organised there, numbering 300 armed men. When he arrived in Cavan town he recorded such hospitality that one suspects he was already known, either in person or by repute. He learned that in the countryside between Bailieborough and Cavan, the Catholics were wealthy, had their own schools – probably hedge schools – where Latin and other subjects were taught. Of the people in this area of north Leinster and south Ulster he noted that the 'vast majority would join the French'. The same journal entries give a hint of Russell's own view of the agrarian 'outrages' much reprobated by the authorities. One notices that he was little inclined to blame the Defenders, whom he saw as reacting to provocation. Closing his journal for 19 January, he remarks: 'Indeeed, when I see the dreadful catastrophe of the Kings, princes and nobles of France, I can't help calling to mind the passage where God says He will visit the sins of the fathers on the children. I think the same fate awaits the great in all the European countries at no very remote period. They will persist in their oppressions till vengeance comes.'[8]

Russell's foot journey to Drumsluice ended on 21 January, presumably at Margaret's little house. Here, reports confirmed what he had gleaned along the road from Dublin. People in Monaghan were said to be discontented with government and very much in favour of the French: 'The common people and middling of all descriptions for French and quite open in their wishes for them.' Around Drumsluice, even the poorest people knew of events in France: 'It is a great thing in their contemplation to see haberdashers, postillions, etc, etc., at the head of armies'. And, he noted, 'They will not fail to apply the lesson.'[9]

Almost as a continuation of his 'E' letter, written the previous August, Russell noted the 'abominable profligacy and folly' of both government and opposition. He described Grattan's stance as that Ireland must stand or fall with England. In the English parliament a sort of madness was displayed by the prosecution of Scottish radicals like Thomas Muir (who was eventually sentenced to fourteen years transportation to Botany Bay). In general, Russell's assessment of the political context was apocalyptic. As he saw it, there was an approaching cataclysm wherein the people, not the government or opposition, must assert themselves: 'The people at last must vindicate themselves and will do it.' The people of no property had outflanked their supposed leaders – Catholic leaders such as John Keogh, the Earl of Kenmare and Archbishop Troy; Whig leaders such as Henry Grattan and, Tone's friend, Lord Moira. In an enigmatic aside, Russell put it: 'Had Mr H's advice and mine been taken it would not be thus.' Presumably, this refers to counsels for greater firmness by the Catholic leadership and the Whig parliamentary opposition. In melancolic vein, Russell mused: 'I have been working, I trust honestly, these now near 3 years for the good of my country and mankind and have ruined myself, but I did my duty.'[10]

It is clear that Russell placed Irish affairs in the broader context of European politics. Despite his hesitations on some aspects of the French revolution, he regarded the spreading war as a conflict between the old forces of corruption and a newer, more democratic, assertion of the rights of every man and woman. There is a religious, even millenarian, overtone to his confidence that ancient wrongs and long-standing injustices were about to be overthrown. As well, in a manner attained by few, even in the United Irish leadership, he had come to repose confidence in the excluded majority of the people. These weeks in the commencement of 1794, when he was on the threshold of new employment at Belfast, were marked by intense political soundings on his part. His awareness of popular discontent and his contempt for officialdom were clear. Hearing that Archibald Hamilton Rowan had been convicted in Dublin, he remarked: 'Pack'd Jury. Corrupt judge and sheriffs.' In his view, the government were

now digging a pit for themselves. Anticipating that the threatened French invasion of England would soon take place, he
wrote: 'The people are in that state of expectation of some great
event taking place in their country which will itself produce it.'[11]

Personal Concerns at Drumsluice

The journey to Drumsluice had at least two objectives. Margaret's
disposition provided her with constant reasons for complaint:
bad weather, lack of company, financial embarrassment, anxiety
about Thomas himself. For his part, Russell's own character had
a developed sense of obligation. Margaret's destitution and isolation worried him deeply. Later in the year, when he had settled into his work in Belfast, he suffered feelings of guilt that his
sister was 'in solitude and want, cut off from any friend whose
conversation could soothe or amuse her'. His own newly settled
condition made him feel uneasy at the contrast: 'I am here in
pleasing society, which at times only aggravates the recollection
of her situation.' More than once, she had obliquely hinted at
joining him in Belfast 'when you get the place you are in expectation of'. The second reason for going to Drumsluice was to
finalise details of Mary Ann Russell's marriage to William
Hamilton. During his visit, Russell procured her marriage
licence and saw to other arrangements for her. On 29 January,
the couple were married. Although the marriage was later attended by difficulties, Russell maintained a close link with both
Mary Ann and William Hamilton. Hamilton and he would collaborate in active political resistance during the years to come.[12]

Work at the Belfast Library

For his new appointment Russell did not lack advice. William
Sampson (with whom he began a satirical review, twice issued,
the *Lion of Old England*) and Martha McTier suggested a course
of lectures in chemistry. Russell's earlier reading fitted him for a
project of this kind and he appears to have outlined the content
of the lectures. However, by November 1794, when the political
situation had become even more complicated, he decided
against the proposal: 'I think the political state of the country
would prevent (the lectures) being beneficial at present, and that
is the only one which could possibly be of service'. Martha
McTier also suggested that he should edit a journal as a means
of earning extra money. This proposal was not taken up either:

perhaps he was too well aware of the difficulties being encountered by the *Northern Star* and the less than successful record of the Dublin *National Journal* in 1792.

Otherwise, he applied himself to the mundane duties of the library. There was management of loan and return of books. Those who wished to join the library were assisted. Robert McGee of Randalstown requested Bunting's music and a copy of the library's rules. The publication of Bunting's work needed supervision. Since March 1793, that proposal had been under way. Yet, by November 1794 the project was in difficulty and even in danger of being abandoned. Russell's journal for 4 November annotates a 'tedious' meeting of the committee. In regard to the 'Airs', Russell felt 'it may go well if managed'. On 6 November, he prepared a letter for Bunting to give the committee. This initiative succeeded, for Russell added: 'By means of the letter etc, etc, the Irish musick went down well and was agreed to be done.' The work was published in November 1797 when he had been in prison for almost a year.[13] There were other cultural pursuits through 1794. As already mentioned, Russell took lessons in music from Bunting and in Irish from Patrick Lynch. A perusal of surviving papers shows his record of loan and return of books, resolutions of the committee, scientific notes (perhaps for the projected lectures), and an incomplete monograph on sociopolitical matters, running to 140 pages. Among the works studied by him was *Histoire des Decouvertes par Divers Voyageurs* published at Berne in 1779 and Rousseau's *Nouvelle Héloise*.[14]

Bereavement and Other Personal Difficulties

Thomas Russell's ostensibly tranquil work at the library was accompanied by personal travail. On the day following his move to the Anne Street premises, he received at the Post Office a letter from India. Its black seal and the handwriting of Nancy Russell immediately gave him cause for alarm. Yet, it required more than one reading to comprehend that he had been bereaved of 'my dearest Ambrose, my earliest friend'. Captain Ambrose Russell had died suddenly at Madras on 3 July 1793. The delay in notification arose for a complicated reason: Tone, at whose Bodenstown house an earlier letter had been delivered, had opened the missive and had refrained from informing Russell until he had settled into the Belfast appointment.

The letter from Nancy Russell, presupposing an earlier one, left Thomas uncertain of the cause of his brother's death. As well as grief, he now had to endure uncertainty. He preserved a brave exterior, dining that night at William Simms' house. Then, a letter from John Russell gave details of Ambrose's death. It reported also the beneficence of army colleagues who had raised more than £10,000, an extraordinarily generous sum, for the support of Ambrose's widow. Despite his grief, Thomas Russell thought of Margaret and ventured to hope – vainly, as it turned out – that Nancy would look after her needy sister-in-law. Later, when Nancy Russell came to England, he travelled to meet her and, perhaps, endeavoured to discover her plans in regard to Margaret.[15]

Russell's grief was deep-set. Only when he set about writing to John did it reach the surface. Then, he 'burst into a passion of tears and wept aloud'. Some days later, he suffered what may have been a mental breakdown – 'The sound of my voice in weeping echoing in the room struck me as so like his (Ambrose) that it redoubled my anguish and tears … I was not well for some days, but my mind felt relieved after it than before.' The imaginative side of Russell's character is discernible when he writes: 'Often since that when musing, the whole of the funeral has been so lively in my imagination as to equal almost reality. I have look'd at him in the vigour of health and beauty and diffusing mirth around him. I saw the hand of death suddenly arrest him and traced its effects on that martial figure, the anguish of his widdow (sic) and the sorrow of his friends.'

Perhaps a sister's intuition caused Margaret to save him further pressure at this time. On 29 March, she told him not to worry about her or Julia, assuring him that there was no need to travel to Drumsluice. With a generous reciprocation of Russell's own concern she wrote: '… you say right, my dear brother, you have not many things to make you happy, you may depend on my doing all in my power to contribute to your ease and comfort.' Tone's letter, when it arrived, was brusque. It explained the delay in forwarding the original notification of Ambrose's death. In a gratuitous piece of advice Tone counselled 'assiduous employment (as) the most effective remedy for grief'. Then it was on to the problem of Arthur Tone, Theobald's youngest brother, who was playing truant from school in Dublin. Tone requested Russell's approach to the McCrackens to secure employment for Arthur on one of their merchant ships – 'a voyage or two may cure him'.[16]

Again, Eliza Goddard

Russell's personal misery was compounded by his difficulties in love. What he termed 'this love affair' recurred with double force. Uncertainty about Eliza's views regained sharper edge. His own words mirror his anguished introspection: '… I have had frequent occasion to remark the truth of Bacon's observation that the times when Love is most powerful is when we are either in great prosperity or adversity, at least the latter, for when my circumstances were most desperate, or any heavy affliction has befallen me, as the death of my ever lamented brother, it is then E. is uppermost in my thoughts.'[17] Months later, in June 1794, Eliza Goddard's memory was troubling him more than ever. On 10 June, he recalled that same date when he and Eliza had visited Cave Hill and had afterwards gone to a social club at the Exchange Rooms. Now, he proposed to retrace those steps, without Eliza, yet tormented by her loss. It was an exercise in nostalgia, a folly he termed it. However, the day was spent otherwise. Russell breakfasted with William Sinclair and visited the McTiers at Cabin Hill. At McTiers, he read an assessment of Anna Maria Bennett's *Ellen, Countess of Castle Howard*. The plot struck him so forcibly 'that all my former agonys revived'. Sinclair, thoughtfully, entertained him to dinner and brought him to view a farm outside the town. When eventually he came home, he still yearned for company. The journal discloses his confusion: ' On my return to my house forget my love, duty and virtue with a woman after having been during the evening conversing and arguing in support of Christianity against Deism.' Once again, his self-criticism is unrestrained: 'Such is man – or at least such am I – so vicious, so imperfect, with wishes and desires for virtue and a firm belief in revelation and yet relapsing into vice on the slightest temptation. I do not improve.' Towards the end of June, Russell penned another tortured memorandum on whether Eliza loved him or not. This oscillation on closely personal matters remains a puzzle in one who was direct and forthcoming in other areas of life.[18]

In the middle of 1794 a coalescence of bereavement, unrequited love and political disillusion may have pushed Russell towards

disorganisation in his everyday life. His friends were loyal as
ever. William Drennan complained to Martha McTier about the
lack of generosity by the Catholic leaders towards one of their
most loyal supporters. He suggested that she should write an
anonymous letter to John Keogh in regard to that fact. Dr
McDonnell, the McCrackens, the Simms and William Sinclair
maintained their hospitality. There are indications that Russell's
state of mind worried some of them. John Russell, writing from
London, put it bluntly: '... by the way, William Sampson says
you are very idle.' One wonders whose influence brought about
the offer of a militia ensigncy (with a lieutenantcy to follow) by a
Lieutenant Fortescue during May 1794. The offer was refused by
Russell on the grounds that it would interfere with his literary
pursuits. It is possible he had in mind the political work which
would cease were he once again in military employ. From
London, John Russell suggested that Thomas's ready pen and
literary culture fitted him for parliamentary reporting to one of
the newspapers. John, whose own financial position was delicate at best, quipped that the only difficulty lay in Thomas's
handwriting, so unclear that the compositors would be unable
to discipher it. There was another, less than discreet, enquiry in
the same letter: 'Does your cheek ever come in contact with a
woman's?' John Russell concludes with an enigmatic reference:
'I am glad to know you are so reform'd. I'm told you never med-
dle with the sex – you have that great model Pitt in your eye.'[19]

Brief visit to Dublin via Drumsluice

Although Margaret Russell's tribulations did not bulk large in
March or April 1794, they reappeared during the summer in
several letters to Belfast. Along with requests for money and renewed complaints about her brother's infrequent visits to
Drumsluice, she enquired: 'How are you getting on with your
old woman and do you like the situation you are in?'
Presumably, the 'old woman' was Judy Clarke, the housekeeper
at Russell's house. He was himself scolded for not sending 'the
ribbon as I bid you'. As well, Margaret requested two issues of
The Lancet for a local doctor who had lost his own copies. In the
background of all these letters is Margaret's desire to live with
her brother in Belfast.[20]

Perhaps it was to please Margaret and to visit the ailing Julia
that Russell took the roundabout itinerary to Dublin in early

August. His journal illustrates the strange mixture of penury yet near-aristocratic ways so much his style of life. The journey brought him through Hillsborough, Tandragee, Armagh, Aughnacloy, Augher and Clogher. Sometimes he rode, mostly he walked. At Hillsborough, he met Vesey Knox, son of Lord Northland, his earlier patron at Dungannon. The first evening of the journey was spent in Hillsborough 'in making some bad verses … and reading a bad novel'. In the morning, he delayed some hours to see Eliza Goddard who, he understood, had arrived at the town. Disappointed, he travelled on to Drumsluice. While there, he accompanied the Reverend Stack to Devenish Island on Lough Erne. His descriptions of colour, tint and atmosphere reach poetic heights at times. The reader will notice developed literary culture in a casual reference to an earlier debate with the polymath, Richard Kirwan, over John Dryden's phrase 'weedy pool'. Now, wrote Thomas Russell, 'if he (Kirwan) saw the rushes at Lough Earn (sic), he would change his opinion.'[21]

In Dublin, Russell joined Tone. Both men dined with William Drennan who informed them that the Catholics had formed a club 'to revive their convention connections'. Russell and Tone visited the Dublin United Irishmen, although Drennan wryly commented: '… it is probable that they will never attend or be of use, as Tone follows, voluntarily or perforce, every turn of the Catholic mind.' Drennan may not have fully grasped the extent of Russell's involvement in the changes taking place in the northern United Irish Society. A Jacobin society, composed mainly of artisans and working men, had already been inaugurated. Although Russell's name does not figure in a report to the British Home Office, it is likely that he had contacts with that society. His availibility to the Mudler's Club, mentioned later by James Hope, and his contacts with people outside Belfast's middle class, render it likely that in the closing months of 1794 he had dealings with the Jacobin society. As well, the United Irish Society in Belfast was itself in process of change. Instead of merchants and professional men, others of less wealth and prominence began to exercise influence within it. Russell noted that 'the young men are far more violent than the others'. One unnamed interlocutor of Russell's mentioned that this new strand were suspicious even of the *Northern Star* group, headed by Samuel Neilson. It was felt the latter were 'not ready enough for the field'. Russell seemed pleased that these younger radicals approved of him – 'They think … he (Russell) would be ready to act'. In his view, this was 'a great compliment as so few are counted'.[22]

Visit to Gracehill Moravian community

From 1759, there had been a settlement of Moravians at Ballykennedy, near Ballymena. Known as the Gracehill settlement, it comprised some five hundred people. Gracehill was a self-supporting community with its own system of trade and credit, its schools and its marriage conventions. With Robert McGee, a fellow United Irishman, Russell visited Ballykennedy on 9 October 1794. He was suficiently impressed by the community to write a detailed memoir for the journal and, some weeks later, to forward 'the Moravian papers' to Whitley Stokes at Trinity College. The journal memoir describes the physical layout of Ballykennedy: its dwellings, chapel, warehouse and parks. Clearly, Russell was favourably impressed by the sense of order and well-being in the community. He sympathetically examines the marriage-by-arrangement convention prevalent at Ballykennedy. An interesting feature is that Russell's attachment to Christianity in its scriptural and ecclesiastical forms went much further than his colleagues, many of whom professed the free ranging speculation of Deism. The sporadic atheism of the French revolution repelled him, although its political principles stood close to his own. Given his religious stance, it is not surprising that Russell's memoir on Gracehill is full of respect for its attempt to build a community around justice and simplicity.[23]

A troubled end to 1794

As 1794 drew to a close, Russell's personal circumstances were far from happy. Despite his commitment to the library and his active political work with the United Irishmen, there remained an unresolved complication to his personal life. Improved circumstances in regard to work, to salary and lodging, an effortless popularity among those who knew him, did not assuage a deeper unhappiness. On 3 November 1794, he recommended a personal diary which, he hoped, would in old age renovate 'the scores and ideas of youth' and, perhaps, show 'a progression in virtue'. Since Russell already kept an intermittent journal, one concludes that this was an attempt to rally by one whose morale was flagging. The opening lines are unpromising: 'My situation is not at present pleasing and (I) can see no effort of mine that can better it.' Ambrose's death, the failing marriage of Mary Ann, Margaret's penury, all worried him. So did his own debts which left 'neither money nor quiet'. Added to these was an extreme confusion about personal relations with women. The attachment of Mary Ann McCracken, patent to subsequent historians, does not appear to have crossed his mind. Eliza Goddard still attracted him, virtually to the point of obsession: 'The emotion I feel when I see her or even hear her name mentioned is so great that I doubt at times whether I would be justify'd in attempting to marry any other.' Here was Russell's dilemma. There was a possibility of marrying another – possibly a sister of Dr McDonnell's wife, Eliza, and of William Sampson's wife, Grace: 'a certain lady with a competent fortune, which would relieve me from the misery I feel on account of my sister rather than myself'. A friendship between Russell and Mary Simms (sister of Robert and William) had also developed at this time.[24]

Russell's less than admirable remark shows his desperation and that peculiar inability to make a choice, to declare an interest, which would ultimately cost him the possibility of a life with either Eliza Goddard or that 'certain lady' to whom he referred. However, the remark also requires the balance of his further hope 'that I should be kind and indulgent to my wife and endeavour to make her happy'. Eliza's attraction was too strong for any other possibility, even though at this stage Russell probably knew that their union could not eventuate. Her father, John Goddard, a bully and a loud-mouthed servant of government, would not allow her to marry a known democrat like Thomas Russell. Unfortunately, after the manner of the time, Eliza's own views are not recorded. Russell, nonetheless, continued to face his self-created dilemma. He argued thus: if he married some one else he could perhaps conceal, and in time overcome, his attachment to Eliza. On the other hand, he felt bound by protestations made to Eliza which might lead her to think he would not marry any other: 'Am I not bound in honour to take care that whatever I might suffer she shall not be unhappy?' The oscillation perdured: '… I fluctuate and ballance (*sic*) and dream, and the prime of my life passes away.' Around this time Russell's pocket books show casual drawings or jottings clearly related to Eliza. And, in his journal, the self-addressed question remains: 'What can or what shall I do?'[25]

Such reflections did not take away Russell's confusion. Even in December, he behaved like a moon-struck youth when in Eliza's presence. Meeting her unexpectedly at a social gathering, he behaved with an agitation visible to all: 'I several times tried to turn about and my courage fail'd me ... I was debating what to do, whether to speak to her or say nothing, and I believe only from what Mrs Montgomery had say'd to me I would have gone.' Although friends might exhort him to marry, although Margaret would write in friendly terms about his settling down, he was in no state, either then or later, really to contemplate marriage with anyone other than Eliza Goddard. There are some indications that the relationship was less than realistic. Russell showed petulant annoyance, perhaps due to jealousy, when he observed Eliza behave with what he deemed less than due gravity. Nor did his friends encourage his infatuation. In the dark month of November 1794, he posed the rhetorical question: '... have I not been told that her understanding is not good, that she never could be qualified to be a companion to me?' When pressed, Martha McTier, who knew both Eliza Goddard and Thomas Russell, would not go beyond some non-committal advice. Perhaps she knew more than she wished to say. In January 1795, Mrs McTier informed her brother that Eliza had met 'a sensible, well behaved young man of 22 and said to have a fortune of £6,000 independent of his father'. The 'young man' was a Captain Kingston whom by September 1795 Eliza had married. With her husband, she went to Dublin where he was stationed. Although Russell did not meet her again, he never forgot this woman whom no one replaced in his affections.[26]

CHAPTER SEVEN

Reorganisation in the North:

'The Man from God knows where' (1794-1796)

Into our townlan', on a night of snow
rode a man from God knows where;
none of us bade him stay or go,
nor deemed him friend, nor damned him foe,
but we stabled his big roan mare;
for in our townlan' we're decent folk,
and if he didn't speak, why none of us spoke,
and we sat till the fire burned low.

On Friday, 23 May 1794, the United Irish Society in Dublin was severely hit by government action. Its premises at Tailors' Hall were raided and, on the instigation of the informer Thomas Collins, its papers seized. As well, the society was officially suppressed. For some months, the fortunes of the Dublin United Irishmen had been at an extremely low point. The 1793 convention Act had already deterred less committed members who reverted either to Whig politics or, in some cases, to fervid loyalism. The Convention Act, facilitated by the Whig opposition, was designed to prevent extra-parliamentary representative gatherings such as the Catholic Convention. Since that time, a climate of menace had prevailed which induced in men of property a new caution. The tribulations of William Drennan and Archibald Hamilton Rowan alarmed all but the most resolute core of the society. Even Tone concentrated his activities elsewhere. When the Reverend William Jackson, a French emissary, was arrested in late April 1794 and it seemed that his companion John Cockaine might testify for the Crown, Tone was forced to make an 'honourable compromise' with government. The society was, therefore, placed in new jeopardy by accelerating events. After its suppression, the initiative in Dublin passed to smaller, more radical groups among Dublin's artisans and to Defender activities which had by now moved to the capital. As to the United Irish society in the city, the first bite of repression seemed to intimidate the somewhat histrionic leadership although the organisation revived later under more competent direction.

The Belfast United Irishmen were less directly touched by the decree of 23 May. Belfast had, indeed, suffered from military repression during 1793 and would again experience concerted military violence in 1797. Yet, the structure of the society in Belfast rendered it more flexible than its Dublin counterpart. Its cellular organisation differed from the top-heavy Dublin society. The popular base of the Belfast society made it less amenable to suppression by an increasingly nervous government. For some time, tradespeople, small farmers, shopkeepers and workmen had greater access to the Belfast clubs than was the case in Dublin. An informant of Dublin Castle gibed at the absence of 'gentlemen of rank or fortune' in the Belfast clubs and the activity of 'a few Belfast Pedlars'. Alongside this honeycombed structure was the Jacobin Club headed by Russell's friend, Rowley Osborne and composed, at least according to Martha McTier, of artisans and mechanics.[1]

The threat of governmental oppression and the acquiescence of the parliamentary opposition had driven many, including Thomas Russell, to view French intervention in Ireland as necessary although undesirable. In regard to this distinction of necessity and desirability, Tone's conversations with the Reverend William Jackson are revealing. The conditions laid down by Tone for any proposed French intervention demonstrate his unwillingness to substitute one set of political masters for another. Nevertheless, by the end of 1794 things had changed yet again. The unwillingness of the government at College Green to envisage reform was more than obvious. As well, the fall of Robespierre with an ensuing respite, albeit temporary, in civil terror and religious persecution, mitigated the hesitations felt by many people about dealing with the French regime. Daily, the ambit of political choices was being restricted. Yet, if French intervention were to be envisaged, it would have to be on a more radical proposal than either parliamentary reform or religious freedom. For these objectives the French were unlikely to trouble themselves.

Hence, the political context of late 1794 and early 1975 indicated new, more radical strategies. The recall in March 1795 of Fitz-william, a Lord Lieutenant who mistrusted John Fitzgibbon's corrupt regime and favoured Catholic relief, drove rank and file Catholics towards extra-constitutional means of redress. In the north, popular feeling was as described in Russell's journal through 1794. In particular, his reference to the younger men, suspicious that their elders were less than 'ready for the field', hints at a developing revolutionary attitude. The original United Irishmen were outflanked by a thrust of which they knew little. The approbation of Thomas Russell, expressed by these younger men, is significant in itself.

What has been termed Russell's personal 'spiral of despair' emerges from his journal at the end of 1794. Yet, early in 1795 he participated in scientific discussions with Dr McDonnell on the invention of the telegraph and improvements in the tanning industry. His knowledge of the French National Convention enabled him to detail the attainments of chemists who were deputies to the convention – Guyton de Morveau, Berthollet, and Four-croy.[2] It is also notable that personal tribulations did not prevent Russell's involvement in reorganisation of the northern United Irishmen. Perhaps Tone's vigorous nostrum about employment being the best remedy for grief had had its effect! Although the journal ceases from spring 1795, there are other indications of Russell's activity at this time. Such activity lay along three axes: internal strengthening of the United Irishmen; forging links with the Defenders, particularly in Ulster and north Leinster; literary work, only a portion of which has survived in an identifiable way.

Re-Organisation in Ulster, 1794-6

When, in 1798, William McNeven attempted to trace the development of the United Irishmen, he solicited information from Thomas Russell on the re-organisation of Antrim and Down. While the special circumstances of McNeven's deposition to a parliamentary committee should be kept in mind, his request is an indication of Russell's part in that re-organisation. Russell's own answer bears the circumspection to be expected from one who was himself a prisoner, whose papers had been confiscated, and whose correspondence might well be used against him. He confirms that the northern society's oath was composed early in the winter of 1794-5. Whereas in 1791 Tone and Russell had op-

posed the requirement of an oath in Dublin, by 1794 the threat of
governmental repression made it imperative that the northern
clubs be secret and oath-bound. When Russell indicated that he
was not 'positive as to the day' the test or oath was composed,
he may be taken at once to imply his own part in it and yet to re-
frain from self-incrimination with the Dublin Castle authorities.
Russell confirmed to McNeven that a new constitution for the
United Irishmen was accepted by the existing clubs on 24 May
1795. Henceforth, leadership in the reorganised society would
arise by elective delegation from the local clubs. Local societies
would depute their representatives to baronial committees
which, in turn, would provide the county leaders. In the same
upward delegation, county leadership would elect provincial
directories. According to Russell's letter to McNeven, the first
county committee to be set up was for Antrim. By 26 or 27 June
1795, the Down county committee had been established. An
Ulster provincial committee, representing a putative 8,000 members in Antrim, Down, Tyrone and Armagh, was set up in August
1795.[3]

This more radical direction and numerical expansion of the
United Irishmen was set in the midst of widespread uncertainty.
With typical arrogance, the government had threatened that the
country would not know peace 'until Belfast is in ashes'.
Although many Catholics were now United Irishmen, including
John Sweetman, Charles Teeling and Richard McCormick, it remained unclear how the Catholic leadership as a whole would
act. The Catholic hierarchy was still eager to show 'loyalty' to
the crown. At the far end of that spectrum were the Catholic
aristocrats, deeply committed to a social order which left them
securely in place. Russell, Tone, Neilson and Drennan were only
too well aware of how easily the Catholic spokespeople could be
'bribed or cajoled into docility'.[4]

There was, however, a very real dilemma for the Catholics. With
the advent of Fitzwilliam as viceroy, there was much hope in
early 1795 that John Fitzgibbon's administration and the penal
laws against Catholics were coming to an end. This hope was
dashed by the recall of Fitzwilliam when the extent of government cynicism was partially revealed. Fitzwilliam wondered if
it was all an incitement of revolt to facilitate Pitt's desire for uniting the Irish and English parliaments. The dismissed viceroy

asked: 'Will a rebellion tend to further that end? … are the means risked such as are justifiable? or such as any man would wish to risk?' Fitzwilliam's recall united Catholics and Dissenters in a common dismay. A town meeting in Belfast deplored the viceroy's abrupt recall and spoke of his character as 'evidently adapted … to make a whole people satisfied, united and happy'. The Belfast meeting designated the occasion of his departure 'a day of national mourning'. And so it was deemed also in Dublin. Thus, in March 1795, disaffection from government policy was shared by all who desired reform, both Catholics and Protestants. The unresolved question was how that disaffection and uncertainty would be channelled.[5]

Meanwhile, United Irish activity intensified in the north. The induction of Henry Joy McCracken to the tenth Belfast society of the United Irishmen gives a clue to the rapid spread of the organisation. About this time, there were sixteen societies in Belfast alone, while in a twenty mile radius of the town there were approximately five thousand members. By 1796, there were thirty eight societies or clubs of United Irishmen in Belfast. Despite his founding role from 1791, Russell took the new oath from James O'Farrell of Larne. The sense of danger which now applied may be gleaned from an exchange between Mary Ann McCracken, her brother Henry Joy, and Thomas Russell. Mary Ann had reminded her brother that, in case of failure, he and Russell would lose their lives. Henry Joy McCracken is reputed to have answered that in any case he and Russell would be the first to fall and Russell is said to have added: 'of what consequence our lives or the lives of a few individuals, compared to the liberty and happiness of Ireland?'[6]

To use Drennan's term, 'mole-work' was under way in Belfast. Whereas Drennan believed Russell was working for the Catholic interest, in reality it was somewhat different. The 'mole-work' was reorganisation of the United Irishmen in Antrim, Down, and further afield. In this, Russell was 'the crucial link between (the new membership) and the original United Irish leaders'. His earlier contacts with people of no property, his easy conversation with those different from him in education and social status, would have proved useful to the highest degree. Besides, he appears to have been trusted by men such as James Hope and those younger men who had been reported as anxious 'to take the field'. A hostile informant to Dublin Castle wrote that 'a Thomas Russell who was formerly an officer in the army and has resided here for some time past corrupting the minds of the lower orders of the people, is said to be now near Sligo, no doubt promoting Union among Irishmen. It has long been a matter of astonishment to the well disposed in this place that their (*sic*) has not been some measure taken by Government or the Magistrates to effectively check this growing evil.' At the beginning of May 1795, a William Johnston wrote to the authorities about a club or society in which 'A Man of the Name of Russell' was most forward.[7]

According to R. R. Madden, in these years of reorganisation Russell was able to combine his library duties with journeys through Antrim, Down, Tyrone and, even, Donegal. On such excursions he set up new cells and inducted new members. Alongside James Hope and Henry Joy McCracken, he is reputed to have undertaken extension work with outstanding success among Presbyterians. A combination of graciousness and flexibility enabled him to overcome sectarian exclusiveness in many quarters. James Morgan, another sympathetic chronicler of Russell's life, details an instance of his ability to cut through petty exclusions. A party of republicans, amongst whom was James Hope, were exhorted by Belfast United Irishmen to join the society. A problem arose when these men objected to an oath. Hope argued that the real test was one's word, even without the solemnity of an oath. Thomas Russell is said to have resolved the dispute in favour of Hope and his companions from Templepatrick. Thus were gained for the society some of its ablest combatants in the rising of 1798.[8]

After its reorganisation, the United Irish Society quickly became 'a mass-based secret society'. Its members were now from diverse sectors of the economic scale. To an extraordinary degree, it also remained a secret society. There were informers and hostile observers, but these had to rely on hearsay. Whenever there was treachery or breach of secrecy, it came, in the main, from a small section of the leaders, not from rank and file members. Despite its 'mass base', the society had a strong central leadership – variously termed a 'grand committee', a 'committee of public welfare', a 'committee of elders' – which approved new societies, oversaw general organisation, and decided on policy issues. The central committee financed and co-ordinated the emissaries who extended the United Irish system throughout the country areas. When the time came for negotiation with the French, the same central committee, in collaboration with the Dublin leaders, exercised a supervisory role. The tradition enshrined in Florence Wilson's 'Man From God-Knows-Where' roots in Thomas Russell's travels through the north 'to examine the societies and confirm them in their republican career'. According to the informer, John Smith, such an emissary would be 'a man of courage and address (who) frequents no public inns (but) goes from the house of one delegate to the house of another.' By 1796, this system of extension had resulted not only in thirty-eight clubs in Belfast but also many others throughout Down, Armagh, Tyrone, Fermanagh and Donegal.[9]

Through the summer of 1795, the United Irishmen in Ulster continued their reorganisation. With membership increasing across the province, there were clubs at Ballymena, Antrim, Larne, Newry, Armagh, Lurgan and Moira. In north Leinster and in Connacht, even in Cork city, new clubs were in process of consolidation. The Jacobin society in Belfast, headed by Rowley Osborne and Samuel Kennedy, would now seem to have merged with the United Irishmen. In other words, the reorganised society of United Irishmen was fast becoming a potent vehicle for political and social change by the dispossessed. In the north, communication between the central committee and the newly burgeoning clubs was maintained through two channels : emissaries from Belfast and delegate conventions at the level of barony, county and province. Within the Belfast directory, long standing members such as Russell, Neilson, the McCabes and Henry Haslett seem to have set the tenor and framed the policy of the renewed society.

A provincial meeting was held on 31 July 1795 about which, despite every attempt at secrecy, a report was sent to Dublin Castle by William Johnston. At the provincial meeting it was resolved 'to promote new societies in the most secret manner'. The informer also mentions a resolution for a general meeting of delegates from the whole country. It is interesting that Johnston, anxious to maximise the import of his information, did not mention anything about emissaries to France. With some realism and not a little hostility, he observes that 'if France does not in-

vade the country, these rebels never dare attempt hostilities'.[10]
On the whole, documentary evidence about the United Irishmen
at this period is scarce. Apart from later testimonies by Tone,
Sampson, Steele Dickson, Addis Emmet and McNeven, evidence is limited to handbills, posters and, signally, the information sent to Dublin Castle by agents or informers. Russell may
now have been too busy to continue his journal, despite his resolution in late 1794. Or else journals for 1795 and following have
not survived.

The testimony of informers such as Andrew McNevin, John
Smith and James McGucken, as well as the examination of people arrested by government forces, afford some picture of
United Irish activity during the years from 1795 to 1797. From
the examination of John Mitchell, a weaver from Ballynashee,
Co Antrim, it appears that even in 1794 local clubs spoke of an
imminent uprising with the help of French troops and arma-
ments. Mitchell's deposition claims that 'James Neilson, John
McCabe, Thomas Russell, Henry Haslett, William Sinclair are
members of the Head Committee at Belfast'. An inaccuracy
about the names of Neilson and McCabe may point up Mitchell's
own distance from the centre of things. Yet, his further remark is
significant – these men were 'frequently mentioned as being so,
at the meetings aforesaid'.[11]

Despite such indications of increased radical activity, it would
be premature to interpret these as a policy for the overthrow of
the state with French help. Even in April 1795, notwithstanding
the disillusion of many Catholics and Presbyterians, 'a republic
assisted by the French was by no means the agreed programme
of the disparate collection of people now forming under the re-
juvenated United Irish banner'. The oath or test proposed in the
reorganised society did not speak of a republic but rather of 'an
equal, full and adequate representation of all the people of
Ireland'. The question of seeking French help had arisen in Dublin
but, as noticed in Tone's discussion with the Reverend Jackson,
had remained unresolved. Thus, it is difficult to estimate the
conversation between Tone, Russell and Thomas Addis Emmet
near Rathfarnham in April or May 1795. Tone revealed his plan
to go to America and, thence, to France in pursuit of French
help. To this idea both Russell and Emmet reacted favourably,
as did John Keogh and Richard McCormick when they were in-

formed. Nevertheless, it would be far-fetched to view this conversation on the road from Emmet's home as somehow the commission of an embassy to France. Yet, the idea was under discussion and when Russell arrived back in Belfast he seems to have mentioned Tone's proposal to an approving Directory.[12]

Tone's Emigration. McArt's Fort

Tone's decision to emigrate was carried through in May 1795 when he, with Matilda and their children, set out for Belfast, en route to America. Doubtless, he had in mind a French mission; yet, he had also been informed that he faced imprisonment if he remained in the country. Arriving in Belfast on 21 May, the Tones were profusely welcomed. Russell and his friends entertained them in a round of visits and excursions. On arrival in America, Tone recorded his thanks for that kindness 'when I so much needed it'. It was a visit, wrote Tone, which 'I shall remember while I have life with sentiments of warmest gratitude'. There were, indeed, many acts of great kindness during that visit: the subscription of £1,500 taken up for the family; the final entertainment organised at the McCrackens on 12 June; the medicine chest prepared by Dr McDonnell. Yet it is the trip to McArt's fort on the summit of Cave Hill which has interested students of Tone and his work. There, with Russell, Neilson, Simms and McCracken, Tone entered a pact 'never to desist in our efforts until we had subverted the authority of England over our country and asserted our independence'.

Russell, too, enjoyed these weeks. Margaret could so forget her own worries as to write: 'It gives me great pleasure to hear that you are well and so happy in the company of your friend.' In high good humour Russell told his brother in London that, due to Tone's presence, for three weeks past there had been 'no lack of whiskey, claret and burgundy'. In February 1796, when depressed and solitary in Paris, Tone would revive this kind of memory – 'What would I have given to have had P. P. with me! – Indeed we would have discussed another Bottle of the Burgundy, or ... some two or three. ... How he would enjoy France, not excepting even her wines!' The hospitality in Belfast was also observed by hostile eyes. Rowland O'Connor urged Dublin Castle to confiscate Russell's and Tone's papers. Despite his accuracy in noting the details of Tone's stay, including visits to 'different parts of the coast and taking plans of it', O'Connor wrongly predicted that Russell would accompany Tone to France. Rowland O'Connor's personal hostility to Russell emerges in his allusion to 'one Russell who formerly had been in the army and who is one of the most violent Democrats on the face of the earth'. Perhaps to underline his own loyalism, O'Connor concluded with the observation that 'the generality of people here wish and are very ripe for a Revolution'.[13]

To claim that there was something like a formal commission of Tone as emissary to France would be an exaggeration. Doubtless, his visit to Belfast was not merely the parting of friends. Political matters would have been examined and proposals made. The state of the United Irish reorganisation in the north would have been noted. The emerging contacts with Defenders in Ulster, Connacht and north Leinster would have been discussed. As to a mission for French help in effecting social and political change, perhaps Marianne Elliott's observation is most apposite: Tone's Belfast sojourn solemnised an informal engagement while 'the influence and encouragement of friends (endowed) his move (to America) with a retrospective sense of national mission'.[14]

United Irishmen and the Defenders

Recent studies in social and political history show that Defenderism was a more complex social phenomenon than hitherto supposed by academic historians. Defenders were not simply rural brawlers who perpetrated mindless 'outrages'. As its name suggests, 'Defenderism' was reactive to land expropriation during the seventeenth-century plantations. At its height, Defenderism was a bulwark against sectarian attacks by Orangemen to whom any sign of Catholic improvement was a pretext for mayhem and even muder. As well, there were some Protestants among the Defenders. It can be argued that, at least in part, Defenderism was a form of resistance by the dispossessed who were declared non-citizens by government policy and made to feel aliens in their own land. While there were many outbreaks of agrarian protest in the late eighteenth century, the most active forms of Defenderism occurred where landlords' arrogance, magistrates' partiality and, ultimately, Orange harassment were at their height. Defender groups in the mid 1790s were particularly energetic in Armagh, Tyrone, Monaghan, Cavan, Louth and those parts of Down where the fiercely anti-Catholic Lord Hillsborough owned extensive lands. Defenderism was also widespread in Leitrim, Roscommon and Galway.[15]

In the course of the years 1790-95, Defenderism steadily adopted more revolutionary political objectives. A rudimentary political and economic programme replaced what had been haphazard expression of resentment. If there had been sectarian overtones to Defender oaths and promises, these began to give way to the more comprehensive ideas deriving from France, Belfast and Dublin. From Armagh, a network of Defender lodges spread across the north-east, remaining in contact with each other through emissaries and agents. Thus, by 1794 'Defenderism had ceased to be merely a spontaneous outburst of Catholic peasant resentment and had begun to assume a truly revolutionary character.'

The Dublin administration was aware of the change. In particular, government feared any link-up between Catholic and Protestant radicals. In July 1795, Lord Camden sent the Duke of Portland a memorandum on the Defenders, including their oaths and catechisms. Thereafter, a campaign of repression, brutal and extra-legal, was initiated by Lord Carhampton with the connivance of both Camden and Portland. Those suspected of Defender sympathies were flogged, sent to the fleet or, on many occasions, murdered. The viceroy's toleration of the 'pacification' of Connacht by these means was commended by Portland as 'perfectly just, manly and liberal'. In March 1796, the Insurrection Act conferred a virtual *carte blanche* for the severest repression in the future and a validation of what had taken place. Magistrates received power 'of seizing, imprisoning and sending on board the fleet without trial anyone found at unlawful assemblies or acting so as to threaten the public tranquillity'. The sectarian intent of these measures is disclosed by the deposition of an Armagh magistrate, Nathaniel Alexander: in the aftermath of Orange attacks on Catholic homes in late 1796, this magistrate reported that the Catholics were the agressors having burned their own homes because of arrears in rent. Earlier, in March 1796, amid reports that Orangemen planned to destroy in Belfast all 'who had promoted the Union of Irishmen', General Nugent brusquely rebuffed local residents who offered their services in defending the town.[16]

In circumstances such as these, the United Irishmen and the Defenders could discern common ground. Given the avowedly non-sectarian charter of the United Irishmen and the suspicion

by some of them that Catholics remained committed to monarchy, this coalition may appear surprising. Yet common ground
was there: opposition to a now ferocious regime, desire for radical change, openness to French help under certain conditions. By
1795, United Irish lawyers were acting for Defenders accused
before the courts. Likewise, funds were set aside by the United
Irish directory to prosecute magistrates whose blatant sectarianism could be proved.

It has been suggested that in 1795 contacts between the United
Irishmen and Defenders had taken place in Louth, with Fr James
O'Coigly representing the Defenders. From these contacts may
have emerged the later agreement by which members of either
group were recognised as members of the other. Samuel
M'Skimmin, not an altogether reliable commentator, claims that
at the start of 1796 Defenders arrived in Belfast from Dublin 'for
the purpose of promoting an amicable arrangement between
that body and the United Irishmen'. As a result, if M'Skimmin is
to be credited, the Defenders were remodelled and a coalition
with the United Irishmen effected. M'Skimmin adds his own
comment that the United Irishmen thereby benefited since 'the
whole peasantry of Ireland (were) Roman Catholics' and ten
thousand of the army were 'sworn defenders'.[17]

By the end of 1795, recruitment of Defenders into the ranks of
the United Irishmen would seem to have been a matter of policy
for the Belfast directory. The 'plan of union', as James Hope
termed it, was conceived by Samuel Neilson and Charles
Teeling, a Catholic merchant of Lisburn. It is probable that
Teeling, along with his son, Luke Teeling, John Magennis and
Alexander Lowry (all United Irishmen) were the links with de-
fenders in the north, amongst whom they were already well
known. Then there was Fr James O'Coigly, recently back from
France and operative in the neighbourhood of Dundalk. Much
of the liaison was done by James Hope and William Putnam
McCabe, a friend of Russell and son of Thomas McCabe. In
Monaghan, Cavan, Armagh, Leitrim and Fermanagh, they
worked effectively to amalgamate the Defenders with the
United Irishmen. Similar work was done by the Belfast solicitor,
Daniel Shanahan, and the tailor, Joseph Cuthbert, who attempt-
ed to enlist militia personnel to the society at Blaris camp, near
Belfast. An informer – perhaps exaggerating the importance of

his communication to Dublin Castle – claimed, in summer 1796, that 'there had been a junction between the leaders of the United Irishmen and the Defenders ... the army was with them ... messengers had been sent to Connaught (*sic*) ... if they could organise the Defenders they could defy government ... there was a complete union between the Defenders and the United Irishmen'.[18]

In this way, the numerical strength of the United Irishmen increased dramatically. At its height, the nominal membership of the society in Ulster reached 100,000. In the months between April and September 1796, the official membership for Antrim had sprung from 5,000 to 12,000. Nor should it be forgotten that Freemason lodges throughout the north provided numerous members of the society at this time. These developments were not without difficulties. The organisation of such numbers posed a problem, mitigated to an extent by the training expertise of some deserters from the militia. Another problem, deemed to have been recognised by Russell himself, was the likelihood of uncoordinated incidents which might incur military repression before preparations had been laid for any general uprising. It has been argued by Charles Dickson that Russell, Simms and the senior United Irish leadership repeatedly opposed attempts to wreak vengeance on members who either informed or, as members of juries, co-operated in the committal of fellow United Irishmen.[19]

The claim by Kevin Whelan that the merger with the Defenders was 'orchestrated and implemented' by Samuel Neilson, Thomas Russell, Henry Joy McCracken, James Hope, James O'Coigly, William Putnam McCabe and Charles Teeling, is difficult to document further. Whelan is surely correct in claiming that the merger created 'the great establishment nightmare of the eighteenth century – the Jacobinising of the secret societies'. The new factor was that the various secret societies were now 'joined to an effective national programme for sweeping political change'. When, in Florence Wilson's poem, Russell is depicted as organising in Co Down during the winter of 1795, this may recreate a tradition of his co-ordination of new recruits to the United Irishmen. Behind the activities of Fr O'Coigly, Charles Teeling, John Magennis and Bernard Coile, who linked Defenders and United Irishmen, was the influential figure of

Thomas Russell. Louis Cullen can argue: 'Coigly and Russell superintended the creation of radical popular organisation beyond Belfast in the Catholic hinterland of Newry, in more distant parts of Antrim and, more unevenly, in less promising territory in Derry, Tyrone and Fermanagh'.[20]

In June 1796, the indefatigably hostile Captain Andrew McNevin was sounding the alarm. According to McNevin, the United Irishmen were now 'ready for a call, they are expecting arms and ammunition in the … bay'. McNevin warned that Russell 'who was an officer in the 64th' was at 'the head of these deluded people … and … now conducts all their plans'. Russell's own view was contrary to McNevin's. In a letter to the *Evening Post* , he dismissed the trumpeting of magistrates and informers as so much special pleading. He downplayed the reports of people 'who have a natural antipathy to those who wish for a reform of Parliament … those petty despots … (who convert) every object into plots, invasions, insurrections and devaluation of property'.[21] On the linkage of Defenders and United Irishmen he does not comment. It should again be noted that his espousal of the Catholic cause was more a commitment to the fundamental rights of all Irish people than any predilection for the church as a clerical institution. For others in the United Irish leadership, the matter was more complex. As already noted, even the instigator of 'the plan of union' with the Defenders, Samuel Neilson, considered the Catholics as 'bigots to monarchy', although he believed there were many enlightened men and true patriots among them. As to the Defenders, Neilson believed that with proper organisation 'they could give very valuable service to the Cause'.[22]

Military organisation in Antrim and Down

Local groups of United Irishmen eluded the strictures of the Convention Act by meeting as book clubs. This was the case at Doagh: one recalls the mention of the club in Russell's journal for July 1793. Documentation was minimal. Hence, in regard to militarisation of the United Irishmen evidence comes from hostile sources: informers and government reports. Much of the information came to Dublin Castle from Andrew McNevin, John Bird, William Johnston and Rowland O'Connor. They stress the expectation of French help by the populace: 'The generality of people here wish and are very ripe for a revolution.' (O'Connor)

The hoped-for invasion would bring not only personnel but also arms and ammunition. In the meantime, people improvised with make-shift pikes and small arms.

The indications are that through 1796 military organisation did progress. Local clubs or societies elected sergeants; three societies elected a captain; ten captains elected a colonel. In Belfast, a military committee co-ordinated the surrounding areas and appointed generals for each county. It would seem that in summer 1796 Thomas Russell was appointed general for County Down. The whole procedure was not without difficulty. In Belfast, some people resented military discipline in what had hitherto been a political organisation. According to the informer Newell, a section believed that 'discipline is not necessary – that they need only give one fire and rush out with the bayonet'. Others were afraid of military discipline as premature because 'it would be attended with the utmost danger, for there is nothing but a pretext wanting to declare us out of the King's peace'. According to a United Irish report for 1796, '... a few counties in Ulster would be unable by force of arms to accomplish an object of such magnitude until our principles are more generally known and better understood'. This hesitation may reflect differences in mentalities between the Dublin and the Belfast leaderships. Did Russell's military experience urge caution? Or was he still with those 'anxious for the field' to whom he had adverted in his journal for November 1794?[23]

Thomas Russell's Personal Circumstances in 1796

Despite his 'strange up country talk', Belfast had accepted Russell with a warmth that far outreached the offices of everyday hospitality. Doubtless, there were many who viewed him with extreme hostility, yet among the now radical middle classes he was regarded with both admiration and affection. As well, his extraordinary readiness for arduous journeys, whether on foot or mounted, gave him a detailed knowledge of the conditions of poor people throughout the north-east. His manifest conviction that a society built upon exclusion of the majority was intrinsically unjust, had forged a bond of respect between him and those who lived in cottages and cabins. His ability, shared with McCracken and Hope, to communicate the necessity for 'a cordial union of Irishmen' gave him an access to rank and file Catholics as well as Presbyterians. It is of interest that

William Drennan disapprovingly regarded him 'an agent on the part of the Catholics … instructed to reside at Belfast, to report what is going on, and to influence, as desired'. Drennan may have misjudged Russell's purpose in Belfast – it went beyond sectional interest to embrace that transcendence of sectarian difference enshrined in the United Irish constitution. Martha McTier noted the bareness of his quarters at Anne Street, the simplicity of his dress and his chronic shortage of funds. Astutely she observed that Russell lacked the money to buy a mourning coat on the death of his brother.[24]

Remarking on the outbreak of fever in Belfast during 1796, Margaret Russell urged her brother to come to Drumsluice. There, he would have the benefit of good air and 'abundance of firing to keep out the damp'. Were Russell's lodgings damp and unhealthy? Earlier in the year Margaret had complained about the lack of information on his movements: 'You tell me you are very busy, but not a word of in what manner nor (sic) how your affair is going on, if it is likely to take place.' Another correspondent from Drumsluice remarked that Margaret and the whole townland were 'loud in declaring the uncertainty of your movements'. William Hamilton, now married to Mary Ann Russell, complained that his uncle-in-law was not answering letters. A further letter from Hamilton gives reason to believe that Russell was writing for the *Northern Star* on political matters, especially in criticism of the courts under the draconian legislation from College Green.[25]

Whatever the circumstances of his daily existence, whatever his preoccupations about developments on the political scene, Russell continued to have many calls on his resources. Constant requests arrived from Drumsluice which he seems invariably to have met. To judge from a letter of Margaret's, on one occasion his patience snapped. Margaret wrote of her sorrow 'to find you have been so much distressed about the Bill'. Nonetheless, she admonished: 'It was partly your own fault as you did not mention the date or sight when you bade me draw on you.' It was hardly a comfort to Russell to be told that Margaret would be 'more careful in future if I should have to (apply for money) which be sure I must towards May'.[26] Another instance of financial embarrassment emerges in a letter from John Russell. Still trying to establish himself in London, he was himself under the pressure of frequent demands for money by his estranged wife.

In March 1796, he reported a visitor who demanded money on the head of an annuity due some years. The visitor, who had 'a bit of parchment in his pocket' and had mistaken John for Thomas Russell, was eventually fobbed off. There is no further evidence as to the nature of the debt.[27]

Another task came Russell's way in regard to young Arthur Tone. In February 1796, Margaret Tone, Arthur's mother, complained that he was 'loosing (sic) his time at present hanging around Dublin being bound to a courier'. Wolfe Tone's earlier suggestion of a voyage or two had not succeeded, since Arthur declared he would rather bind himself to a sweep for seven years than go to sea. There is some evidence that Russell had introduced Arthur to Robert Simms, whose tanning business he may have entered for a while. At the end of February, Peter Tone wrote to acknowledge 'with the most grateful sense the many obligations both myself and my family are under to you and the good people of Belfast'. Arthur Tone, however, did not share these views. Despite the attention of Russell, Simms and the McCrackens', he did not prosper any more in Belfast than he did in Dublin.[28]

Through spring 1796, Russell played intermediary between Whitley Stokes and Patrick Lynch. Stokes and Lynch were translating parts of the bible into Irish but seem to have had difficulty in establishing direct contact. They corresponded through Russell, at the Belfast Library. Stokes appears somewhat arrogant in regard to Lynch: having failed to reply to letters, he then sends 'a charge to keep the text clean and not to let it go out of his (Lynch) own possession …'. When the work was eventually published, it was without acknowledgement of any involvement by Lynch.[29]

Political Writing: Pamphlets, Songs and Articles

Among the United Irish leadership were political writers of accomplishment. Most notable in Belfast were Samuel Neilson, the Reverend James Porter, William Sampson and Thomas Russell himself. With considerable ability they made use of the democratisation of political culture which had been under way since the 1750s. The stock-in-trade of United Irish endeavour to raise political consciousness among the people were handbills, broadsheet papers, ballads and catechisms. Independent studies by Jim Smyth and Nancy Curtin have traced the development which led one correspondent with Dublin Castle to lament: 'The Society of United Irishmen use every ingenious device to promote discord and sedition. Addresses, odes, songs – in short every species of literary mischief is resorted to and circulated ... to every part of the kingdom and amongst all the lower orders of the people.' The Reverend James Porter's 'Billy Bluff and the Squire', a satire on Castlereagh and the Reverend James Cleland, enjoyed wide popularity and was probably the reason for Dr Porter's execution in 1798. From 1793 Russell had set himself the task of writing political analyses either as letters in the *Northern Star* or as pamphlets of an independent kind. Around that time he and William Sampson began to collaborate on 'The Lion of Old England', which lampooned government policies in a most effective way. In larger context, Russell had composed several anti-slavery poems, the best-known of which is 'The Negro's Complaint', published in the *Northern Star*. With two other poems of Russell (*The Dying Negro* and *The Captive Negro*) this was republished during 1798 in 'Paddy's Resource or The Harp of Erin'. Consonantly with United Irish policy, Russell had proposed in 1794 to write a book on political issues. However, it appears that his roving life-style in subsequent years did not allow the project to be completed.

A passing remark to John Templeton suggests that Russell may have written several political tracts during 1796. Towards the end of summer he went to Newry for the purpose of finishing one such pamphlet. Newry was the home of Eliza Goddard until she married Captain Kingston and thereafter moved to Dublin. Several United Irishmen lived there, including the McGennis family whose family home was at Dromantine some miles outside the town. By early September, the pamphlet was ready for publication under the auspices of the *Northern Star*. Entitled *A Letter to the People of Ireland on the Present Situation of the Country*, the tract was signed by 'Thomas Russell, An United Irishman'. Bearing the mark of haste, its style emulates neither Russell's 'E' letter against Grattan nor the anti-slavery letter subsigned 'G'. The focus and impulsion of these shorter pieces are somehow absent from the *Letter to the People of Ireland*. Yet, the pamphlet remains a valuable aid to understanding Russell's political views on a range of topics in late 1796. Although it reiterates several positions taken in the journal, nonetheless it clarifies allusions which were incomplete in diary form.[30]

These issues include maltreatment of Catholics and Defenders, Whig perfidy on Catholic emancipation, the war with France, slavery, and – as a dominant theme – the necessity for union among Irishmen of all religious backgrounds. In Russell's view, the relief of Catholic grievances was lost not because Protestants were ungenerous but because excessive trust had been placed in 'men of the first lordly and landed interests in Ireland who shamefully and meanly deserted the people'. People such as Henry Grattan, Lord Moira and Lord Charlemont had failed to push through reforms which they knew to be just and timely. In the mid-1790s, when it seemed that popular pressure would ensure the redress of Catholic disabilities, the Whig opposition proved treacherous to the people despite fair words by Grattan and his associates at an earlier time. When, as in 1793, Catholic demands were insistently pressed, the Whigs entered common cause with the government against the Catholics. As Russell put it: 'No persons reviled the Rights of Man or the French Revolution, or gabbled more about anarchy, and confusion, and mobs, and United Irishmen, and Defenders, and Volunteers, or coincided more heartily in strengthening the hands of that government which they had opposed, and riveting the chains of the people ... than the gentlemen of the opposition.' In other words, despite the liberal-sounding rhetoric of Grattan, Moira and Charlemont, both government and opposition regarded the people of Ireland as their common enemy to be vigorously resisted.

Russell's pamphlet also analysed the inaction of the Catholic leadership, such as it was. Neither senior clergy nor the Catholic gentry opposed governmental repression of rank and file people. Instead, they hastened to prove their loyalty by condemning the 'partial disturbances' enacted by those who demanded redress of wrongs. The slave mind was operative here: 'A century of slavery had divested them (senior ecclesiastics and landed gentry) of political courage or a wish for political disquisition.' As to the bulk of the people, they were subjected to savage laws which they had no part in framing. If they disobeyed these laws 'death, exile or such punishment as the framers thought proper to annex to the action was certain to follow'. While due process might be availed of by the ascendancy classes, these did not apply to Catholics and Defenders.

In government circles, the idea that Dissenters and Catholics should unite in a common demand was regarded as 'unnatural'. (It is of interest that the Catholic Bishop of Ferns, James Caulfield, referred in 1798 to 'the accursed business of uniting'.) Thomas Russell saw this reaction as the rabidly anti-democratic stance of an establishment which fostered divisions to consolidate its own power. As opposed to the fulmination of government and hierarchies, his pamphlet spelled out the programme of union. The only way to halt widespread oppression was effective union to demand political reform and religious emancipation for Dissenters and Catholics alike. Divisions, carefully fostered by government, ensured defeat. Union among Catholics, Protestants and Dissenters would create an alternative to the regime of force and corruption. It would give 'political integrity and virtue to their government, and liberty, peace and happiness to themselves'. Russell's *Letter to the Irish People* cleverly detailed the ploys of the administration to destroy every attempt at union. Up to 1791, College Green had kept the Catholic leadership at bay by pretending willingness to help them but insisting that Protestants and Dissenters would not tolerate Catholic emancipation. When, in 1791, a fragile union of Catholics, Protestants and Dissenters seemed to emerge, new tactics were employed.

Now, every effort was bent towards disassociating the Catholic leadership from the more radical Dissenter movement in the north. According to Russell, the Dublin administration tried to buy off the Catholic leadership with reforms well short of what was required. When it seemed that a partial repeal of penal laws would satisfy the more conservative Catholics, government pressed home its advantage. Thus, the administration set itself to repress the northern radicals who sought political as well as religious reform. On this, Russell's words recreate the disappointment of radical Dissenters who felt betrayed by the Catholic leadership. He could also have added that many Catholics also felt betrayed by the same leadership. Gradually, they too moved towards a more radical position. Middle-class Catholics led by John Keogh, Richard McCormick and John Sweetman moved closer to the United Irishmen. In rural areas, Defender activities began to increase in face of repression until a virtual merger with the United Irishmen occurred later in the decade. On the views of northern Dissenters Russell had a particular authority when he wrote:

'That any of the Catholics should be satisfied with a partial repeal of the penal code, or even make the total repeal their ultimate object was sufficient to betray a want of unity in the design. From the instant that the government saw this, the cloud which hovered over them was dissipated as if by enchantment; that instant they took their ground; the Catholic bill was procrastinated; strong measures were adopted with the greatest harmony and unanimity by Parliament; part of the people was attacked; the most spirited part of the north was dragooned; proclamations were issued; volunteers were disarmed; arbitrary imprisonments were inflicted; prosecutions were instituted; the gun-powder and militia bills were passed; the nation was foiled in its pursuit and put down; terror was the order of the day; it could scarce be believed ... how rapid the change was in the spirit of the metropolis, and so completely was the common enemy, the people, subdued, that long before the end of the session, some of the opposition again ventured to rail at the government.'

Through several pages Russell drove home the futility of political action without union among the groups demanding reform. Likewise, he blamed Catholic gentry and hierarchy for leaving ordinary people exposed to government terror: 'Witness the severities exercised on the lower orders of Catholics, which continue to this day, and of which it is imposible to hear the true account without indignation and horror.' The tragedy was compounded by the Militia act which the government now felt free to impose and which pitted one section of the populace against another. Russell's own military background should be kept in mind as one reads his complaint: 'A formidable Irish army was raised, armed and disciplined, to keep Ireland in subjection; the armed peasantry of one county were employed to subdue the peasantry of another, who were resisting real or imaginary grievances that they had felt in common.' Awareness of this anomaly later caused Russell to believe that the militias could be persuaded to join in a projected rising, even as late as 1803.

The *Letter* is noteworthy for its examination of the warped social structures of the decade. The excluded majority were ridiculed if they showed any interest in politics. Political endeavour was reserved for members of the ascendancy. Likewise, the rank and file were prevented from analysing the deeper roots of their oppression. The exigencies of tax-collectors, tithe-proctors and landlords prevented them from seeing the remote cause of their woes, viz. a thoroughly corrupt government. Meanwhile, an 'aristocracy or oligarchy governed Ireland with despotick sway'. Keeping the people disunited and, therefore, impotent, the ruling class could 'plunder and insult the country, and even quarrel among themselves for the division of the spoil with impunity'. Ireland was, in effect, governed by a clique for a clique. Russell argued that whenever a union of the people took place – 'when they once considered all Irishmen as friends and brethern' – the power of the aristocracy would vanish. The arrogant claims of the ascendancy was based neither on superior virtue nor on contribution to society. As to virtue, Russell believed that in Ireland (as elsewhere) power had long since corrupted its holders. As to contribution to the wellbeing of the country, he argued that the same ascendancy had taken far more than they ever gave. A strongly worded paragraph speaks of the aristocratic class as 'fungus productions who grow out of a diseased state of society and destroy as well the vigour and the beauty of that which nourishes them'.

Towards the close of his essay, Russell addressed several points which coalesced in the question of the war with France. One of these points is the right of all people to political freedom and, then, their duty to exercise it responsibly. Here, he reiterated his earlier criticism of those, some of them United Irishmen, who derided the *sans culottes* as 'the mob, the rabble, the beggars on the bridge, the grey-coated men whose views are anarchy and plunder'. As he had done in the small towns and villages of Antrim and Down in 1795 and 1796, Russell now argued that everyone had a duty to assess what government was doing in their name. One hundred and fifty thousand Irish soldiers were engaged in the war. Nearly a third of the British navy were Irishmen, many of them conscripted to the fleet. The very excise duty on shoe leather and the tax paid by anyone who drank more than water implicated even the most peace-loving in the war. Hence, the morality of the war with France concerned everyone. In Russell's view, the war was neither for religion nor freedom. It was for 'cloves and nutmegs and contracts and slaves'. Thus, he returned to the cause for his persistent refusal of sugar-based foods, viz. slavery and the slave trade. Slavery, Russell argued, was now the issue of 'the greatest consequence on the face of the earth'. The slave trade created barbarism and misery; it prevented the spread of civilisation and religion. It was, he wrote, 'a system of cruelty, torment, wickedness and infamy ... the work of wicked demons rather than men'.

Although Russell's pamphlet went to a second edition, it never had the impact of Tone's earlier *Argument in Favour of the Catholics*. Yet it remains a valuable measure of radical thought in the mid-1790s. The thrust of the *Letter* is entirely political. It gives no clue to the military arrangements which had been developing *pari passu* with political organisation through the years 1795 and 1796. As a political treatise, the *Letter* was eloquent on the need for union among all Irish people, for the extension of democratic rights to all, and for the application of moral principles to such abuses as slavery. The closing paragraphs give the first extended indication of Russell's tendency to make religious sensibility the clinching argument in political matters. He adduces repeated biblical citation to insist: 'The great object of mankind should be to consider themselves as accountable for their actions to God alone, and to pay no regard or obedience to any men or institution, which is not conformable to his will.'

Reception of the pamphlet was mixed. Writing to William Drennan, Martha McTier refers to various criticisms made even by Russell's friends. Some months later, chief secretary Thomas Pelham gave Russell to understand that he had read the tract. However, the author of the *Letter* did not have much time to estimate reaction to his publication. Within days of the *Letter*'s appearance, Thomas Russell's life altered dramatically for reasons outside his control.

CHAPTER EIGHT

Newgate

John Jeffries Pratt, Earl Camden, was a reluctant viceroy. By character unsuited to the troubled context of Ireland, he depended on a coterie of ascendancy politicians for advice and guidance. These hard-line officials included John Fitzgibbon, John Foster, John Toler (later known as the hanging judge, Lord Norbury), Lord Downshire, and Camden's own nephew Robert Stewart, Lord Castlereagh. Castlereagh was young, ambitious and able. Having dabbled in reform politics, he then attached himself to William Pitt, renouncing his earlier associations. Castlereagh's influence was paramount in the repression from 1796 to 1798 even though he was nominally assistant to the chief secretary, Thomas Pelham. It was Castlereagh who judged 'that the Presbyterian element in the North was the real centre of genuine republican sympathy and (that) once and for all the North must be rendered ineffective'.

On 16 September 1796, some days after the publication of Russell's address to the Irish people, Castlereagh, Lord Downshire, Lord Westmeath and John Pollock (now a government attorney) carried warrants to Belfast for the arrest of the leading republicans in the town. With detachments of cavalry and artillery from the Belfast garrison, they set guard upon a number of houses, including the home of Samuel and Martha McTier. The offices of the *Northern Star* were raided. A search-party entered William Sampson's house to arrest Samuel Neilson. Although Mrs Sampson was close to childbirth, every room was ransacked by Lord Westmeath and a Captain Coulson of the local garrison. Meanwhile, Neilson heard of the raid while walking on the Exchange. Straightaway, he presented himself at the Artillery Barracks, declared he was not evading arrest, and asked only for a speedy trial.

The Belfast library was also raided – this time by Pollock and
Lord Downshire. Not finding Thomas Russell, they seized his
papers and – fortunately for historians – had them sealed by the
High constable of Belfast, William Atkinson. Like Neilson,
Russell was doing business in the town when he learned of the
search-parties. Returning to the library he gave himself in
charge to the chief magistrate or Sovereign of Belfast, Dr Bryson.
Russell declined even to examine the warrant punctiliously
shown by Lord Downshire. He insisted on handing over the
keys of the library to Dr Bruce, a member of the library committee. Other well-known radicals were arrested at Belfast and
Lisburn: Rowley Osborne and Samuel Kennedy of the Jacobin
club, John Young, Henry Haslett, Daniel Shanahan, Charles
Teeling, Samuel Mulgrave and James Bartley, all United
Irishmen. William Orr, later executed, was arrested at his home,
outside Belfast. The show of strength was designed to intimidate
Belfast and, doubtless, to deprive the radicals of their leadership.
Nevertheless, the *Northern Star* retained its nerve. The paper's
editorial criticised the bravado of the aristocratic magistrates as
an exercise of repression and 'a contemptible invasion of the
peace'. No other reason, said the *Star*, could explain their osten-
tation in effecting what 'the meanest constable in town could
have done as well'.[1]

To Newgate and Kilmainham

On their arrest, the prisoners were immediately brought to
Dublin under heavy security. Each man was placed in a separate
post-chaise. Four troops of cavalry and two King's messengers
travelled with them. To Russell's distress, the cavalcade halted
at Newry, near the residence of Eliza Goddard. Late in the
evening of 17 September, the prisoners arrived in Dublin. Russell,
Musgrave, Young and Shanahan were lodged at Newgate.
Neilson, Haslett, Kennedy, Bartley and Teeling were placed at
Kilmainham or, as the *Freeman's Journal* put it, 'in the county jail,
newly built upon Gallow's Hill'. Not content with reporting the
prisoners' arrival, the *Freeman's Journal* berated 'a legion of political devils called the United Irishmen with the arch demon Tom
Paine in their van (who) threw the most destructive tares in the
promising harvest of our prosperity.' The report went on to excoriate kindred societies in England who wished to subvert 'our
envied and inestimable constitution'. In the opinion of the *Freeman's*

Journal, these societies wished to create 'a democracy in its (the constitution's) ruins'. To his credit, William Drennan remembered his own imprisonment and called at Newgate. There he was refused admission and could only send a message to Russell through the intermediacy of a warder.[2]

On Sunday morning, the prisoners were brought before Judge Boyd for committal. Charles Teeling later described how Neilson mocked the judge, to the amusement of the prisoners. Not, however, of Russell. Teeling records: 'No man regarded etiquette and the punctilios of politeness more: He looked solemn, stroked up his fine black hair and with a sweetness of countenance peculiarly his own ... begged of Nelson (*sic*) to respect the dignity of the Bench and the personal virtues of the learned judge.' On return to Newgate, Russell and his companions were put in separate cells. To date, they had received treatment which compared most favourably with that meted out to people not deemed 'gentlemen' by the authorities. Although the prisoners had been arraigned on a charge of High Treason, and despite Neilson's request for a speedy resolution of their case, they did not come to trial. Instead, they were destined to remain imprisoned without either bail or trial. In effect, it was a form of internment. Russell was to become the longest-serving political detainee of the time. Was this due to lack of evidence? Was it due to reluctance by government to expose informers who had insinuated themselves among the United Irishmen?[3]

Shortly after the arrests, one such informer – John Smith, alias Bird – forwarded a memorandum to Dublin Castle about Russell, Shanahan, Neilson and Osborne. In Russell's case, Smith wrote: 'Of him I know nothing but by report. He was always spoken of as a man of the strictest republican principle on whose integrity the committee reposed the greatest confidence and who had by his writings done very essential services.' The report on Neilson is more bitter: 'A presbyterian of the most rigid cast – a great affecter of consequence, gloomy and pedantic. He is at the head of the conspirators, knowing everything but ... he'll suffer death rather than tell anything.'[4] Inexplicably, Arthur Wolfe, the attorney-general and future Lord Kilwarden, precluded Russell's lawyers or agents from visiting him. Wolfe, a man of considerable courtesy and integrity, ordered: 'I cannot for the present agree that Mr Russel's (*sic*) counsel and agents should have access to him, the consideration of this should be deferred.' Thus, during the first days of his imprisonment, Russell endured solitary confinement, dependent on the uncertain mercies of Newgate's keeper, Tresham Gregg, for the provision of basic necessities. Meanwhile, the attorney-general permitted Neilson and Haslett to receive visits from their wives, while Teeling was allowed to see a Catholic priest. The reason for this especial severity towards Russell is unclear. It is of interest that the state attorney, Pollock, had inscribed upon the warrant for his arrest an injunction to particular vigilance by the escort.[5]

Conditions at Newgate

Despite its name, Newgate or New Prison, was an epidemic-ridden institution, due to faults in its construction. Located at the Little Green, not far from the north Dublin quays, its sinister entrance was furnished with a gibbet and dominated by a hangman's gallery. The prison was badly managed by Tresham Gregg about whom the Inspector General of Prisons made severe complaint. Whereas political prisoners like Russell were entitled to an adequate subsistence allowance (fixed at half a guinea per day), this was seldom paid. There were suspicions that Gregg indulged in peculation at the expense of his prisoners. Thus, detainees were cast into the power of warders, some of whom abused their power unscrupulously. Shortly after their arrest in February 1797, Robert and William Simms applied to the under-secretary at Dublin Castle for an increase in their daily allowance to the half-guinea 'which the other state prisoners have'. In their application the Simms' brothers complained of being obliged to pay nearly double for their requisites. At Kilmainham, some short time later, Henry Joy McCracken wrote of living expenses when 'plundered by turnkeys etc. and still more so when confronted with others who cannot support themselves nor yet be left to themselves'. Nonetheless, it appears that two major officials of Newgate – the medical officer, Dr Mitchell, and the chaplain, the Reverend Gamble – were meticulous in attention to duty and humane in its exercise. McCracken described the Reverend Archer, Inspector of Prisons, as a gentleman and a person of humanity. It should also be noted that Russell would insist, some years later, that 'during the whole course of my confinement (setting aside the injustice of it) I have always been well treated by Government and by

those in whose charge they placed me, with respect and propriety'.[6]

Early months at Newgate

This comment of Russell may be seen as an expression of his
own unwillingness to bear personal grudges. Yet, it cannot be
discounted as purely the forgiveness of a generous spirit.
Despite the hostility of pro-government newspapers which
urged stern action against Russell and his colleagues, the administration visited no further severities on him than protracted imprisonment without trial. In most other respects, the authorities
observed the legal proprieties and courtesies. Russell's status as
a 'gentleman' and former army officer was recognised even to
the meticulous appellation of him as 'Captain Russell'. There is
some ground to the suggestion that highly placed individuals in
Dublin society approached the chief secretary, albeit unsuccess-
fully, for his release. In any case, the initial restrictions in regard
to visits, association with his colleagues, and the receipt of
books, were lifted after some weeks.

A paradox of the times is that while Newgate and Kilmainham
were typical of 'the eighteenth-century criminal code's deter-
rence by terror' (Elliott) yet people like Simon Butler, Oliver
Bond and Archibald Hamilton Rowan had been kept in relatively
comfortable circumstances. Otherwise, inmates of scant means
were imprisoned in dank cells with tiny apertures for light and
alms bags to garner the expenses of their survival. There is scant
clue to Russell's conditions of confinement or, for that matter, to
his mental state in these early weeks. Later communications indicate that his political convictions enabled him to deal resolutely
with imprisonment. Many who wrote to him displayed their
own character rather clearly. For example, William Russell, the
youngest member of the family, showed an emotional superfi-
ciality: 'You cannot expect condoling with you in any flowing
stile (sic), a son of Neptune knows not how.' In October, the bluff
but somehow more admirable John Russell rejoiced to hear that
Thomas was in good health. Perhaps disingenuously he added
that good spirits 'are ever the result of innocence and rectitude
of conduct'. Thomas Russell may have been enquiring about
Digges, his debtor, for John commented: 'The person you allude
to is still in Dunree but not detained there for what he owes
you.' John Russell also spoke of money to accrue from the will of

a relative or close friend named Harman. Demands from Drumsluice continued even into the first year of imprisonment – Stephen Hamilton persevered in drawing on Russell while Margaret wrote that Hamilton had been in great need of what Russell had sent and 'more if he could get it'![7]

The first clue to an improvement in the conditions of Russell's imprisonment comes from Dr McDonnell. Writing to Newgate, McDonnell recorded satisfaction that Russell now had access to books. The doctor had found two books requested by Russell and would procure any others he might require. James McDonnell's didactic traits emerge as he lists the principal sources of happiness for anyone 'in a situation like yours': religious sentiments or virtuous dispositions, awareness of interested friends and 'a turn for literary pursuits. The suggestion is that Russell had all three advantages. McDonnell also mentioned the Belfast librarianship. Some evidence exists that the library committee generously paid Russell's salary even while he was in Newgate. In this early letter, McDonnell referred to John McCoutry (McCautry) who had offered to act as substitute until any trial should eventuate. Another letter from McDonnell signalled that the library might have difficulty in retaining McCautry's voluntary services much longer. As well, the Reverend Abernethy, a New Light clergyman, proposed to rent the unoccupied part of the library and to pay the incumbent housekeeper. In requesting a speedy answer to this suggestion McDonnell pointed out the advantages – rent of eight pounds per annum and economy of the six pounds stipend to the housekeeper.[8]

Damaging rumours

Apart from deprivation of their liberty and the not unreal terrors of Newgate, the state prisoners had to contend with rumours outside their control. Some weeks after the arrests, an English newspaper, the *Sun*, claimed that Thomas Russell – 'better informed of the intended proceedings than all his associates' – was about to give evidence against his fellow-prisoners. The *Sun* also claimed that he had signed a communication with the French government and was himself strongly tainted with 'Jacobinical notions'. Although the allegation was published on 18 November, Russell did not learn of it until mid-December. He wrote to the Dublin *Evening Post* which published his lengthy response

with an editorial rider. The editor introduced Russell's letter by
regretting that 'such a monster of ingratitude, as well as disloy-
alty, is likely to escape the punishment he so well deserves'. The
'ingratitude' refers to a claim by the *Post* that Russell had been
'particularly favoured by government on many occasions'.[9]

In his letter, Russell admitted that he had no personal complaint
against government. As well, he rejected any suggestion that he
had acted from 'private pique or resentment'. In regard to his
giving evidence against his colleagues, Russell declared that to
do so he would have to cast off 'every sense of shame, of honour,
of virtue and religion'. Describing informers as 'nefarious and
execrable pests of society', he reaffirmed the central tenets of the
United Irishmen – 'from these principles I shall, I trust, never
swerve'. Several other points made in the letter are of interest.
For instance, Russell denied that there was any insurrection 'in
that part of the north in which I lived'. Again, he rebutted the allegation that he had 'in any other manner held communication
with the French'. Scares about insurrection came from two
sources: the 'distempered imagination' of people wishing to
magnify their own zeal, or petty despots who converted everything 'into plots, invasions, insurrections and devaluation of
property'. The sole object of such people was 'a government of
force and not of affection'. To his denial that there was an insurrection in the north Russell made one exception. There was an
insurrection in parts of Armagh, carried on by 'those fanatics
styling themselves "Orangemen" whose principles and actions
are equally detestable and who are ... tools in the hands of
wicked men'. This reference was to the outbreak of sectarian attacks in Armagh following the institution of the Orange Order
in 1795.[10]

Russell's letter furnished the only information he wished to
give. He admitted his conviction 'of the fatal effects of religious
prejudices on the liberty, morals and happiness of our country'.
Again, he admitted that he had worked to create 'a spirit of
union and brotherly affection among the people'. And he reiterated a foundational principle of the United Irish movement that
'no man should be deprived of his civil rights on account of his
religious opinion'. His list of political grievances was also coherent with the policy aims of the United Irishmen: restriction of
Ireland's commerce to serve English interests, excessive taxation

squandered by a rich ascendancy, lack of effort to educate, in-
struct or help the poor, readiness to commit the country to an
unnecessary, unjust and disastrous war. The only answer to
these grievances was reform of the House of Commons where
representation should be 'in the hands of the people and not ...
of a bigoted, corrupt, rapacious and ignorant Aristocracy'. The
letter ended with a flourish – neither imprisonment nor exile
would prevent him from prosecuting 'by constitutional means
that great object, so essential to the liberty and happiness of
Ireland'

This protestation from Newgate is interesting in the biographical
frame of Russell's life. Even more it is noteworthy as comment
on the political situation in the north during 1796. The letter
should be read against the backdrop of Russell's incarceration
and, in particular, of his care not to incriminate himself or others.
Yet, his habitual refusal to dissimulate impels the historian to
read the *Evening Post* letter more or less at face value. Russell
knew of, and despised, the petty informers who served, and
sometimes misled, Dublin Castle. Without doubt, he would
never join their numbers. Again, it is noteworthy that he identi-
fies the Orangemen as the chief disturbers of the peace. Behind
them he accurately discerned more powerful individuals who
used Orangeism for their own purposes. Russell clearly reiterates the United Irish diagnosis of the 'fatal effects of religious
prejudices'. And he does no more than repeat the policy of the
society when he spoke of 'a spirit of union and brotherly affection among the people'

His disavowal of a French connection and of insurrectionary
conspiracy merits close attention. In a sense, both were realities.
On the day his letter was published in the *Post* a French expedition under Lazare Hoche was virtually foundering in Bantry Bay
with Tone on board. The Reverend William Jackson's visit to
Dublin from France had occurred in 1794. Intermediaries such
as Fr James O'Coigly had visited France. Very shortly after the
letter was published Robert Simms and George Tennent knew
about Lord Edward FitzGerald's plan for a new mission to the
French government. Tone had already spent months in France
where he had regretted the absence of Russell, his friend and
mentor. There was, therefore, a connection with the French of
which Russell will have known. Yet, many United Irishmen – at

this stage, Russell was most likely one of them – saw French intervention as problematic for Irish freedom and independence. It can be taken that, at this time, Russell had no direct involvement in any project for an invasion of Ireland by the French. At a later time, Russell would acknowledge that 'this design of inviting the French was framed by the executive and withheld from the people at large a very long time, nor did it become much known until after the expedition to Bantry Bay'.[11]

Russell's denial of any revolutionary groundplan in the north is more complex. The tradition, articulated by R. R. Madden, that he was appointed commander of County Down in Summer 1796 cannot be overlooked. Reports to Dublin Castle had already identified United Irish clubs where people spoke of 'getting the work done in one night'. Granted the self-serving nature of much information, it is nonetheless clear that quasi-military organisation went side-by-side with political clubs throughout the north. Much of this was defensive strategy, in view of threats from military and sectarian attacks. In addition, there is reason to suppose that the United Irish directory at Belfast was aware of the danger of uncoordinated incidents. From all that is known of his character, it is unlikely that Russell would fabricate a version of events while knowing things to be exactly the opposite. Thus, given his mentality, given also the implications of his oath as a United Irishman, it can be inferred that by summer 1796 no insurrection had been planned in detail. On the other hand, a substructure with strong revolutionary potential did exist in many parts of the north. And on that Russell would never inform.

The fear of the *Evening Post* lest 'this monster of ingratitude should escape the punishment he so well deserves' was unfounded. There was no pact. No turning of King's evidence. No release. Not even a trial. Russell was informed that although nothing had been proven against him it was thought better to keep him confined. This internment of Russell and Neilson incited even John Smith to remonstrate with the viceroy: 'Why keep ... honest men in captivity without even the shadow of a crime to adduce? Why irritate the public mind, already goaded nearly to desperation? ... give peremptory orders for the instant liberation of the persons before mentioned.'[12]

Illness at Newgate

Early in 1797, the fever which recurrently afflicted Newgate inmates attacked Russell. In March, John Templeton regretted that the most effective remedy, air and exercise, was unlikely soon to be forthcoming. Drawing upon a report from Russell, he rejoiced 'to find your sufferings alleviated by the intercourse of Dr Mitchell'. In the same generous letter, Templeton offered to go bail for his friend. Dr Mitchell's attention and Russell's own relative youth – he was now in his thirtieth year – brought him through the fever. Neilson, too, fell ill, with some suggestion that a nervous breakdown had occurred. As imprisonment stretched into months, talk about early releases caused strains between some of the prisoners. At Kilmainham, deep tensions emerged between Henry Joy McCracken, Henry Haslett and Samuel Neilson. Mary Ann McCracken noted with relief that '... our friend Thomas Russell is well and in good spirits'. Her further comment is of interest: 'I was much afraid that he had no companions to his taste and ... that his spirits would flag; he still continues to be the first of men in the esteem of his young friends the Tombs, especially Isabella ...'[13]

Preliminary conversations with government

In the case of one so literate as Thomas Russell it is to be expected that he should write about his case to the Castle authorities, when the necessary materials became available. Governmental reluctance to try him or admit him to bail is difficult to interpret. There is a suggestion that he would not accept bail since that might insinuate a guilt which he did not admit. John Templeton, while offering to provide sureties, gently rebuked him for a perceived fastidiousness. On this, Russell temporised: bail would apply only in Dublin and friends there would vouch for him. There is an overtone of defiance in his stance, almost as if he were determined to carry the justice of his case into the heart of government. In October 1797, he once more addressed Arthur Wolfe. Writing to the attorney-general, he reminded Wolfe that since his arrest two assizes and a special commission had occured without his being tried or admitted to bail. With an habitual courtesy, Russell then wrote: 'From this statement ... I hope you will esteem me justified in requesting you to bring me to trial or to order that I be admitted to bail.' Immediately, Wolfe responded in similarly courteous terms although without relief for the prisoner: 'What you desire is not in my department and ... I have not authority to comply with your request.'[14]

Another bout of illness affected Russell in January 1798, an attack of the fever endemic to Newgate. From Belfast, Robert Simms, who had been released the previous summer, sent items of clothing and slippers to aid Russell's convalescence. Perhaps the rigours of Newgate winter impelled Russell once again to request the Castle for a resolution of his case. To chief secretary Thomas Pelham, he reiterated an earlier demand for return of his papers and admission either to trial or bail. In a letter of March 1798, Russell made an uncharacteristically personal complaint that 'in the meantime my life and my health are wasting in a prison'. All who were arrested with him in September 1796, with the exception of one, had now been released. Arguing from his voluntary surrender as a sign of confidence in his own case and in the justice of government, he challenged Pelham: 'Of the first of these I am as much convinced now as I was then. It remains, Sir, for you to show me that I was not mistaken on the last.'[15] Pelham's reply is not extant. However, a narrative of his imprisonment written by Russell in 1800 suggests that he would not have been surprised by a refusal. It appears that shortly after his arrest he had rejected a proposal that he should emigrate to England if released. Perhaps there was more to this proposal – a suggestion that he should inform on the United Irishmen – which may have been the basis for the allegation in the *Sun* newspaper in November 1796. When certain high ranking individuals, including the renowned scholar Richard Kirwan, approached Pelham for his release they found that, while Pelham spoke favourably of Russell at the personal level, the government proposed to hold him in prison for the duration of the war. In his narrative of December 1800, Russell delicately put it: 'Mr Pelham spoke handsomely as to my private character ... but (that) from my public character and conduct (government) were determined to keep me in prison during the war, at the same time expressing very exaggerated notions of my talents and influence ...'[16]

Very soon after Russell's application to the chief secretary, Pelham was replaced by his assistant, Lord Castlereagh. On 3 May 1798, Russell applied to Castlereagh once more for trial or bail. A second time he mentioned the detriment to his health in-

flicted by prolonged imprisonment. Castlereagh answered immediately to refuse the application: 'Having laid it before the
Lord Lieutenant I am desired by His Excellency to acquaint you
that he is sorry he does not feel himself enabled from existing
circumstances to comply with your wishes at present.' Behind
the polite formalities can be discerned a determination to hold
Thomas Russell in prison, at least for the duration of the war
with France.[17] Nor did Russell confine attention to his own case.
A fragment in his handwriting is clearly the draft of a memorial
to Lord Camden in favour of a hard-pressed Newgate prisoner.
The possessions of this unnamed man had been sequestered and
Camden's intervention was sought. Again, Russell befriended a
female prisoner at Newgate and enlisted one of his lawyer
friends – perhaps Thomas Addis Emmet – to act for her. His concern was sufficient to earn Mary Dalton's gratitude. On her release, she wrote to Russell enquiring about his own bail: 'The
only comfort the world can give me is to hear and know how
you are and at all times to pray to God to … send you well and
safe from your confinement.'[18]

Moral Stock-Taking

On November 21, 1797, his thirtieth birthday, Russell drew up
an examination of conscience. It was a lengthy memorandum
and, in the manner of such documents, heavily self-critical. In
view of his close confinement at Newgate some of his inculpa-
tions are surprising: 'Relapsed into fornication and lust and become more irritable, my respect for veracity not so great, and
swearing has increased upon me.' Russell's biblical predilection
is evident from his remark that in proportion to his daily reading of the bible he had lived more virtuously. On the other hand,
when he acted in a less than upright way, he was 'ashamed and
afraid to open that book'. His lack of opportunity for intoxica-
tion would enable him 'to guard more against women'. He
hoped that, when freed, 'to be able totally to abstain from them
till marriage'. Today, our sensibilities correctly recoil from this
language in regard to relationships with women. Yet, its tormented intensity may afford some clue to Russell's difficulties
in his relationship with Eliza Goddard. As the examination of
conscience moved to resolutions for amendment, Russell undertook 'to gain a compleat (sic) mastery over my passionate temper'.
He would study more in order 'to serve mankind and engage in

some work of utility'. A marked difference with 'enlightened' philosophers such as Paine and Godwin emerges when Russell proposes to write a study of 'the insufficiency of reason'. This distinction between the necessity of a divine revelation and the incapacity of human reason to discover a deity preoccupied Russell throughout his adult life. The memorandum concludes with a mysterious reference to 'the worst action of my life to which ... my own Lust ... betrayed me'. Since Russell does not specify further, this enigmatic reference must be allowed to stand without elaboration.

A good insight to the author's religious sentiments can be gained from the prayer with which this extraordinary document concludes:

> O Lord God ... it is not from thy justice
> before which I stand condemned
> that I expect salvation,
> but from thy mercy that I expect pardon and forgiveness,
> my Lord and Saviour Jesus Christ.[19]

CHAPTER NINE

Repression and Reaction (1797-98)

Two winters more, then the Trouble year,
when the best that a man could feel
was the pike he kept in hidin's near,
till the blood o' hate and the blood o' fear
would be redder nor rust on the steel.
Us ones quet from mindin' the farms
Let them take what we gave wi' the weight o' our arms
from Saintfield to Kilkeel.

With the arrest of Russell and Neilson, the United Irish Society had lost its most determined leaders. Shortly thereafter, other prominent members were imprisoned. In a matter of weeks, Henry Joy McCracken and William Orr were committed to Kilmainham and Carrickfergus jails respectively. After the wave of arrests, the northern leadership became more cautious and less decisive. When the fleet of Lazare Hoche reached Bantry Bay in December 1796, there was virtually no response throughout the country. The government, taken largely by surprise, had a narrow escape. Intermittent communication with France and uncertainty about the fleet's destination ensured that the north remained quiescent. Neither the time nor the place of intended landing was known to the Belfast leadership. Thus, news of a French expedition left the directory undecided: Was the report a trick by government to provoke an unprepared rising? Was the expedition a decoy for another flotilla, directed either to Galway or to somewhere in the north?[1]

By March 1797, in the aftermath of Bantry Bay, the north was feeling the edge of military repression. The Habeas Corpus Act had been suspended. The Insurrection Act legitimated widespread raids, burnings and arrests. General Lake's order for confiscation of arms was brutally executed by violently excited troops and yeomen. The *Northern Star* remarked that with so many people of integrity in prison 'it looks as if the felons alone are to remain outside the gaols'. With scant exaggeration, Tone – who had regained the safety of France – remarked that 'the system of Terror is carried as far in Ireland as ever it was in France in the time of Robespierre'. Despite Thomas Pelham's claim that the oppression of Catholics in Armagh 'had been greatly exaggerated', drunken troops and yeomen were visiting men, women and children with what the Bishop of Down termed 'every species of indignity, brutality and outrage'.[2]

It is, therefore, all the more difficult to trace the operation of the United Irishmen in the north during the months after Russell's arrest. Agents of government had infiltrated the upper leadership to sow confusion at the most strategic junctures. The Newry-based informer, Samuel Turner, had instigated the arrest in September 1796 of William Orr, executed a year later in a signal travesty of justice. In February 1797, Robert and William Simms were taken to Newgate. So, too, were the Reverend Sinclair Kelbourne, William McCracken and Dr Alexander Crawford. The new, more timid, leaders responded uncertainly. Writing to her brother at Kilmainham in June 1797, Mary Ann McCracken gave a hint of the pressure on the leadership about the correct response to repression. Her letter detailed how Belfast had 'lost the confidence of the country from being prudent and cautious on a matter of great importance'. 'Visible timidity' and 'the diabolical suggestions of some traitors' were at the root of the disarray. As a result, many people spoke of 'a desertion of their cause'.[3] About this time, a meeting of United Irish leaders was informed that the only thing preventing a rebellion was the unwillingness of County Antrim to rise. The same meeting heard that the colonels for County Down were unanimously in favour of a rising but that French arms and men would not arrive for at least six weeks. The uncertainty was compounded by reports that Tone's arrangements were being impeded by treachery among French officials.[4]

For all his undoubted sincerity, Robert Simms (the United Irish commander for County Antrim until his arrest in February 1797) was cautious in the extreme. In all justice, it should be noted that he was reluctant to expose his people to the consequences of an unprepared, unaided insurrection. Yet, as the months passed and repression became ever more severe, rank and file members grew restive. Notwithstanding Russell's denial of a French link on his own part, anticipation of a further expedition was general throughout the north. So, too, was a readiness to assist the French, seen by many as potential liberators. Russell's estimation was accurate: people joined the 'system' – the United Irish network – either from principle or, in many cases, as a refuge from the distress now visited on the country. Even Dr McDonnell predicted that any disturbance would occur 'between the scythe and the sickle'. In the event, McDonnell was only a year too early.[5]

Contact with Dublin was maintained through Robert Simms and William Tennent. In February 1797, a special committee of the United Irishmen appointed an envoy to France. The committee – Lord Edward FitzGerald, Thomas Addis Emmet and Richard McCormick – opted for Edward Lewins, a colleague of Tone in the now defunct Catholic Committee. When Simms was imprisoned in Newgate shortly afterwards, he would have informed Russell of all that had occurred hitherto. The suffering of a people harried beyond endurance, the pressures to revolt, the incursions of Orange mobs, the defeat in Parliament of all resolutions for conciliation, would have been of major concern to Russell. Henry Joy McCracken's letter to his family in June 1797 discloses this awareness: '... every day we hear such reports from the North that often I have supposed ... that ... the next post ... would bring an account of your being burned out ...'.[6]

Further personal circumstances

At a personal level, Russell continued to bear his imprisonment well. To judge from an account for victuals sent him by a local trader, he and his colleagues had a more than satisfactory diet – at least, when they could afford to have foodstuffs sent into the prison. Soup, fish, veal, mutton, potatoes, sweetmeats and fruit are the major items detailed by the grocer. For Russell, accustomed to physical exercise and enamoured of the countryside, the greatest deprivation was confinement in unsanitary conditions. The prisoners did enjoy some form of handball, albeit in a narrow space. On return to Belfast after being granted bail, Robert Simms enquired: 'Have you had ever a ball since we left you?'; and admonished: 'you were generally a lazy performer'.[7]

When Simms left Newgate in June 1797, he brought a letter from Russell to Mary Simms. A close friendship between her and

Russell had developed, especially after hope for marriage to Eliza Goddard proved fruitless. Russell's imprisonment and, perhaps, earlier hesitations on his part did not allow this relationship to reach full term. Writing from Ballymena, Mary Simms now acknowledged the missive carried by her brother. She expressed a double pleasure in Russell's 'kind and affectionate letter' and Simms' liberation. As well, she encouraged Russell: 'I know your great understanding and the cause in which you are engaged will prevent your spirits getting flat ...'. Alluding to his scientific work, Mary Simms assured Russell that his 'flower seeds and fossels (*sic*)' had been passed to John Templeton. Perhaps exhilarated by her brother's release she wrote: '... the dog days I hope are surely over – never to return again.' Robert Simms' mood was less cheerful. He reported that in Belfast 'no business of any kind – except arrests – is going on'.

Despite Mary Simms' optimism, Russell's freedom was by no means near. The release of Robert Simms, Arthur O'Connor and Charles Teeling, the rumours that 'Neilson and co.' (Drennan's phrase) were to hear something from government, caused anxiety in Kilmainham. Was some sort of pact in train? McCracken's letters to Belfast give a hint of the tension among the Kilmainham prisoners. Russell's own correspondence indicates no sign of compromise with the administration but maintains his demand for either trial or liberation. At the end of summer 1797 Robert Simms' concern for Russell led him to write: 'I was in great hopes when I left you that you would have seen the green fields before now ... I don't however despair for I have little doubt but that your liberation will soon take place.'[8]

Difficult times in Belfast

On 10 August, Simms wrote yet again. The Belfast summer assizes had just ended; there was a respite for William Orr; 'General Clark' (a mysterious emissary of the southern United Irishmen) had passed through Belfast en route to Dublin. Simms asked for a 'full and accurate account of Clark' through Russell's friend, McDowell. This request suggests a relatively free access to Russell by his friends. Simms' further admonition strengthens that suggestion: 'I would strongly recommend you to be more on your guard with respect to drink for I really think you give way to it too often.'

Simms reported on the Belfast Library, the committee of which

had just met. James Munford was proving to be an excellent secretary. John McCautry still acted for Russell as librarian.
Although the committee had been shaken by arrests and the dis-
ruption of trade, Munford had rallied his colleagues: the library,
wrote Simms, 'is now rapidly amending under the auspices of
Munford'. Commenting ruefully on the destruction of the
Northern Star, Simms thought Arthur O'Connor's *Irish Press* was
now in some degree supplying the place of the *Star*. A comment
by Simms on the battle of Aughrim (1690) discloses in an interesting way the intellectual background of some Belfast republicans. Whereas Russell had a romantic Jacobite view, and saw the
defeat at Aughrim as the collapse of the Irish nation, Simms proposed a different interpretation. For Simms the defeat of James II
was not a tragedy: 'It was happy for the world that the English
government succeeded.' A Whiggish understanding of the
'Glorious Revolution' emerges as Simms continues: 'If Louis
had been able to have James on the throne of Gt Britain and
Ireland, despotism would have reigned ... and ... instead of our
seeing a government patronise Locke on government we should
have seen then passive obedience.'[9]

It is symptomatic of the current ambiguities that John Smith,
even though he was in contact with Dublin Castle, should write
to Russell about hardship in Belfast. The Reay Fencibles had
clashed with the Monaghan Militia. The regional commander,
General Nugent, blamed the townspeople and threatened to
blow up the town in two hours! Smith mentioned 'acts of cruelty
committed in various parts' and ended his doleful script by
telling Russell: 'I think you who are at present in confinement
are better off than those who are in the way of being abused and
insulted every hour.' Military repression was not the only peril
threatening Belfast in summer 1797. Dr McDonnell had opened
a fever hospital but it quickly became what John Templeton
called 'a Seminary for disease'. Within three months, Dr
McDonnell, the housekeeper, the apothecary and the surgeon
had all caught fever. Although the dangers of the hospital were
predicted by many, McDonnell had persisted in his charitable
endeavour. When Russell answered Templeton's letter he offered some quasi-scientific reflections on how to deal with cont-
aminated air. With an overtone of irony he stressed that, at
Newgate, he understood the problem![10]

The letter from Templeton is interesting for other reasons. Already mention has been made of his offer to stand for Russell's bail. Templeton, an unfailingly gracious correspondent, also remarked that every flower bank in his garden was a reminder of his imprisoned friend. Every excursion to Glenarm and 'the sublime rock of Rathlin' provoked nostalgia for their joint field trips to those parts. This remembrance pleased Russell. Writing on 10 September, he admitted that at Newgate he had not seen 'even a bush or blade of grass except a few that grow in the corner of the prison'. Yet, he insisted on his firmness of purpose with an almost religious fervour: 'nor do I repent or would I alter any part of my political conduct, for I acted … for the good of my country and of mankind and I know that I shall ultimately be tried by an infallible, just and merciful judge.' Responding to Templeton's good report of the library's fortunes under Munford and McCautry, Russell accurately predicted that it would ultimately be 'a fine institution for the province, perhaps for the whole country'. As to the fossils he and Templeton had collected, Russell hoped they were arranged properly, safe from 'meddling ignorant people'. Already he had heard that Bunting's work had been completed. Now he wished success to the publication, for Bunting's sake and for the enhancement of the library, Bunting's sponsor.[11] Incarceration did not shield Russell from continued application by the mysterious Stephen Hamilton. Several times during 1797, this self-centred young man virtually demanded money. As well, Mary Ann Hamilton (nee Russell) importuned him for 'whatever is in your power'. Her husband, William, was not supporting her and she lamented that 'the first misery in this life is seeing a child's distress and hearing their cry…'.[12]

Circumstances at Newgate and Belfast in early 1798

In the winter of 1797-8, Russell fell victim to Newgate's parlous sanitation. Once more, he contracted fever and, this time, a severe bowel complaint. The medical officer again distinguished himself by careful attention in prescribing a special diet and an allowance of wine. Now at Ballyclare, Co Antrim, Robert Simms procured the remainder of Russell's wardrobe from the library premises and, as already mentioned, sent clothing appropriate for convalescence. William Simms promised to send a copy of Bunting's new book in the preparation of which Russell had so effectivly helped. Robert Simms disapprovingly noted Catholic resolutions of loyalty to the crown 'from the lower parts of the county … owing to the influence of the priests'. These letters advert to continuing harrassment by government forces and their associates. Samuel Musgrave returned from Newgate to find his house and shop at Lisburn 'dreadfully plundered'. Near Belfast, at Crumlin village, houses were burned by Orangemen. Robert Simms added further detail: 'Such inhabitants as dared to complain before a magistrate have been threatened with further vengeance'. In yet another letter of January 1798, William Sampson remarked: 'Croppies lie down is now the word and we do lie down.'[13]

A contradiction in Thomas Rusell's character is gleaned from an intensely charged letter from John, his brother. Still in London and in a close liaison with his former housekeeper, John Russell appears both anxious to secure his brother's approval and expectant of disapproval. He wrote to Newgate in October 1797: 'I have mentioned a name that probably you will not like … only know her and then you will approve of her … you will see a perfectly well-behaved, well-looking woman with a manner and countenance open, generous and modest. God send you may see her and love her'. In view of Thomas Russell's own 'adventures', one notices with some surprise John's anticipation of his brother's stricture.[14]

Perhaps due to illness, Russell fell behind in correspondence during the winter of 1797. Templeton complained of not hearing from him for weeks. Margaret Russell protested that, although she wrote every week, he never said whether he received the letters. Simms wrote frequently while attending to practical matters like clothes and footwear. Rowley Osborne, chairman of the Jacobin Club, was released sometime in January 1798. Soon afterwards he wrote hoping that Russell was 'in better health than when I saw you'. Osborne felt unsafe in Belfast. At Linenhall Street he had been accosted by yeomen who insulted him as a 'croppy'. In the town, he reported, all businesses except breweries and distilleries were at an end.[15]

Despite applications by prominent individuals, including an unnamed military officer of high rank, Russell would become the longest-serving political prisoner among the United Irishmen.

All indications point to *raison d'état* as the ground of his prolonged detention. Thus, pressure from Templeton and others to
sue for bail was misplaced: Russell's liberation was impeded in
high quarters. In 1797 he became aware that Pelham's assessment of his importance indicated prolonged detention. Perhaps
his unusual popularity and his earlier military experience
caused the administration to deem it necessary that he be interned without trial.[16]

In February 1798, William Drennan heard rumours of impending releases. Prison doors were to open on condition that the
prisoners took an oath of allegiance and promised good behaviour. Neilson was about to be liberated although, as Drennan
wrote, 'whether this is in consequence of the quarrel among the
informers or his conversations with Pelham and Castlereagh ... I
am not so well informed as to say'. Further, Drennan understood that Neilson had refused liberation unless Russell were
also released. Sometime in February 1798, Neilson was released
on health grounds. From a base in Dublin he continued to organise the United Irishmen in Leinster and parts of Munster.
Meanwhile, the directory bickered over the circumstances in
which a rising should take place. Then, in March, a swoop on
Oliver Bond's house decapitated the leadership since virtually
all the high-level officials of the society were meeting there.[17]

The Rising of 1798

The events of summer 1798 cannot be taken up in detail here.
They passed Russell by, incarcerated as he was throughout their
tragic duration. After the arrests in March he would have had
opportunity to meet the leadership of the United Irishmen,
many of whom were committed to Newgate. Just before the rising, Neilson, who escaped the swoop on Bond's house, was re-
arrested almost at the walls of Newgate while planning the rescue of Russell and other prisoners. Tensions between a Dublin
faction, amongst whom were Thomas Addis Emmet and
William McNeven, and a wider Dublin-Belfast group organised
by Samuel Neilson and Arthur O'Connor, did not prevent the
rising whether in south Leinster or in Antrim and Down.

Events in the north were beset by problems of communication
with Dublin. Yet, the rising of May 1798 was neither unplanned
nor unorganised, as is frequently claimed. Later, Robert Simms

and Robert Hunter who stood down as high-level commanders gave their reasons for not acting decisively. Belfast was to await the non-arrival twice of the Dublin mail-coach as signal that a rising had taken place in the capital. When the mail functioned as usual, Simms resigned as adjutant-general. In a later explanation, Hunter claimed he had 'craved from the Executive even one month to put the north in preparation, which was refused'. In Down, when the United Irish colonels met at Banbridge Fair they decided not to attempt a rising 'unless there was a general rising or unless there was an invasion'. Reports from that county indicated that there were plenty of pikes along with cannon and sixty thousand stand of arms. The arms had been smuggled in fishing vessels and then secreted throughout the area.[18]

According to the leaders who deferred action, 'McCracken, Munro, Thompson, Orr, Dickey and the other violent young men who had not the confidential information attempted to bring out the people'. McCracken's view was otherwise: noting the caution of the leaders, he remarked that 'the rich always betray the poor'. With James Hope and Henry Munro, he attempted to co-ordinate an insurrection in Antrim and Down. Its brief vigour was suppressed brutally and savagely. Yet, it engaged the bravery of many whom Russell so much admired – small farmers, fishermen and at least one woman, Betsy Grey of Comber, Co Down. Florence Wilson's lines stand as tribute to them all, Protestants, Catholics and Dissenters:

> In the time o'the Hurry, we had no lead –
> we all of us fought with the rest –
> an' if e'er a one shook like a tremblin' reed,
> none of us gave neither hint nor heed
> nor ever even'd we'd guessed.
> We men of the North had a word to say,
> an' we said it then, in our own dour way,
> an' we spoke as we thought was best.

On the eve of the projected rising, Lord Edward FitzGerald, said to be the supreme commander of the United Irishmen, was apprehended in Thomas Street, Dublin. In the affray, he was wounded and taken to Newgate in severe pain. At the prison, Russell remained with him 'most of the first night of his imprisonment until I was separated from him by order of government'. It is of interest that Russell believed FitzGerald's death resulted not from his wounds, but 'from inflammation and water on his lungs'. From Russell's papers it also emerges that he spoke with Henry and John Sheares after their trial and sentence to death.[19] It is uncertain when Russell learned of the collapse of the senior United Irish leadership in Antrim and Down. There is no hint of disapproval in his subsequent correspondence with Robert Simms. Nor is his opinion extant of McCracken's and Munro's courage. McCracken evaded arrest after the rising collapsed. Some weeks ensued before his arrest and execution on 17 July 1798. One of the most poignant documents of the time is Mary Ann McCracken's account, written on the day after her brother's death, to inform Russell ('his dearest and valued friend') of what had happened. The closing words of her letter disclose her extra-ordinary spirit and her regard for Russell:

> That the cause for which so many of our friends have fought and died may yet be successful, and that you may be preserved to enjoy the fruits of it, is the wish of one who remains with the truest regard your sincere friend.[20]

Other friends of Russell – James Dickey and John Storey, a printer at the *Northern Star* – had been executed a few days before Henry Joy McCracken. James Hope was not captured and survived to join Russell in another attempt at revolution in 1803. Henry Munro was captured and hanged outside his own house in Lisburn. Thousands of others died in Ulster and Leinster leaving a testimony of bravery which has remained alive through subsequent generations. The words of Mary Ann McCracken summate the pathos and glory of 1798: 'In considering the unsuccessful struggle in which my brother was engaged, many are too apt to forget the evils of the time: the grinding oppression under which the people laboured; the contempt in which public opinion was held; the policy which prevented its expression and intimidated the press. The only means then existing of stemming the torrent of corruption and oppression was tried, and they failed, but the failure … was not without its beneficial effects.'[21]

The Kilmainham Pact

The circumstances of this 'pact' caused major difficulty for Russell's straightforward character. Late in July 1798 he was asked by Samuel Neilson to sign a document which would save

William Byrne and Oliver Bond from imminent execution. Both men had been sentenced to death, with their execution fixed for 25 July. Neilson's document committed its signatories 'to give whatever information they individually possesst(*sic*), without implicating others and to leave the country provided the lives of Messrs. Byrne and Bond were saved.' The subsequent complications of the proposal give rise to the suspicion that larger purposes than even the safety of the sentenced men were at work. The troubled history of the 'Kilmainham Pact' motivated Russell's later 'narrative' framed in December 1800.[22]

According to his narrative, Russell demurred from Neilson's proposal. He could not advise 'anyone who had engaged in the contest to withdraw even for a moment from it'. A protracted discussion took place among the Newgate prisoners, rendered all the more difficult by their own powerlessness and the proliferation of rumour. Neilson urged the propriety of halting useless bloodshed. He argued that 'the turn the war in the country had taken rendered it expedient to endeavour to effect some general measure of amnesty which would put an end to unavailing exertion and misery'. Russell continued to oppose compromise with government but agreed 'to do anything or make any sacrifice consistent with my conscience and honour to save the blood of any individual'. Ultimately, he was persuaded that to sign the document could save Byrne and Bond, ameliorate the condition of the United Irish leaders under threat of execution and 'save the people from the struggle'.

Also present at this tortured discussion were Francis Dobbs, a member of parliament and a religious enthusiast of millenarian bent, as well as a city sherriff named Archer. Their role is difficult to estimate: were they well-intentioned individuals or agents of higher powers? According to Russell's later account, Dobbs insisted that the idea of a signed document 'did not proceed from the government but from the prisoners'. Dobbs also claimed that the initiative would help to stop bloodshed. For Russell and, doubtless, for the other prisoners it was a harsh choice – to sign the document and, perhaps, be represented as having compromised or to refuse and, possibly, ruin the chance of avoiding further bloodshed. When at length Russell agreed to sign he wished to express in writing his own reluctance in the matter. Dobbs insisted that this would put the whole process in jeopardy. In the circumstances, the only demur Russell could make was oral. Later, he recalled its format: '… it is evident from my long imprisonment … that (I have) nothing personal to apprehend, that for the same reason I have nothing to declare, that my sole motive (is) to save the blood of others'. The whole event of 24 July caused him 'the greatest mental anguish' he could ever have to endure.

Yet the affair had not terminated. After the paper had been signed, Dobbs, Archer and an official named Pasley returned with a second document. The government was reported to have accepted the proposal – by now the unfortunate William Byrne had been executed – and wanted the new document signed by the prisoners. Neilson, Russell and 32 others signed it on the understanding that it meant 'general amnesty for all who chose to accept the same terms'. Some time afterwards, Thomas Addis Emmet, William McNeven and Arthur O'Connor were brought to a meeting at Dublin Castle with Lord Castlereagh (now chief secretary), John Fitzgibbon (chancellor) and Edward Cooke (under-secretary). It was agreed that Emmet, McNeven and O'Connor would draw up an account 'as to arms, ammunition and plans of warfare … so far as ourselves individually are concerned, so as no other individual whatever may be implicated'. The whole transaction came to be known as 'the Kilmainham treaty' since negotiations were mainly with Emmet, McNeven and O'Connor, all of whom were imprisoned at Kilmainham.[23]

The protracted saga of these negotiations fits within a larger scene of political intrigue. Directly, it affected Neilson and the prisoners against whom evidence could be brought on a capital charge. Against Russell, government seemed unable to secure or unwilling to adduce sufficient evidence. He later commented that although no one more than he was in the power of the rank and file of the people – 'whom it is the fashion to revile under the epithets of common people and mob' – yet no information was obtained against him from that source. It remains true that he might reasonably have expected to benefit from any amnesty following on the document's signature and the account of events prior to the rising, which Emmet, McNeven and O'Connor were to furnish. A larger canvas was being drawn by the new viceroy and his chief secretary. In June 1798, Charles, Marquis of Cornwallis had replaced Camden as viceroy. Of considerable military renown in India and America, he was now deputed to unite military and civil government in Ireland. His long-term purposes were not always to the liking of the Dublin Parliament or of high-ranking officials at Dublin Castle. Even in summer 1798, plans were already being laid for the legislative union of Ireland and Britain: it would seem that this plan, conceived by William Pitt, was to be fostered by Cornwallis and Castlereagh. In such a context the lives of the state prisoners would be little more than pawns in the *haute politique* of Dublin and Whitehall.

For all his grim reputation in Irish oral tradition, Cornwallis was neither inhumane nor unintelligent. Shortly after his arrival in Ireland he had formed his own ideas of the country's distress. Although he was now at the head of government forces, he recognised the brutality of the 'national troops' and the venality of the Irish ascendancy. Of the militias Cornwallis wrote to his friend, General Ross: 'murder appears to be their favourite pastime'. As to the politicians and the Irish gentry, the new viceroy judged that their fiercely anti-Catholic and anti-priesthood bias 'would drive four-fifths of the community into irreconcilable rebellion'. He came to believe that amnesty and not extirpation was the preferable way to deal with the insurrection. More than once in dispatches to Whitehall he outlined such a strategy for detaching ordinary participants in the rising from their leaders. Cornwallis inclined to banishment of the leaders rather than a policy of wholesale executions.

Thus, the proposal, however originated, that the state prisoners should come forward with 'a full confession of their sins, every information respecting the conspiracy and treason both at home and abroad' admirably suited the viceroy's purpose. As Cornwallis saw it, 'the establishment of the traitorous conspiracy by the testimony of all the principal actors in it (was) of much more consequence than the lives of twenty such men as Oliver Bond'. However, so virulent was the hostility of the ruling party in Dublin that 'nothing but blood will satisfy them'. Viceroy and chief secretary (Castlereagh) proceeded carefully. Late on the night of 24 July, Castlereagh presented the viceroy the initial statement signed by Neilson, Russell and others. According to himself, Cornwallis regarded the statement as deserving 'the most mature consideration'. However, he needed the support of

the Dublin administration. In the absence of Fitzgibbon, he convened the attorney general (John Toler), the solicitor-general
(John Stewart), the prime serjeant (James Fitzgerald), as well as
Lords Carleton and Kilwarden. Kilwarden (Arthur Wolfe, former attorney-general) and Toler rejected the proposition lest it
should 'irritate almost to madness the well-affected part of this
Kingdom'. Whereupon, Cornwallis declared his interest in the
matter at an end.[24]

More was to come. William Byrne was executed on 25 July. It is
difficult to avoid the conclusion that his death was also part of a
war of nerves with the object of wringing further concession
from the prisoners. As Cornwallis remembered the train of
events, the prisoners were told simply of the rejection of their
proposition. According to Cornwallis, this resulted in 'a much
more extensive (proposition) as to confession and information'.
Reporting to Whitehall, Cornwallis now adduced the full con-
sent of the senior government lawyers whom he consulted as
warrant for his acceptance of the prisoners' second offer and his
postponement of Oliver Bond's execution. The viceroy took particular care to mention that William Sampson, Hamden Evans
and Arthur O'Connor were now among the signatories.
Cornwallis' longer purposes may be gleaned as he asks rhetorically: 'What will the gentlemen who appeared at Maidstone say
to this?' In other words, the Whig opposition, both in Dublin
and London, would be grievously damaged. It is interesting
that what Cornwallis interpreted as a victory was understood by
Russell as an avenue towards amnesty.

The minutiae of further discussions between the prisoners and
Dublin Castle cannot be enumerated here. Emmet, McNeven
and O'Connor worked hard to trace the development of the
United Irishmen through the 1790s. Their document remained
mid-way between an account so weak as to spell capitulation to
government or so strong as to invite rejection by Cornwallis. In
the event, the memorandum was rejected in early August as
'containing many gross misstatements of facts and much unwar-
rantable invective against the government'. Privately, Cornwallis admitted that the document was ably written but in the
style of a controversial pamphlet. It did not yet serve his purposes. As the viceroy put it: 'This would be a very inconvenient
paper for us to receive.' When under-secretary Cooke returned

the memorandum to the Kilmainham trio they, rather than break off the deal, offered to give information before the secret committee of the House of Lords. It is difficult to judge whether Cornwallis was being self-congratulatory or astute to a Machiavellian degree when he wrote to Whitehall: 'This was exactly the point to which I wished to bring them, as it will prevent the necessity of our taking any notice of the secret information in the report.'[25]

Although the transaction worked well for Neilson and Bond, both of whom were in danger of execution, for Russell it meant chagrin, self-doubt and even humiliation. Ever since his imprisonment he had avoided all temporising with officialdom. In September 1798, some inkling of government duplicity emerged. An emigration bill, to cover the banishment of named state prisoners, was introduced to the house of parliament. Of the signatories to the July document it was stated that 'they had confessed their guilt, retracted their opinions and implored pardon'. It was a monstrous prevarication, totally at variance with the document itself. For Russell, it was utterly damaging to his sense of honour and contrary to what might have been expected of him. Threats by Samuel Neilson to publish the details of the prisoners' transaction met with counter-threats to recommence executions. Finally, the prisoners backed down, motivated by the desire still to avoid bloodshed. Eventually, Emmet, McNeven and O'Connor did appear before the secret committee. They, too, felt that their appearance before the committee had been traduced by the public press. On 27 August, they inserted a joint protest to the newspapers alleging gross misrepresentation directly contrary to the facts. The advertisement reassured the prisoners' friends 'that in no instance did the name of any individual escape us.'[26]

Although demands were raised in parliament for trial of Emmet, McNeven and O'Connor, and although Castlereagh prescribed solitary confinement at Kilmainham, Cornwallis took a cooler view. On 23 September, he asserted to the Duke of Portland that all his aims had been achieved. The 'treason' had been proved by incontrovertible evidence from the prisoners' document and subsequent testimonies. Ominously for Russell and the other state prisoners, Cornwallis argued that government still had 'the power of detaining the whole of the state-prisoners ... as long as the war lasts, or as it shall be thought necessary'. Then, wrote Cornwallis, they could be banished for life 'instead of turning them loose on the public to pursue their treasonable practices'. The viceroy's own view was that the prisoners should be sent out of the country as soon as possible. Drawing on his American experience, Cornwallis doubted if that country would be willing to receive 'such a cargo of sedition'. At the conclusion of his memorandum, he suggested that the state prisoners might be sent to Fort George or other of the forts in the Scottish highlands. There, wrote Cornwallis, they could have liberty to walk a mile or two from their place of detention.

On the whole, the government venture had reaped some rewards. Were it not for Russell's own observation that the initiative had come from the prisoners, one would incline to view it as engineered by government through Francis Dobbs. Cornwallis' view that it was preferable to banish rebel leaders than engage in wholesale slaughter may well have been taken up by Neilson and developed through Dobbs. Whichever hypothesis is adopted, the benefit accruing to government was clear to Edward Cooke, no enthusiast for Cornwallis' administration. In a memorandum to William Wickham on 28 July (just as the negotiation about signatures was coming to a close), Cooke stressed that even if no new information were disclosed 'what we have will be ascertained'. In addition, as Cooke put it boastfully, 'we will get rid of 70 prisoners, many of the most important of whom we could not try, and who could not be disposed of without doing such a violence to the principle of law and evidence as could not be well justified'. As to the 'zealots and yeomen' who made 'a fine buzz' about compromise, their 'tone softened' when they learned that Fitzgibbon approved of the measure.[27]

The prisoners' sense of betrayal will have been all the greater when Alexander Marsden, another under-secretary at Dublin Castle, informed them of those permitted to emigrate and those to be further detained. Russell was among the prisoners denied release. Verbal courtesies were observed as Marsden, a not unsympathetic man, reported that the viceroy was sorry 'the circumstances of the times did not enable him to include them in the liberation, but he hoped soon to be able to do so'. The reasons for this further delay are not stated. Hostility to Emmet, McNeven and O'Connor lingered since their public criticism of the select committee's report. Nevertheless, the potential embar-

rassment for Cornwallis passed almost unnoticed and is hardly
the reason for delay in liberating the state prisoners. Claims that
a document composed by Russell and other state prisoners to
seek French assistance deferred their release remain unverified.
It is notable that Rufus King, the American minister in London,
was strenuously opposing the state prisoners' entry to America,
as had been predicted by Cornwallis. This opposition led the
viceroy to advise the postponement of arrangements for their
passage to America until 'his Excellency is furnished with further information on this point'.[28]

It was a difficult chapter for the prisoners in which their powerlessness was abused by government for its own purposes. Later,
the 'Kilmainham treaty' would be criticised by some French al-
lies. Yet, when Tone heard of it he was overjoyed: 'Is poor Russell
at last out of the scrape ... would he were in Holstein ... he
would break parole and come to Paris, if it were only to see you
(Matilda Tone) and Maria. If that should happen, take care of
him, and let him imbibe.'[29]

The mysterious Francis Dobbs

Francis Dobbs, a former governor of North Carolina and then a
member of parliament, played an ambiguous role not only in
these conversations but later in Russell's imprisonment. He was
a religious enthusiast who shared with Thomas Russell an abiding interest in the apocalyptic prophecies of the bible. Dobbs'
political acumen may be measured by his later opposition to the
Act of Union not on political grounds but rather because it ran
counter to biblical prophecies. In regard to the 'Kilmainham
treaty' he was, at best, a meddlesome interferer or, at worst, a
duplicitous agent of Dublin Castle. Even after the conversations
in regard to the document signed in July 1798 he again visited
Russell and gave him to understand that the administration was
not averse to his liberation. This probably sincere yet trouble-
some meddler importuned Russell to write a letter on how he
(Russell) proposed to fulfill his engagement to leave the country.
Russell's stance was that he needed three months at liberty to
put his affairs in order. Thereafter, he would emigrate to whatever country was agreed. As guarantee, he would give whatever
security was required. Perhaps with the painful experience of
July-August in mind, he refused any verbal agreement which
might be liable to misunderstanding.[30]

Hence, on 14 September 1798 Russell sent a letter to Dobbs for conveyance to government. Between the letter and the earlier conversation with Dobbs there were some changes. Russell asked for four months' liberty rather than three; he now asked to go to the continent of Europe since he had 'a strong dislike to America'. Perhaps of greater interest is his insistence on explaining his motives in the state prisoners' transaction with government. Through the letter conveyed by Dobbs he published his own stance in such a way 'as by no possibility to affect others, with respect to the Emigration Bill'. Reaffirming his willingness to emigrate, Russell also emphasised that he had 'never retracted any political opinion or confessed any political guilt'. Even more, in signing the document of agreement he had 'no motive in mind but to save the lives of others'. Dobbs subscribed to the letter his own view that Russell as a man of honour would carry out all he had undertaken to do. Thomas Russell's argument would have been inconvenient for the purposes of Cornwallis and Castlereagh. Perhaps it was this letter which ensured Russell's further detention. Certain it is that within days of the letter's composition the cells of the state prisoners were raided and their papers confiscated. Writing to Newgate in December Dobbs had the grace to admit that, despite his best efforts, the scheme had not worked: Castlereagh had insisted that Russell was one of the prisoners to be detained until 'the place of destination was fixed.'[31]

Despite his brush with high officialdom, Russell had more pedestrian concerns. On 17 September, he asked for the restoration of an allowance of wine, prescribed by Dr Mitchell, but discontinued 'in these last few days'. On 2 October, he requested permission to visit prisoners in other jails – perhaps to speak with Emmet and McNeven on the consequences of the Emigration bill. Throughout October, he demanded the return of his papers confiscated by Oliver Carleton the previous month. And he continued his application for either bail or trial. Concern for Margaret occupied him during these weeks. At the end of October 1798 he admonished her to use for herself the remittance of five pounds he had sent. Selflessness did not distinguish Stephen Hamilton who demanded twenty-five pounds. Russell confided to Margaret that he could not meet this request: due to his long confinement he had not been able to attend to his affairs. There is a despondent note as Russell concludes his letter: 'I am as well

as can be'. Just before Christmas Margaret wrote of her surprise
to see 'by chance in a late paper that you and other gentlemen are
to be detained during the war ...'.[32]

Tone's arrest and death

In late October 1798, a French expedition to Ireland foundered
off Lough Swilly. Wolfe Tone, holding a general's rank in the
French army, was arrested and sent to Derry jail. Early in
November, he was brought to Dublin where he was committed
to the royal prison. From Newgate Russell endeavoured to rally
help. First he requested the barrister Peter Burrowes to act on
Tone's behalf. Despite political risk for himself, Burrowes engaged John Philpot Curran to lead Tone's defence and sought to
raise money for expenses. Writing to Newgate, Burrowes –
whose gallantry is all the more remarkable in view of his political disagreement with Tone – promised to give every possible
assistance, remembering 'how estimable a man he was and how
much he was my friend'. The barrister did not hesitate to specify
difficulties. A letter to Cornwallis in which Tone claimed the
rank of a French general was not helpful. Neither was the nature
of Tone's departure from Ireland in 1795. Nor would his case be
helped by the character of the expedition on which he was engaged. Hence, Burrowes estimated that the most to be hoped-for
was postponement of court-martial until trial by jury could be
obtained. With considerable humanity, Burrowes promised
Russell that 'if I have anything consolatory (of which I despair) I
will put you in possession of it'.[33]

Russell also wrote to the principal state prisoners at Kilmainham. One can judge the character of his letter from the wounded
dignity of Addis Emmet's reply. Emmet's letter to Russell re-
sponds to an accusation of not doing enough to save Tone.
Clearly, Russell had over-estimated the leverage which Emmet,
McNeven and O'Connor enjoyed at Dublin Castle since their
testimony before the parliamentary secret committee. Were
they failing to utilise their purchase with Castlereagh,
Fitzgibbon and Cooke? Certainly that is the implication Emmet
took from Russell's letter: '... it seems to imply that your fellow-
prisoners imagine some such thing could be done'. Emmet
pointed out that any application by the state prisoners in favour
of Tone would only do harm. When they sued for Bond's life
they had something to offer – their own banishment and some

information. No such bargaining power now existed. In fact, the contrary was true: 'I assume government hate us and if we had asked such a favour they would doubly rejoice of their opportunity in gratifying their own vengeance against him and dislike against us.' With some realism, Emmet reported that the Chancellor, John Fitzgibbon, had warned that Tone before his emigration 'signed such a confession of his own treason, as could and was intended to hang him in the case of his ever returning'. The Kilmainham prisoners, therefore, did not intend to undertake mediation: '… we can see nothing we can do'.[34]

Burrowes and Emmet were right. The court-martial went ahead. Tone was sentenced to death. For Russell, Tone's death in doubtful circumstances on 19 November would have counted as yet another personal tragedy comparable to the execution of Henry Joy McCracken on 17 July 1798.

CHAPTER TEN

Internment at Fort George
(1799-1802)

By Christmas 1798 the prospect of release had dimmed considerably for Russell and his colleagues. This is reflected in Margaret's
answer to her brother's letter of 20 December. Margaret regretted that 'all hope of your being liberated is at an end'. It would
seem that Russell had attempted to boost her flagging morale.
On the political level, the prisoners still hoped for yet another
French expedition. That, at least, was the claim of an informant –
probably Leonard McNally – who had access to them. Writing to
John Pollock on 3 January 1799, the informer stressed that
'Russell is confident that a fleet will be ready for sea by the end
of the month'. Its arrival would be supported by four thousand
men led by Francis Blake, allegedly resident at Capel Street,
Dublin. With particular vindictiveness the informer advised that
the daily five shillings now allowed the prisoners should be reduced to two shillings. This benign correspondent was of the
opinion that the surplus three shillings was being 'put to mischief'.[1]

Political optimism is a consistent feature of Russell's complex
personality. He remained convinced that a war of liberation in
Ireland would easily succeed, provided the people as a whole
were involved. In his retrospective account he avowed, in
December 1800: 'I had and have the most perfect confidence of
the easiness of accomplishing the object wished for by the people'. For Russell the defeat of the rising in south Leinster and
east Ulster did not spell the end of the cause. Significantly,
Leonard McNally adverted to diverse stances among the prisoners on the legislative union between Britain and Ireland now
mooted in official quarters. Whereas the Kilmainham prisoners
recommended opposition, the Newgate detainees tried 'to get
their friends to support the union in order to influence the orange men'.[2] Yet another informer, James McGucken, recom-

153

mended that the state prisoners be deported as soon as possible. McGucken complained of their ability to communicate both within and without the prisons, even if 'there were a thousand soldiers to guard them'. The same letter suggests defiance among the state prisoners: 'It appears to them that government are either afraid to send them abroad, or are keeping them as hostages, in case the government should have occasion to redeem themselves'.[2]

Deportation to Scotland

On 18 March 1799, Tresham Gregg, still keeper of Newgate, informed Russell that on the following day he was to embark on ship. No further information was given. Yet, during the evening Russell sent a letter to Margaret informing her that the state prisoners were to be sent to England. With typical consideration he assured her that 'your bills shall be paid ... I will take care that you shall not want money'. Early on the 19th, Russell, along with fifteen other prisoners, was taken to the Dublin quays. There they boarded the *Ashton Smith* under a guard of Angusshire Fencibles, commanded by a Captain Ewing. In the evening the ship left for Belfast Lough. Turbulence at sea made the prisoners severely ill, especially Samuel Neilson. At Belfast they were joined by Robert Simms, William Tennent, Robert Hunter and William Steele Dickson, the Presbyterian clergyman so actively involved in the United Irish Society. After a brief delay in Belfast Lough, the *Ashton Smith* headed for the firth of Clyde where adverse winds and tides prevented disembarkation for some days.

Only on 30 March were the prisoners brought ashore at Gooroch, near Greenock. Here they were taken in charge by Colonel Hay and a detachment of infantry. Their destination was Fort George, an extensive fortress some miles north of Inverness. On the way, the prisoners' every need was seen to by Colonel Hay. Inhabitants of the towns through which they passed treated them with unfailing courtesy. On one occasion, Scottish merchants spoke of the recent Catholic rebellion in Ireland. Dr Steele Dickson vigorously rejected any suggestion that the rising could be defined on sectarian lines. To illustrate this, Steele Dickson instanced the religious professions of the twenty prisoners: ten, including Russell, were Anglicans, six were Presbyterians, four were Catholics.[3]

After a journey of nine days, the prisoners arrived at Fort George. The fortress was commanded by Colonel James Stuart, a man of refined manners, honourable principles, and not a little courage. Stuart ensured the state prisoners were comfortably lodged. He allowed them considerable freedom of association and ample opportunity for exercise. They were provided with a satisfactory diet which they were permitted to take in common. To Russell, so long confined in the noisome confines of Newgate, this situation will have been a dramatic improvement. Thus, in his first letter to Drumsluice he could inform Margaret of his 'perfect health and spirits'. As ever, he thought of remittance for her and of arrangements to cash it. Of Fort George he had no complaint, 'except the distance from you and my friends'. When the prisoners settled into the routine of their detention they found the governor amenable to every reasonable suggestion. Eventually, they were allowed to swim in the sea and given the facility of a ball alley. This was a boon not only to the athletic Russell but also to his fellow-prisoners.[4]

Due to the liberality of Colonel Stuart, the Fort George prisoners settled into an even pace of life. The accomodation was good, the diet excellent, the prison staff humane. A time came when the state prisoners were treated almost as friends by Stuart. Their greatest deprivation was exile and the inevitable removal from such politics as continued in the aftermath of the 1798 rising. On 4 August, not three months after his arrival in Scotland, Russell sent a courteous letter to Edward Cooke at Dublin Castle. He reminded the under-secretary of a promise the latter had made to return Russell's confiscated papers. This brief letter concludes: 'The first time that you have leisure I should esteem it a favour if you would order them to be sent to me'.[5] The prisoners still at Newgate were not so fortunate. For them, overcrowding persisted as a fact of life. Despite the transfer of Russell and his colleagues, despite the resulting vacancies on the floor they had occupied, the remaining nine prisoners had only six beds. Fruitless application was made to the keeper of Newgate and to the inspector of prisons. As a final measure, the prisoners sent a remonstrance to under-secretary Marsden on 21 May 1799.

Correspondence at Fort George

Russell's surviving correspondence of this period is mainly with his sister, Templeton, and McDonnell. Throughout his imprisonment Russell assiduously wrote to Margaret. His concern for her poverty was unremitting. She, too, was generous in performing services for him and, at times, his colleagues. Mary Ann McCracken and James McDonnell kept contact with her and, when necessary, endeavoured to rally her spirits. Russell's Belfast friends dissuaded her from travelling to Fort George on grounds of expense and uncertainty of access to the prisoners. In October 1800, Margaret returned to Dublin to live at Fitzwilliam Place, Grangegorman, financially dependent as ever. Thomas hoped their brother John would 'not now neglect you'. However, John Russell showed no sign of becoming enmeshed in Margaret's woes. Already he was pressed for funds by his daughter, Mary Anne, and his son-in-law, William Hamilton. Virtually nothing could be expected from him.

One notices Russell's self-reproach on Margaret's isolation when he writes: 'Your distress of which I have been partly the innocent cause has only the effect of increasing my affection and I feel confident that I shall have the means of showing it.' Albeit unwillingly, he contacted Dublin friends to advise her and perhaps to aid her with gifts of money. As well, he sent remittances when he could do so. In one of his letters, Russell became almost enthusiastic about Fort George and its environs saying that he had never seen a more healthy place. As a consequence of these new conditions he was able to reassure Margaret that 'I never was better and in particular the pain in my heart which I used to have occasionally has quite disappeared.'[6]

In September 1801, Margaret, now at Wood Street, was planning to embark on her own small business. Thomas wished her well in her 'scheme of independence' – it may have been the small school she eventually did run for a while. By October she had moved to 2 Henrietta Place where Mary Ann McCracken visited her during business trips to Dublin. At this stage, talks of peace between England and France gave hope that the state prisoners might soon be released. With a good sense of realism, Russell advised Margaret that there was 'no use writing to government as the letter might be overlooked'. Yet, he was sufficiently attuned to her anxiety for him to add: 'I just mention the last lest you should think I was remiss on a business which so much concerns me'. In the same letter he mentioned papers relative to the mineralogy of Antrim as especially relevant to him. These were still retained at Dublin Castle.

Margaret Russell was generous in helping other detainees at Fort George. One of the prisoners, Matthew Dowling, was anxious at not having heard from either his mother or sister. Russell asked Margaret to call on these women at Golden Lane, to find how they were and to inform Dowling of their welfare. This service she discharged promptly much to Dowling's relief. By November 1801, Russell was happy to note that their London brother (John) had sent help to Margaret ('tho' so little') and that 'your scheme is likely to succeed'. There was still talk of liberation – 'some letters arrived from London, received this day, speak of our liberation as likely to take place'. One wonders if Colonel Stuart had not permitted a judicious 'leak' from his dispatches! On his thirty-fourth birthday Russell noted that this was the sixth he had spent consecutively in prison. As some years earlier, he hoped 'every year I shall improve in or out of prison'.[7]

In March 1802, Edward Cooke agreed to release the confiscated papers from Dublin Castle. They were to be given to Francis Dobbs, still on the fringes of Irish politics. This time, Dobbs proved an effective intermediary. On Russell's instructions, Margaret received the papers from Dobbs and retained them at her lodgings. To Margaret, then, is due the survival of her brother's pocket-book and many other documents which remained intact through the intervening centuries. Perhaps the release of these papers, perhaps the improvement in political circumstances which Margaret observed, caused tension for her. By May 1802, Russell was somewhat piously advising: 'the anxiety you express about my liberation is very natural, but it is our duty to keep these feelings within bounds – providence orders all for our ultimate good and we should patiently wait its decisions'.[8]

Strains at Fort George

Despite the civility of the regime, relationships among the state prisoners exhibited ambiguities. At one level, polite interaction remained unbroken among these men of idealism, education, good manners and long-shared experience. The arrival at Fort George during 1800 of Mrs Emmet and, in particular, the months of her pregnancy, evoked the courtesies to be expected from men of cultivation. More than once Russell spoke of the Emmets in letters to Margaret. The happy outcome of Mrs Emmet's confinement came up for extended mention. At this time Russell's poetic interests revived as he crafted verses somewhat in the style of Thomas Moore. When the eight-years-old son of Samuel Neilson came to live at Fort George, a small faculty of education was set up to benefit him and the Emmet children. Russell (mathematics), Emmet (history), Neilson (English) and Steele Dickson (Latin) were the ad hoc professors!

However, at another level difficulties subsisted among the state prisoners. Differing analyses of Irish politics probably reflected old differences. The northern United Irishmen, like Neilson and Russell, were more radical than the cautious, institutional approach of the Dublin leadership. Neilson observed that some of his colleagues 'would not set the Liffey on fire'. Although there is no documentary evidence of it, it is probable that the transactions in the 'Kilmainham pact' may have planted a seed of disunity. The question of future directions, their own and those of United Irish politics, would have been a matter of debate for the prisoners.[9]

More complicated is the view of Thomas Addis Emmet that Art O'Connor was an informer. Emmet suspected that O'Connor was an agent of government, planted to gather evidence against his fellow prisoners. As a result, relations between the two men were unfriendly. It is true that O'Connor's behaviour during the Maidstone trial of Fr O'Coigly was ambiguous. If O'Connor was an agent, it is unlikely to have been at the instigation of Colonel Stuart. In the absence of documentary evidence of perfidy on O'Connor's part, one has to consider that long imprisonment fuelled exaggerated suspicions among some of the prisoners. Even in the relatively confined space of Fort George Emmet and O'Connor avoided each other. On their deportation, en route to Hamburg, a duel between them was prevented only with difficulty.[10]

On the other hand, some informing did occur, although not through the governor of Fort George. Robert Hunter claimed to a Belfast magistrate that he had informed Thomas Pelham (now at Whitehall) of a plot among the state prisoners. Angling for permission to return to Belfast or Liverpool, Hunter told the magistrate that Neilson and Emmet were at the head of a plot 'for the dissemination of republican principles in Scotland and especially for sapping the loyalty of Scottish regiments of militia in view of a French invasion of great Britain'. A sad feature of Hunter's communication is his attempt to incriminate those who had shown kindness to the prisoners: Colonel Stuart was charged by Hunter with negligence while of an officer's wife, Mrs Cameron, he alleged that she was 'an Irish patriot'.[11]

The Russell prison narrative

These circumstances should be connected to the lengthy memorandum sent on 10 December 1800 to John Russell. In essence, it explains Thomas Russell's own motivation when reluctantly he entered conversation with government in July 1798. The narrative, which has already figured in discussion of the 'Kilmainham pact', probably arose from sporadic criticism of the 'pact' in 1799 and 1800. Russell is careful to record his migivings and implies an awareness that it worked to government's advantage. The transaction with government was, clearly, weighing on his mind as he composed the detailed narrative and arranged for its delivery to his brother. A covering note is noteworthy since it gives a clearer view of his political stances at the end of 1800 than can be gleaned from the allusive style of his other letters.[12]

In this note, Russell reaffirmed the political principle for which he was imprisoned. A little rhetorically he insisted that his belief in that cause increased every day: 'The numbers who have fallen and among them many great and good … imposes a greater obligation on the survivors to persevere in the great cause.' Without doubt, he refers here to Tone, McCracken and the many unnamed people who had died in 1798. At a time when many – even among his friends and comrades – were tempering conviction to expediency, he remained adamantly attached to the principles of the 1790s. A broader thrust emerges when he links the good of Ireland with the good of all peoples. In Ireland, the contest was not 'for relative power or riches (but rather) between the two principles of Despotism and Liberty'. In that contest there was no compromise, no *via media*. To Russell, it was clear which principle must ultimately triumph. Such confidence is a recurrent feature of his political thought, so strong that it becomes problematic. It is an optimism based not upon calculation of probabilities but on a vision that approaches messianism. He appeals to biblical principles rather than political analysis: an impending judgement awaits individuals and nations which persist 'in supporting injustice and tyranny by fraud, cruelty and superstition'. God had made all people equal: to depart from that divine ordinance led to folly and confusion.

In clear reference to the 'reconciliation' mooted by Lord Cornwallis, Russell protested: 'neither can I conform to the notion that usurpation is defensible because the usurper professes great talents or uses his power with clemency'. In his view, government would always claim to act for the people who, conveniently for government, were not deemed wise enough to act for themselves. Russell's personal charity is notable in his heartfelt compliment to Colonel Stuart: 'He is a gentleman who if somewhat older might put you in mind of our late father. He unites politeness and humanity with a discharge of his duty.' In terms which speak much about his chivalry, Russell added: 'I have always been treated with respect and attention on the part of government since my first imprisonment ...'. In similar fashion he concluded by referring to his great pleasure 'in the society of my friend Emmet's delightful family'.

Gradual releases

In December 1801, five of the Fort George prisoners – Steele Dickson, Simms, Tennent, Harper and Dowling – were allowed home. In his Christmas letter, Russell hoped that Margaret and he would spend the next Christmas together. Yet he discounted rumours of further releases until something definite was known. An earnest of good news came in March with the release of his papers to Francis Dobbs who sent them for safe-keeping to Margaret. By May, he expected imminent liberation. Somewhat pressingly, he asked Margaret to get from Richard Kirwan (then at Rutland Square in Dublin) introductory letters 'to some of the literary men on the continent'. In the same letter he asked her to procure money from an otherwise unidentified Mr C. This composite request evidently distressed Margaret. In a letter of acknowledgement, Russell apologised that he could not give his reasons except that 'no one perhaps has a more natural invincible repugnance to incur obligations than I'. On the eve of release he was again asking Margaret to ensure that 'what I wrote to you the day before yesterday' was given to a Mr Sweetman for transmission to Hamburg.[13]

There were other requests. On 3 June Russell wrote to John Templeton for letters of introduction in France and Holland. These were necessary as he wished 'to see something of the present state of science, after so long a seclusion from the world'. With an overtone of embarrassment he confessed that he had written to Dr McDonnell for money but had no reply. On 5 June a further missive asked Templeton and McDonnell for a letter of credit in the amount of twenty pounds. Templeton sent the money although he could not give introductory letters for the continent. Meanwhile, William Drennan caustically alluded to Russell's letters 'in the manner of Greek philosophers' for a supply of fifty pounds and leaving 'the support of his sister to his friends'.[14]

Drennan may have had some reason for his barb. During these closing weeks of his imprisonment there was an air of unreality to Russell's letters. Shortage of money and uncertainty for the future weighed heavily on him. Six years had shielded him from dramatic changes in the temper of those who had earlier shared his radical politics. William Sinclair had forsaken radical politics to concentrate on his own business affairs. Robert Hunter was now endeavouring to avoid further trouble. For middle-class Belfast Presbyterians, the abolition of the Dublin Parliament spelled a new opportunity for equality in the broader context of the Act of Union. Russell may have underestimated how things had changed when he emphasised that his soul was 'still on fire' and that the defeat of 1798 was no more than a 'temporary miscarriage of the Cause'. He remained confident that the people had not abandoned their ideals and that, hence, 'the cause will succeed'. Once again, the admixture of religion and politics recurs as he wrote: 'The only true basis of liberty is morality and the only stable basis of morality is religion.'

By now, Russell had become sharply critical of French politics or, more particularly, of Bonaparte's notable turn to self-aggrandisement. This would-be emperor, according to Russell, 'tramples on liberty in France, suspends its progress in the world, and madly attempts its total destruction'. Disillusion impelled Russell to regard it as fortunate that no revolution under French auspices had occurred in Ireland. As he put it, there would have been no change except an exchange of masters. The fact that atheists and deists now governed France and, what Russell

termed, 'boundless profligacy of marriage laws' convinced him
that the French people were being bound to the feet of tyranny.
A portent of Russell's future action is given when he informs
Templeton that he will stay in Europe so that 'all the faculties I
possess should be exercised for the advancement of the cause'.
Every generous mind, he thought, should be motivated by 'the
widows and orphans of my friends, the memory of the heroes
who fell and the sufferings of the heroes who survive'. In a personal conclusion to his letter Russell sent affectionate remem-
brances to the McCrackens, particularly Mary Ann, and to
Edward Bunting whose 'Airs' he had kept with him throughout
the prison years.[15]

Almost by return, Templeton told him his idealism was misplaced. Templeton was himself a United Irishman whose affection for Russell was undimmed by separation. Nevertheless, he
stressed that there would be no revolution until the recent past
was forgotten and a widespread jealousy healed. The poor
would not readily trust the rich, nor the rich the poor. Each suspected the others' motives. The rising had exposed the dispositions of many: now, selfishness had begun to prevail. Russell's
memory of those who died was not matched in Ireland. People
had forgotten 'the blood which flowed from their friends ... and
with exultation (they were now submitting) to a fortunate
usurper'. While Templeton's sincerity is undoubtable, events
would show that in north and south the aspirations of the 1790s
had not been utterly extinguished. Russell maintained the view
that in Antrim and Down people waited only for proper leadership to essay once again the 'cause' for which they had suffered
so much.

Release and exile

On 31 May Russell told his sister that the remaining prisoners
were being sent to Hamburg. Despite his suspicion of
Bonaparte, Russell wished to go to France. Of Hamburg he
knew virtually nothing, except some Irish people already there.
Perhaps with a prescience of his further activities he advised
Margaret to rely on providence 'even should our separation be
permanent'. On 26 June 1802, Colonel Stuart received instructions for the releases facilitated by the Peace of Amiens. Stuart interpreted his orders in the most liberal sense since he included
Thomas Addis Emmet, for whom a remit had not arrived,

among those to be released. Later, he would be penalised for his generosity and removed from his post. For Thomas Russell, six years of imprisonment had now ended.[16]

CHAPTER ELEVEN

Exile and Return

What with discourse goin' to an fro,
the night would be wearin' thin,
yet never so late when we rose to go
but someone would say: 'do ye min' thon snow,
and the man who came wanderin' in?'
and we be to fall to the talk again,
if by any chance he was one o' them –
the man who went like the win'.

As Thomas Russell emerged from his long imprisonment, amongst all his colleagues he remained 'the most determined to revive the (United Irish) movement'.[1] Approaching thirty-five years of age, in good health and spirits, he was eager to resume the work interrupted by his arrest in 1796. The shift towards imperialism in France rendered him suspicious about what could be expected from that quarter. Templeton's pessimism about war-weariness and mutual distrust in Ireland did not alter his desire to assist in any further attempt at revolution there. His confidence in the 'men of no property' may have led him to distinguish middle-class acquiescence from the longer memories of a populace which had suffered the brunt of repression.

The newly released detainees had no choice of their immediate destination. They were taken to Cuxhaven, near Hamburg, where they disembarked on 4 July. Their arrival at Hamburg was observed by Thomas Ridgeway who dined with two of them ('one of whom was a Captain Russell'). By all appearances, the ex-prisoners were activating Irish contacts at Hamburg. To Russell's chagrin, money he expected was not available. After a few days the new arrivals left again for Amsterdam. This journey was difficult: it took twenty days to cross the Zuider Zee in contrary winds. Even at Amsterdam, the funds long awaited by Russell had not arrived. It is possible that here he met Robert

Emmet who had come to meet Thomas Addis for the first time in years.[2]

Thereafter, the erstwhile state prisoners went different ways. Thomas Addis Emmet went to Brussels with his family. William McNeven travelled to Vienna while Arthur O'Connor joined Irish emigrés at Paris. Russell, too, headed for Paris. By the end of August 1802 he was living at the Hotel d'Angleterre in the capital's Rue Colombier. Pressed for money, he signalled distress to Margaret: 'I have been here now a fortnight and am quite vexed at not having got the cash which was promised me … I beg of you to let me know by return of post if any such has or will be sent to me'. Margaret's anxiety will doubtless have been compounded by the further necessity to sue for him once again among his friends in Dublin. John Russell, still in London and making fragile progress in literary work, promised a visit to Paris. He also sent letters of introduction to Parisian writers – earlier he had recommended Thomas for parliamentary reporting. Thomas Russell was eager to meet him to discuss what could not be put in writing – 'when we meet I will tell you what it was hurried me'. While pressing John to come he concluded on a political note: 'wishing and expecting to see you in a free Ireland'. As to his own finances, it is possible that his literary skill – not his calligraphy ! – along with introductions to 'literary men' procured some income during the Parisian autumn and winter of 1802-3. According to information given to Dublin Castle in late 1803, either Robert or William Simms sent credit to Paris after Russell's discharge from Fort George. John Russell did spend some days at the Hotel d'Angleterre, a sojourn which nearly resulted in his arrest some months later.[3]

Political contacts in Paris

The Irish community in Paris was an intensely political one. Unfortunately, a penchant for intrigue made it a seed-bed for internal bickering and, at least in one case, a source of information for Dublin Castle. This group included Surgeon Lawless, a near relative of Lord Valentine Cloncurry, James J. McDonnell, a Mayo barrister who had participated in Humbert's ill-fated expedition of 1798, and Michael Quigley, a captain during the rising of the same year. Others in this circle were Malachy Delany, formerly an officer in the Austrian army and Lyndon Bolton, a Dubliner whose home was a meeting-point for Irish political emigrés.

A visitor at McDonnell's house in the Rue de Bussey was Jean Joseph Humbert, McDonnell's general from the expedition which landed at Killala in Autumn 1798. This extraordinary officer seems to have been fired by the idea of another expedition to erase the ignomy of his earlier defeat by Cornwallis. At McDonnell's, Russell met Humbert and noticed that, although the general spoke much about America and the West Indies, yet 'the freedom of Ireland occupied all his allusion'. Talk about an expedition to Louisiana and about the liberation of the West Indies seemed a cover for mounting an unofficial sortie to Ireland. The French seemed to expect that Irishmen in France and America would join these projects 'if they were not employed in liberating their own country'. Russell was unconvinced – Bonaparte wanted the Irish as mercenaries rather than on an expedition to Ireland. However, he viewed Humbert differently and hoped that the goodwill of this former Jacobin would offset the dangers of Bonaparte's private ambitions.

Allowing for the credentials of General Humbert, an enigma remains as to Russell's quick immersion in revolutionary politics. Templeton had warned about the impossibility of another rising. Russell's own doubts about French involvement persisted. He had not been in close touch with Irish affairs for years. Was not this new pattern of activity irresponsible to the point of folly? Was it the activity of an incurable dreamer? Was it the delirium of one unhinged by long imprisonment and driven by the executions of his close friends? These criticisms have been levelled even by those sympathetic to his perseverance. Yet, to answer such questions requires consideration of a further enigma – the origins of Robert Emmet's insurrection of 1803. During the months of his brief stay in Paris, Russell would again have encountered Emmet who at that very time endeavoured to enlist French help for another rising. Emmet did have a plan which, through General Augereau, he presented to Bonaparte. In Emmet's strategy, the French were to land at Galway and from there march on Derry. Here they would await reinforcement by northern insurgents. Emmet hoped the south would rise in the rear of government forces. Russell's presence would be crucial to a new insurgency in Ulster. Emmet's own confidence about the feasibility of a new rising may have been misplaced and, perhaps, may have arisen from what today would be termed *agents provocateurs*. Yet evidence can be adduced that across

Leinster and into Munster, people awaited a concerted plan to rise against government. In that framework, Russell's belief that he could mobilise the north is not nearly so far-fetched as it was portrayed.

Despite these ambiguities, Russell took the discussions at Rue de Bussey with sufficient urgency to prepare an arms depot at Le Havre. John Swiney, an ex-prisoner of Fort George, had set up a factory at the port. When Russell learned from Humbert that old cast arms from the French army could be purchased in bulk, Surgeon Lawless set about collecting money to buy them. Swiney's factory at Le Havre would provide a convenient storage-point. Meanwhile, Russell acted as a sort of quartermaster in giving sums of money, provided by Robert Emmet, to Irishmen en route home. Through the closing months of 1802 and early in 1803, there was frequent to-and-fro between Paris and Dublin. William Hamilton, Russell's nephew-in-law, made two journeys from Paris to Dublin. Returning to Paris on his first trip he was spotted by government agents in London. Money, albeit in small quantities, was provided by Emmet and sent to Russell for disbursement. The enigmatic William Putnam McCabe – Russell's friend of Belfast days – moved between Le Havre, Rouen and Paris. Early in March 1803, he instructed several Irishmen, including Michael Quigley, to leave immediately for Ireland. When Quigley enquired about the force to be employed in Ireland and whom else was to travel there, McCabe refused to answer. Nor was further information afforded by Russell when he gave thirty pounds for Quigley's and another's travel expenses.[4]

Russell's arrival in Ireland

Quigley and Hamilton were not the only ones Ireland-bound. At the end of March 1803, Russell set out for Dublin. Having passed six months, almost all in revolutionary preparation, he may have understood it was time to leave. With a passport in the name of Agar, issued by the British minister at Paris, he travelled by Calais and Dover to London. James Hope later claimed that the Irish exiles were told by associates of Talleyrand that Bonaparte was in league with the British government to deport them, 'their residence there not being considered favourable to Napoleon's imperial views'. In London, Russell spent some days with his brother through whom he met James O'Farrell, a

former United Irishman now prospering in the city. At West-
minster bridge he recognised, and was recognised by, John
Claudius Beresford, a virulent enemy to the republican cause.
Immediately, he set out in rudimentary disguise for Dublin via
Liverpool. From his re-entry to Ireland, his presence was known
to Dublin Castle. Later, William Wickham, the chief secretary,
referred to alarm caused in official circles by news of Russell's
arrival. Information from William Turner, dated 31 May, will already have been known to Castle officials: 'From every circumstance ... I am satisfied that Russell or some others of the Fort
George exiles have returned and are at present in Dublin.'[5]

Emmet had been warned of the risks attached to Russell's premature arrival. Officially, the former state prisoners were
banned from entering the country. Nevertheless, Thomas
Russell's near-legendary reputation would render his presence
of major benefit. And so, early in May, Russell joined Emmet,
Hamilton and William Dowdall at a rented house in Butterfield
Lane, some four miles south west of the city. Here he lived,
rarely leaving the house except under cover of darkness or disguised. From Butterfield Lane, links were quickly established
with veterans of the 1798 uprising.

In the Wicklow mountains, Michael O'Dwyer and his followers
had become a symbol of resistance after Vinegar Hill, Wexford
and New Ross. With the caution that had ensured his safety
hitherto, O'Dwyer refused to attend meetings at Emmet's headquarters. Now, through 'Big Arthur' Devlin (who had been a
soldier in Fort George during Russell's imprisonment there),
O'Dwyer agreed to visit Butterfield Lane for discussion of proposals for a rising. The Wicklow guerilla's condition was that
whoever entered the house should not leave until he (O'Dwyer)
had first departed. For several days, Russell, Emmet and
O'Dwyer considered the organisation of an uprising. It was
agreed that once Emmet had taken Dublin Castle, O'Dwyer
would mount a diversionary campaign from Wicklow. In
Kildare and Carlow veterans of 1798 were contacted by Michael
Quigley. He informed them of an impending event which
would require both manpower and whatever arms remained
from the earlier rising.

Difficulties

At a planning conference attended by thirty officers, Russell outlined the problematic nature of French intervention. Napoleon's pretensions ran counter to everything for which republicanism stood. Russell also appears to have mistrusted Talleyrand. This cynical manipulator of revolutions was now Napoleon's Foreign Minister. Many of the Irish in Paris believed he had provided British officers with vital information on earlier expeditions to Ireland. The only high-ranking French officials in whom Russell had any confidence were the ex-Jacobin generals, such as Humbert, now mistrusted by the would-be emperor. At Butterfield Lane, Russell raised difficult questions. Would French help eventuate? If it did, how was its potential for despotism to be countered? The dilemma was clear: French assistance was needed; yet, it could lead to a new, even worse, tyranny. Russell's own instincts were consistent with his mistrust of Bonaparte. The Irish people should strike for their own freedom. If help came from France then a strategy to confine the ambitions of the First Consul would have to be devised.

Other problems emerged as the days passed. It became clear that Emmet had been tricked by certain highly-placed individuals into a false estimation of success. The possibility of treachery presented itself. Emmet's facile reassurance that 'some of the highest men of the land had invited him over' now appeared in its true worth. When Russell saw the plans unravelling he is reputed to have said: 'This conspiracy is the work of the enemy: we are now in the vortex – if we can swim ashore let it not be through innocent blood.' His usual estimation of the people's strength led him further to argue: 'If the people are true to themselves, we have an overwhelming force; if otherwise, we fall, and our lives will be a sufficient sacrifice.' It was all very noble. Yet, in view of the changes that had occurred since 1798, it was fatally romantic. Russell's view on the power of the rank and file of the people was not a new discovery on his part. Before leaving Fort George he had written: 'Who that knows that colossal power was shaken from its summit to its base by the gallant peasantry of a few counties, ill armed and ill led, could ever cease to promote a general and effectual movement?' In the same letter he had argued, mistakenly, that the Irish people were now more united than ever. In the crisis of 1798 they had discovered who were their friends and who not.

There was also the question of northern support, crucial to any strategy for a rising. The enthusiasm for democracy, the universalism on 'the rights of man', so evident during Russell's stay at Belfast, had made Antrim and Down his spiritual home. Despite warnings to the contrary, he still assumed that thousands in these counties were ready for an insurrection. While his warnings about Napoleon impressed the meetings at Butterfield Lane, his confidence of raising tens of thousands in Ulster did not convince his hearers. Even Emmet, a visionary rather than an empirically-minded realist, was surprised at Russell's attitude. To the credit of the leaders, a fact-finding mission was sent to Ulster. The later report by James Hope and Michael Berney was enthusiastic and seemed to bear out Russell's optimism. The north would rise if Dublin was captured: Russell's presence in Ireland had revived confidence. However, Hope and Berney may have posed the wrong question: would people rise in support of a French invasion? The possibility that French help might not come was not considered. As well, the emissaries had moved among people who lacked experienced leaders – since 1798, officers of the United Irishmen had either been executed or imprisoned or grown tired of the struggle. Later, Russell found that absence of French help and dearth of trained local officers had destroyed all chance of a mass uprising.[6]

Preliminary journey north and other movements

It should, however, be noted that Russell did inspect local preparations and calculated the chances of success. He later told Ellen Rabb of his travels 'in the principal part' of Ireland since his arrival in March. On one occasion he had travelled, unrecognised, in a stage-coach with a woman who had been his hostess at Belfast. Perhaps his military training enabled him to estimate troop strength in the country: there were only 18,000 regular troops in Ireland – as to Yeomen and Militia, they would 'fly to our standard' once a battle had been gained. There is some evidence that he utilised his army experience to propose drilling manoeuvres and an outline for the use of munitions. Towards the end of May, Russell visited the north. Little is known of how or with whom he travelled. The precise reason for the journey remains uncertain. Was it to confirm, for those who looked to his personal leadership, that he had in fact returned? Was it to contact groups unavailable to Hope and Berney during their earlier

visit? According to James Hope, Russell's stay was brief: two
nights in Belfast, a day in the county Antrim. Perhaps contact
was also made with sympathisers in north Down, for example,
James Witherspoon of Knockbracken. Perhaps Russell spoke to
activists such as William Farrell at Carnmoney, and others at
Broughshane and Ballymena. In these areas he later was given
support. The ever-perceptive Martha McTier heard rumours
that he had visited Belfast and 'saw several of his old friends'.
Writing to William Drennan, she also noted, a month before
Emmet's rising, that the friends on whom he called 'disappointed
him much (in) in not mounting when he wished'. Captain J. A.
Russell, Thomas Russell's nephew, played down these meetings
somewhat and wrote to his uncle's first biographer: 'After privately hearing the opinions of several friends separately,
Thomas Russell and his agent returned to Dublin.[7]

It has been suggested that Russell may have contacted the
McCrackens during this trip northwards. During May, the presence in Dublin of Frank McCracken and William Tennent was
noted by an informer who wrote to Dublin Castle: 'Their being
in town at this juncture is somewhat extraordinary, as they bore
very conspicuous characters in fomenting the late Rebellion'.
Otherwise, the details of Russell's preliminary activity are obscure. With such little reconnaissance it is difficult to envisage
how he could have expected a successful rising in the north. As
an ex-officer, he could hardly overlook the need for a sufficiency
of arms and a body of trained leaders. Yet he seems to have returned to Dublin in expectation that the north would rise when
given the signal. Meanwhile, other plans developed from
Emmet's headquarters at Rathfarnham. It is possible that contacts had been established with Defender elements in Cavan
through James Hope and William Hamilton. Since Hope's nomination to lead O'Dwyer's men, Wicklow had benefited from
Hope's organisational ability. In Carlow and Kildare, detachments were primed to converge on Dublin city. At the centre
were the arms factories in Dublin's Liberties and nearby Thomas
Street. Nonetheless, in far retrospect, such apparent inattention
to detail for a rising in the north remains a puzzle. Were Emmet
and Russell misled by false information about a French landing?
Or were they fatally inept in their preparations?

That Russell persisted in these arrangements may be yet another example of his loyalty to 'the cause' of which he so often spoke. It was typical of him to remain loyal to colleagues, even in the throes of difficulty. And he consistently believed that government forces were vulnerable in the event of a popular uprising. Yet, there is another feature of his character, implicit hitherto, which may explain his continued optimism. His strongly religious inclination extended to a theory of history where the dual principles of good and evil remained in constant struggle. Even in 1800, he interpreted political events in a millenarian way by insisting that the dominance of injustice was coming to an end, to be replaced by a more humane social order. Nor can his association with Francis Dobbs, whose bizarre reliance on biblical prophecies led to an unrealistic view of politics, be discounted at this point. With these reserves in mind, the judgement may be well-founded that the rising of 1803 was prepared by 'leaders lately returned from France and out of touch with the country'.[8]

Return to Antrim and Down

Final arrangements saw Russell appointed commander for the north and member of the provisonal government. James Hope was now asked to resume his task as Russell's assistant in the northern counties. William Hamilton was to take charge of the Cavan area. As well, Emmet drew up a proclamation to be issued simultanously with the rising in Dublin. Early in July, Russell, Hope and Hamilton left Butterfield Lane. The date for the rising being set for 23 July, they had disastrously short time to finalise arrangements. As the three leaders quitted Dublin, they attended a meeting, in Crow Street, at the home of Philip Long, treasurer for Emmet and his colleagues. In high spirits Russell declared that he would raise 50,000 men in the north. Then he embarked on the journey northwards. In his luggage was a military greatcoat which Emmet had pressed on him in token of his rank as General for Antrim and Down. He also carried the proclamation establishing a provisional government until the people could elect a more permanent structure. Unanswered questions remain to tantalise historians of the rising. Was the date set precipitately ? Had an eventuality occurred which rendered haste necessary? How was communication between Dublin and the remote areas to be maintained?

Somewhere on the route, Hamilton parted company with Russell and Hope. His task lay in Cavan where the Defender movement was still active and where, nine years before, Russell had noted strong pro-French sympathies. On 15 July, Russell wrote a brief letter to Mary Ann Hamilton showing a mixture of elation and apprehension. He told his niece that, with her husband and James Hope, he was going 'to triumph in the cause of our country or to fall'. Everything to ensure success had been done 'as far as possible man can do'. With something of a flourish he assured her that 'I thought of you at the last moment'. Russell and Hope traversed Collon, Dundalk and Newry. Many years later, Hope recalled that as they passed Eliza Goddard's home Russell became agitated. He recalled that when he was being brought to Newgate in 1796, the cavalcade halted exactly opposite her residence. Now, as then, he was deeply affected. The unresolved love for Eliza Goddard was still on his mind after almost ten years in prison and exile.[9]

Other problems beset the two travellers. At Newry, a pre-arranged meeting did not materialise. After two nights, with expectations already disappointed, Russell and Hope went to James Witherspoon at Knockbracken, closer to Belfast. Witherspoon, a veteran of 1798 and intensely loyal to Russell, placed his house at the disposal of the travellers. Several activists came to Knockbacken, including Robert Simms, Russell's old friend and ex-general for Antrim in 1798. Even though Simms expressed reservations, others returned to their districts to mobilise support. Most likely, at this time Russell learned of the explosion at Emmet's munitions depot in Thomas Street on 16 July. The information will have caused doubt as well as alarm. Had the conspiracy been discovered? Had the rising been precipitated in Dublin before due date? Would a general alert now make the north's task even more perilous? In fact, Dublin Castle either did not realise the significance of the Thomas Street explosion or else was playing a game of cat-and-mouse for its own purposes. Isolated in county Down, Russell had no means of making a confident judgement. On 19 July, he left Knockbracken for Belfast. In this town of his former popularity, some of the leaders from the 1790s met at John Swiney's public house. The meeting was highly unsatisfactory. Some, already agents of Dublin Castle, were ready to plant doubt and confusion. In addition, a profound scepticism was expressed not only by Robert and William Simms but also by several others. The most that could be agreed was a further meeting, set for 22 July.[10]

A letter to William Hamilton, dated 15 July, sets a problem for the narration of Russell's activities in Antrim and Down. Its tone of pessimism raises questions about its date: it was after the 15th that plans for the rising started to unravel due to the Thomas Street explosion. Despite this, the letter signals a major problem and is, in effect, a recall of Hamilton to Belfast. Very clearly it shows the near-desperation Russell felt as people, for perfectly understandable reasons, refused to answer his call. At times, the letter verges on an incoherence unlike Russell's normally lucid prose. He speaks of mistakes which he would now endeavour to rectify. With the religious overtone already noted, Russell avows: 'Whether I fall or succeed is in the hand of God, but the cause I will never relinquish'. This new pessimism begs the question of whether he had encountered unforeseen obstacles: 'God has for the present stopt (*sic*) our projects for purposes no doubt wise. Courage alone was wanting here ... to render our success not only certain but easy.' A note of foreboding is clear as he informs Hamilton: 'I am going to join anybody I can find in arms in support of their rights and that of mankind.' As if writing to colleagues in struggle, Russell enjoins: 'Let me request of you not to suffer yourselves to be despirited, the cause will succeed, tho' individuals may fall.' It is an interesting circumstance that the letter was conveyed through Ellen Rabb of Ballysallagh, near Bangor, to Mary Ann McCracken for transmission to Hamilton.[11]

CHAPTER TWELVE

Debacle

And he told me that Boney had promised help
to a man in Dublin town.
Says he: 'If you've laid the pike on the shelf,
ye'd better go home hot-fut by yourself,
an' once more take it down.'

For a wheen o' days we sat waitin' the word
to rise and go at it like men,
but no French ships sailed into Cloghey Bay
and we heard the black news on a harvest day
that the cause was lost again.

This narrative left Russell and Hope at Swiney's Belfast house on Tuesday, 19 July. It also noted the disintegration of Russell's high expectation of a spontaneous reaction to his call. From Tuesday to Friday both Russell and Hope travelled into north Antrim by Ballymena, Kells and Connor. Only in Kells and Connor did they receive an encouraging reception. Elsewhere, the indispensability of French assistance was emphasised. Local people had no more than hidden pikes or small arms. To questions about French help neither Russell nor Hope could satisfactorily reply. And yet, both popular tradition and information to government attest widespread expectation of a French landing. Informers recurrently adduced rumours that a French expedition, perhaps the San Domingo fleet, would enter Clough Bay or Dundrum Bay. At Russell's subsequent trial, Baron George rebuked him for giving the impression that French forces would land at Ballywalter, Co Antrim. It is not clear when Russell made this claim: he had spoken at Anadorn of an arms-landing at Kilkeel while admitting that French troops were not to be expected. The circumstances of trial did not permit him to respond to the judge's rebuke.[1]

It is not surprising that at Ballymena, Carnmoney and Brough-shane there was less than enthusiastic reaction to Russell's call. At Carnmoney, memories of savage repression in 1798 were too fresh for another rising to be contemplated without arms or for-eign help. Nevertheless, there were people who listened to Hope and Russell. Several copies of Emmet's proclamation were later affixed on public buildings in Carnmoney. William Rogers, aged fourteen, was arrested while carrying the proclamation.[2]

Government agents, some of them former United Irishmen, at-tended these meetings. James McGucken was at once informing Dublin Castle and sowing confusion in Belfast. His ploy was that no rising should be attempted in the north until success in Dublin had been established. As in 1798, the signal of a success-ful Dublin rising would be the continued interruption of the Dublin stage-coach. As well as the operation of informers there were other factors militating against Russell's expectations. While at Fort George, he had been warned by John Templeton that mutual suspicion prevailed in Ireland. Not heeding this, he believed that a union of hearts persisted after 1798. Yet, differ-ences did exist, marked along an economic axis. Behind the hos-tile words of McClelland, the solicitor-general, a bitter truth can be discerned: 'The only description of people who are at all in-clined to join Russell are the lowest orders of the Catholics. Their clergy and the higher orders are generally considered here as loyal. This opinion … has operated powerfully on the minds of many of the Presbyterians, who from former habits might otherwise have been still adverse to the Government.' Men of property and clergy as a whole consulted narrower interests than the union of Protestants, Catholics and Dissenters, so much part of the United Irish ideal. Despite McClelland's words, those who attempted a rising were by no means confined to Catholics. Yet the benchmark of economic and institutional interest, which caused Henry Joy McCracken to remark that the rich always be-tray the poor, still applied.[3]

The meeting arranged for 22 July did take place in Belfast. It was one of the more effective gatherings of that troubled week. No evidence exists as to whether Russell's old friends Templeton, Simms or Rowley Osborne were present. Some veterans of 1798 did attend, not adverse to attack on Belfast as part of a broader strategy. An erstwhile member of the Tipperary militia, Stephen

Wall, was nominated as commander of the area. Once again, however, there was no detailed response to questions about strategy for capture of the town. It is little wonder that, on the day fixed for the rising, Wall had to inform William Hamilton that 'Belfast will not rise'.[4]

From Belfast, Russell and Hope went separate ways. It was now the eve of the projected rising and dangerously little had been achieved. Hope rejoined Hamilton who had returned to Antrim from Cavan. Russell headed back to County Down. His thoughts at this juncture can only be conjectured. As yet, he had no definite following. Little more than vague possibilities had been discussed. No coordinated policies had been agreed other than attacks on Dublin, Belfast and Downpatrick. No reports were to hand from Dublin, except of a premature explosion in Thomas Street. His own army training will have alerted him to these grave difficulties. And what of Hope, veteran of 1798 and erstwhile instructor to O'Dwyer's insurgents? Did he fear that insufficient communication would again lead to the confusion which reigned at Antrim in 1798?

A detailed letter from the rector of Lisburn, Dr Samuel Cupples, to the Reverend Foster Archer gives an external view of Russell's operations in Antrim and Down.[5] Cupples' account, to be read through the filter of his own hostility, is based on reports from people arrested near Castlereagh. Nevertheless, it sketches the broad pattern of Russell's activity in the days before the fateful 23 July. According to Dr Cupples, Russell spent almost a fortnight in a house near Castlereagh where he met 'the chief agitators among us'. In the course of several meetings, he called for a rising to shake off an 'abject slavery and bondage'. His recommendation was that 'if fifty or a hundred would assemble they would increase rapidly, the very fields and hedges as they passed would supply recruits and they would soon reckon thousands in their ranks'. Cupples' letter re-echoes the dearth of precision which must have alarmed those interested in Russell's proposals. He would not give an exact hour for the proposed rising. His argument was that 1798 was lost through lack of secrecy. Only thirty-six hours before the due time in Dublin would people be informed. Thereafter, a coordination with Dublin would operate. In the south a force of over 100,000 would strike. With the assistance of the north, Ireland could be wrested from gov-

ernment control even without the help of Bonaparte. This calculation should be seen in conjunction with Russell's own estimate
that there were only 18,000 regular troops in Ireland, while the
militia would come across to an organised rebel force.

Cupples mentions that Russell barely escaped arrest at
Castlereagh on Wednesday – he had left only fifteen minutes before a local magistrate raided his lodging. Later accounts, most
of them from people constrained to give evidence, give some insight to Russell's isolation as he moved southwards on Friday,
22 July. Although these accounts were given under duress, they
offer a broad picture of his actions near Downpatrick. Early on
Friday 22 July, Russell headed for Saintfield along with James
Drake. At Saintfield, he hired a horse from a yeoman named
Cosby. From there, he went through Ballynahinch and by late
morning had arrived at James Smith's tavern in Anadorn, near
Downpatrick. Here, a meeting of eight or ten gathered.
According to James Keenan, later a crown witness, Russell
bluntly asked him what he (Keenan) could do in regard to a ris-
ing. Keenan said that he knew ten or twelve men and boys in
Downpatrick 'but if I asked them about it I do not know but that
they would hit me in the face'.[6]

Still at Anadorn, a messenger told Russell that he could raise
'some 100 or 150 men'. James Corry, a Downpatrick shoemaker,
was cited by Keenan as willing to assist Russell in the town.
Corry also undertook to procure a map of Antrim and Down. A
strange feature of Keenan's evidence is his insistence, elicited by
the prosecution, that Russell wore a military coat with edging
and epaulettes during the Anadorn meeting. Henry Smith, son
of the innkeeper, 'remembered' being told by Russell that 'there
was to be a general insurrection all over Ireland'. Dublin, Belfast
and Downpatrick were to be captured on the evening of the
23rd. Every parish was 'to lift the arms of the yeomen and
Orangemen in that parish'. Prominent gentry were to be made
prisoners, their arms taken, and they themselves to be held
hostage against any threat to rebel forces. Russell argued that
'the Catholics were oppressed by the Orangemen and the people
ought to rise and release them'. When Smith asked if there
would be French help, he was told that 'there were not any
French to come but … there were 30,000 stand of arms expected
soon to be landed at Kilkeel from France'. It is notable that the

Smith's evidence confirmed the government line that Emmet's rising was a sectarian affair orchestrated by disaffected survivors of 1798.

At a late stage in the Anadorn meeting, Patrick Doran argued that none but fools would join a revolution of this kind. In Henry Smith's 'recollection', Russell became agitated and said to James Drake: 'James, this will not do.' Then, Russell is said to have donned a military coat claiming it was that of a French general. Smith also alleged that Russell mentioned seven leaders who had come to Ireland with him. Dublin was to be taken and, for the rest of the country, there were sufficient people to capture the towns. In addition, thirty thousand pounds were available to the rebel leaders in Dublin for purposes of the revolution.[7]

With little support at Anadorn, Russell went to Loughinisland which was then a stage on the road from Ballynahinch to Downpatrick. It was a mainly Catholic area where lived Patrick Lynch, his teacher of Irish at the Belfast library. As Russell arrived sometime in the afternoon of Friday, he met the parish priest and curate who were playing quoits. After desultory conversation with the priests, he went to James Fitzpatrick's public house. This was known as 'The Buck's Head', a thriving hostelry where travellers were received and where locals congregated. Initially, Russell passed as Captain Shields, a dealer in horses. Soon, however, Father McCartan heard of the stranger's green military coat and talk about a French invasion. According to his own deposition, when the priest went to Fitzpatrick's, he was told the visitor had already left. While Father McCartan was a hostile observer, it was otherwise with Patrick Lynch. In reluctant evidence for the crown, Lynch described his embarrassment at recognising his friend of the Belfast Library. Knowing there was a hue and cry, he did not want 'to have it in my power to hurt him'. Thus, on Friday evening, he managed to avoid the visitor. On Saturday morning, having heard of Russell's purpose, he tried to dissuade him. Russell, who now seemed fatigued, told Lynch that he had been in Belfast and 'had slept but little for some days past'. Acording to Lynch, Russell mentioned that the people seemed 'backward' and unwilling to strike for their freedom. In the same testimony Lynch recalled that, when some men came into Fitzpatrick's, Russell asked them if they did not want to get rid of the English. He seemed to regard his immediate task as the capture of Downpatrick which would spark a general uprising in the county.

Another official witness, Patrick Reneghan of Clough, spoke of his own refusal to join the revolt: 'I said I would do no such thing and if they did they would be hanged like dogs.' Reneghan argued that since the priests had told the people to re-main quiet, no rising could be expected. His testimony discloses nervous excitability on Russell's part: 'If there was to be no ris-ing, he would stay no longer in that place … he would go to Antrim or Belfast as the people would act there.' To the repeated question about arms Russell is said to have recommended peo-ple to use 'forks and spades and shovels and pickaxes'. Lynch remembered that, when asked about the capture of Downpatrick, Russell seemed 'as if he did not know which way it was to be or as if he did not wish to give a direct answer'.

An insight to this episode of disarray is given in the evidence of John Taite at the trial of Michael Corry, perhaps the son of James Corry and also a Downpatrick shoemaker. On Saturday night, about ten or eleven o'clock, Corry and Tate went to Vianstown (less than two miles from Downpatrick) where they met a dozen men. Corry had listened attentively to Russell's plans for he in-formed the others that a general uprising was set all over Ireland, with Dublin and Belfast being attacked simultaneously. Their task was to capture Downpatrick. The circumstances em-phasise the tragedy of these men: armed only with pitchforks, they waited two hours for a signal-fire over the nearby Seaford. It would announce the commencement of the rising and the house arrest of Matthew Forde, the county sheriff. No fire ap-peared. Neither did the five or six thousand men expected to march on Downpatrick. According to Russell's hasty letter to Mary Ann McCracken, he arrived at Vianstown to find all had gone except three. Clearly, at this stage there would be no rising in Down. All he could do was return to Loughinisland and raise Emmet's standard at the dolmen near the 'Buck's Head'. In the early hours of Sunday morning, Thomas Russell quit Loughinisland to set out 'on his keeping' for Antrim.[8]

Yet, something did happen on the night of 23 July. In Dublin's Thomas Street, and in the Liberties, there were encounters with government troops. Lord Kilwarden, a humane official and one who had distinguished himself for even-handedness in his treatment of Wolfe Tone, was killed. In Belfast, men gathered near Malone; one wonders if John Templeton from nearby Orange Grove did meet the group! At Carnmoney, a sizeable number responded to the call of William Farrell, a calico-maker in the town. Copies of Russell's proclamation were affixed on public buildings and, as already mentioned, young William Rogers was arrested carrying the same proclamation. From Carnmoney, men went to Broughshane, but found no general movement there. Nor was there movement in Belfast itself, even though armed men were reported on the road to Ballymena. Stephen Wall's communication was accurate : there would be no rising in Belfast.[9]

Confusion in official circles

Mutual recrimination between Dublin Castle and Whitehall would continue after Emmet's rising. The tortuous development of that controversy enters the larger scene of British imperial interests. Was Emmet's rising allowed to proceed by Wickham and Marsden in order to consolidate imperial aims through destroying the remnants of 1798?[10] Panic among loyalist burghers and in some parts of the army discloses the uneasy stability from 1798. Dr Cupples provides good evidence of the insecurity. Writing to the Reverend Foster Archer he spoke of 'your old acquaintance Russell who is now skulking about this country'. Notwithstanding his bias, Cupples was close to the truth in arguing that men of property among the Presbyterians had changed their opinions since 1798 and that Catholics were too few to excite apprehension. From Cupples' point of view it was a cause of fear 'that there are among us a number of villains, who having no property will be ready enough to forward any system of sedition that may be set on foot if opportunity offers'. A magistrate, Robert Browne, reported of having been 'out all night' and that 'Rebels did certainly meet at Loughinisland'. On Sunday night, 24 July, Earl Annesley was 'alarmed by an express from Dundrum of an insurrection having taken place at Saintfield'. Annesley continued to worry. On 27 July, he warned that 'The French fleet is expected off the coast. Arthur O'Connor, Emit (*sic*) and Nelson (*sic*) with French officers are about the town'.

It was left to an arch-loyalist, Thomas Whinnery, post-master in Belfast, to boast that the 'desperate desperadoes' were quiet around the town. Yet, Whinnery was not fully at ease: 'Accounts from all quarters of the country agree that Russell has been using every effort to promote a rising but has not yet succeeded.' Believing that Russell was still in Belfast or its neighbourhood, he suggested a reward of a thousand pounds should be offered for his capture. The notion of a reward was also mooted by General Colin Campbell who, in terms more moderate, wrote: 'I do not despair of getting hold of Russel (sic), a Reward I think would bring him in'. Expectation of a French fleet persisted. The captain of a coal-boat bound for Youghal reported that four young men boarded his ship 'looking out for a vessel that was to call in this (Dundrum) bay. A charitable informer from Rostrevor, who longed 'to see Dixon's neck stretched', reported that the Reverend Steele Dickson awaited near Clough Bay the arrival of 30,000 stand of French arms. A similar expectation had been expressed by Russell at the meeting in Anadorn.[11]

Refuge near Belfast

Despite these flurries by nervous magistrates, clergymen and officers, despite the possibility that Russell may have issued a second proclamation, the revolt in the north had ended. He travelled into Co Antrim, to the house of James Green, near Cave Hill. From there he returned to James Witherspoon at Knockbracken. Nevertheless, he was reluctant to involve his friends in his precarious state. Did he know that, to the disapprobation of Templeton and Mary Ann McCracken, Dr McDonnell had subscribed fifty pounds to the reward offered for his capture? It is unclear when he accepted the obvious fact that Belfast was not going to answer his call. Reports came to Martha McTier that he had lived for some days in bad circumstances immediately above the city, perhaps in the vicinity of Cave Hill. Mrs McTier's loyalty to her erstwhile guest persisted, despite political differences. Writing to Dr Drennan she lamented: 'When I think of this man lying in hovels and ditches on a hill from which he could view the habitations where once he was the most admired, the most loved among the gay, the witty and fair ... I cannot forbear wishing that if such cursed events as revolutions must be, they might be brought about by open, fair, well-fought battles in the field.' It was a generous thought made all the more poignant by her detail of Russell's visit to a house near Antrim: 'As a beggar Russell went to Mrs Ferguson's window and when he could not get money, he asked for a drink.'[12]

Meanwhile, at Loughinisland, arrests were taking place. It was from among those arrested that the crown lawyers managed to extract the story of 22, 23 and 24 July, in mid-Down. Father McCartan, the parish priest, was endeavouring to limit damage to his flock. On behalf of 1300 Catholic parishioners he expressed to Matthew Forde, the local landlord, 'abhorrence of every attempt towards rebellion or anarchy'. McCartan further emphasised: 'We were not tampered with by any French incendiary, or by any person whatever, except by a man who called himself Russell.' If any other 'incendiary' should come by, Fr. McCartan promised, 'we will seize him and deliver him in safe custody to the next Magistrate'. With less excuse, Thomas Beatty, vicar of Garvaghy, hastened to inform Dublin Castle that Russell had been in Garvaghy but was now in Armagh 'lurking in the dress of a peasant somewhere between Tandragee and Newtownhamilton'.[13]

The Reverend Beatty may have been correct. Perhaps Russell did go to an area he knew well from his journeys to Drumsluice. Yet, the last days of his stay in the north were spent with Daniel and Ellen Rabb, near Ballysallagh. Once again, the influence of Mary Ann McCracken is apparent since Daniel Rabb, a weaver, worked for her. Russell came to the Rabbs late at night in the company of three others. Ellen Rabb noticed their fatigue and willingly gave them shelter. Russell was permitted to remain at Ballysallagh while the other three returned via Hollywood to Belfast. The young housewife observed that Russell was 'under the circumstances ... wonderfully contented'. Years later, she recalled 'how incredulous he was as to the hopelessness of his cause'. Apparently, he discounted the gloomy reports from Belfast: only when he read in the newspapers of Emmet's capture did the harsh reality sink home. Ellen Rabb also noted Russell's determination to resist capture.[14]

By now, the newspapers carried Russell's description and details of the immense reward for his capture. As to the description, it can hardly have displeased him: 'A tall handsome man about five feet eleven inches high, dark complexion, aquiline nose, large black eyes with heavy eye-brows, good teeth, full chested, walking generally fast and upright, and having a military appearance, about forty eight years, speaking fluently, with a clear distinct voice, and having a good address.' Martha McTier observed: 'The description of Russell in the papers is nearly accurate and will gain him female protectors.' It says much for the loyalty of those around him that he was not arrested in Down, Armagh or Antrim. Dr Cupples ruminated bitterly that although Russell found so few followers in the north, yet he had remained perfectly safe there, being detected only by accident in Dublin.[15]

As to William Hamilton and James Hope, they too were in hiding. Hamilton eventually made his way to Cavan, while Hope moved from place to place until the search for rebel leaders died away. With his description posted 'on every corner' and with the extraordinary sum of £1500 offered for his capture, Russell felt it unsafe – not least for his hosts – to remain at Rabbs'. In addition, he had resolved to find some way of rescuing Emmet, now a prisoner at Kilmainham. Most likely it was to the Rabbs' house that Mary Ann and Margaret McCracken came to see Russell and to hear an account of the failed rising. Perhaps, too, they discussed plans for his escape to Dublin. Certain it is that Mary Ann McCracken had found this safe refuge for her brother's closest friend.[16]

Daniel Rabb arranged with a boatman to bring Russell southward to Drogheda. While these arrangements were in train, Russell moved to the home of James McCutcheon at Craigavad. Under the cover of night he left on board a trawler for Drogheda. Once there, he was assisted in making his way to Dublin. A little more than five weeks had elapsed since he promised Philip Long to return from the north at the head of 50,000 men.[17]

Safe keeping in Dublin

In Dublin, Robert Emmet was the centre of attention. At Dublin Castle, the chief secretary William Wickham and the under-secretary for civil affairs Alexander Marsden were anxiously surveying the aftermath of the July rising. Behind them was the chief of police, Charles Henry Sirr. These men controlled a 'battalion of testimony', a network of loyalists, disenchanted radicals and purely venal bounty hunters. Every day, a stream of information and denunciation crossed the desks of Wickham and Marsden. The none-too-gentle Major Sirr laboured to entrap the working men and women of the Liberties who had provided the backbone of Emmet's conspiracy. Yet, above all, the efforts of the Castle and its network of spies were directed to encompass the destruction of Emmet.

The eagerness of Castle informants did not lead to accurate reports. While Russell was still hiding at the home of Daniel and Ellen Rabb, a 'gentleman of loyalty and honour who resides beyond the Black Rock' thought he saw Russell enter a house near Blackrock, Co Dublin on 13 August. The same informer spoke of Dr William Drennan and a Surgeon Wright as frequent visitors to the same house. Yet, Russell went to ground successfully in a city where many people, in the Liberties and in other more affluent areas, were ready to hide him. According to his nephew's later memorandum, these fugitive days were directed towards Russell's escape, disguised as a priest or minister, to the Isle of Man. While in Dublin, he moved about furnished with a false travel-permit. James Hope came from the north to confirm that Hamilton was still safe, although a fugitive in Cavan.[18]

CHAPTER THIRTEEN

Arrest

For some twelve years Daniel and Mary Muley (née Harrison) had lived above their gunsmithry at 29 Parliament Street, Dublin. The house was substantial, situated almost at the gates of Dublin Castle and only a few steps from College Green. It was, therefore, at the very administrative centre of government. Daily, senior officials such as Wickham and Marsden would pass the door. The indefatigably hostile Major Sirr worked nearby. As to the Muleys, they were not *personae gratae* at the Castle. They were known to be United Irish sympathisers and Mary Muley's family in Kildare were reputed to have assisted Emmet's uprising. Further, it was alleged that Daniel Muley had supplied arms for the insurrection in Dublin. Yet, he continued to do business in hand-pistols and other weapons even with British army officers. The Muleys supplemented their income by letting the upper floors of their house. Already, they had rented shop space to John Fleming, a shoemaker. By summer 1803, Fleming and his wife also occupied rooms in the higher reaches of the house.

On Wednesday, 7 September, Daniel Muley was requested by an intermediary, 'who looked more like a citizen than a countryman', to provide three rooms for a Mr and Mrs Harris.[1] One room on the first floor and two on the second, were taken for a week at a guinea's rent. Without luggage and dressed in a surtout, Harris arrived in the late evening. It was understood that Mrs Harris would not arrive for some days. Daniel Muley observed curfew regulations by affixing the names of Mr and Mrs Harris to the mandatory door-chart. Thereafter, the visitor did not leave his room, although he seemed to expect a caller. During the next two days Muley provided his guest with meals, the newspaper and some magazines. He noticed Harris's interest in the second volume of Thomas Paine's *Geography*. Mary Muley attended the rooms only when Harris was in another apartment. She did not meet the visitor face to face.

During the evening of Friday, Muley brought a case of pistols to a Captain Harmsworth, then lodging at an hotel in James Street. When he returned home he discovered that the house had been raided and that Harris was in the custody of Major Sirr. Later, the Muleys were informed of their visitor's real identity. He was Thomas Russell.

Betrayal

The Muleys' probably knew this already. Daniel Muley's evidence at Dublin Castle on the following day shows a man who knew more than he cared to tell. Above all, he would not incriminate his wife. He insisted that he brought all meals to 'Harris', that he interviewed the man who rented the apartments and that only *he* spoke to the mysterious guest. Muley insisted that he forbade his wife to have anything to do with the visitor. And he denied all knowledge of the original intermediary. One suspects that Muley knew the man in the surtout coat was Russell. A hint of Daniel Muley's sympathies is given in his admission that he thought the mysterious lodger might be a debtor and that, in such a case, he would not have shown a bailiff to his room.[2]

How did Russell's presence become known to the Castle authorities? The remote answer is that Dublin was a city of divided allegiances. There were many, such as the residents of the nearby Liberties, who were fervently sympathetic to Emmet and Russell. Yet, there was also a myriad of petty informers and rabidly loyalist snoopers eager to make denunciations to the Castle. The more proximate reason for Thomas Russell's betrayal is that an ambitious young lawyer named John Swift Emerson was keeping an eye on Daniel and Mary Muley. He was a place-hunter who had repeatedly curried favour with Charles Henry Sirr. Perhaps the 'dubious' reputation of Daniel Muley activated Emerson's instinct for self-advancement. Perhaps the loose-mouthed Watty Cox who worked nearby had let slip that profit might be made from observing the gunsmith's premises. In any case, Emerson noted that the pattern of activity at Muley's had altered. A certain room was kept shuttered. A visitor whose meals were brought to him remained there. When the room was swept or dressed the visitor was first escorted away by Daniel Muley. Here was a chance of further ingratiating himself with Major Sirr and, more important, with senior Castle officials.

While Russell awaited his visitor and, perhaps, read Paine's *Geography*, Emerson frantically pursued town-major Sirr. Four times he called on Sirr and twice was rebuffed. He also called on Marsden at Dublin Castle with the message that 'there is a traitor concealed in Mr Muley's house in Parliament street'. Emerson's note shows remarkable knowledge of the house. It details exactly the room of the suspicious lodger: 'The stranger's room is next to Waddy's house and the second room over Muley's own shop. I say his own shop as a shoemaker occupies the other half of the shop.' Even as he wrote, Emerson waxed impatient: 'the stranger is there now, the shutters of the window of his apartment are kept generally closed.' Major Sirr was neither at the Castle nor at home. He was trying to incriminate Robert Emmet even further by a search for letters at John Philpot Curran's house in Rathfarnham. Thanks to a daughter of Curran he was foiled, and returned late to the city. When Emerson's request for another raid was put to him, Sirr reacted irritably. Perhaps it was fatigue, perhaps it was scepticism about Emerson's judgement that made him hesitate about going out again. Only sustained pressure from Emerson made Sirr convene a guard and with Humphry Minchin, a sheriff, converge on Parliament Street.[3]

It is clear that Emerson was a coward as well as a sneak. When, at length, Sirr agreed to raid Muley's house, Emerson insisted on remaining in the street. Having arrived at Russell's lodging about half past nine, Sirr went directly to the room designated by Emerson. Here, he took Russell unawares. The official version of the arrest was that Russell went for his pistols, but seeing that Major Sirr was unarmed, did not fire. Ellen Rabb, who had spoken at length with Russell when he sheltered at her house, later professed surprise that Russell had allowed himself be taken without a fight. In any case, Sirr and Minchin disarmed him and took him prisoner. He was brought to the Castle in a matter of less than five minutes. At the Castle yard, a group of officers who had dined with Wickham crossed the path of the arresting party. One of these officers who had served with Russell in India saluted him by name. Only then did Major Sirr, Attorney Emerson and Sheriff Minchin recognise the importance of their capture.[4]

Aftermath of Russell's arrest

Why did Russell, with an enormous price on his head, choose a

rendezvous at the Castle gates? Those most hostile to him suspected a plot, like Colonel Despard's in London, to assassinate
either the viceroy or the chief secretary. This allegation is based
on little more than the fright of Dublin loyalists and can be discounted. R. R. Madden, on the other hand, suggests that he had
arranged to meet Henry Grattan, prior to escaping abroad. Given
his long disenchantment with Grattan's politics, this supposition remains doubtful. A third possibility is that he was laying
plans to free Emmet from Kilmainham. On slender evidence,
Helen Landreth claims that he was awaiting David Fitzgerald,
an associate of Emmet's, with funds to organise a rescue. The
hypothesis that Russell was planning Emmet's rescue is coherent with his own stated resolve when quitting the north about 25
August. His subsequent meeting with James Hope and the
choice of a house so close to the Liberties would suggest that he
had re-established contact with Emmet's Dublin followers. In
the Emmet family, the tradition remained for generations that a
rescue attempt at the scene of Emmet's execution was planned
and that Russell was part of it. Whichever hypothesis is adopted, he had come too far into dangerous territory. The irony is
that he was ultimately captured almost by accident through the
prying attentions of a minor bounty-hunter.[5]

Sirr and Emerson quickly recognised their good fortune. Almost
by accident, a sizeable reward had come within their grasp. In
the months to come their strange association would break under
the weight of their own rapacity. A ghoulish wrangle ensued in
late 1803 as each man claimed his blood-money for Russell's
capture. After several bitter disputes, they received £500 each.
The senior Castle officials, Wickham and Marsden, stood aside
from these quarrels. Yet, they also realised the importance of
Russell's apprehension and tried to extract political gain from
that seemingly fortuitous event. As to Russell himself, he remained defiant. He is reputed to have said on arrest that he was
as ready to die on the scaffold as on the field. A short while afterwards he wrote to an unnamed friend: 'I mean to make my trial,
and the last of my life, if it is to close now, as serviceable to the
cause of Liberty as I can.'[6]

Despite various stratagems on the part of his captors, Russell
gave no information. Wickham believed that he was fully con-
versant with the Irish emigrés in Paris and could make 'the most

important discoveries'. Yet, personal safety mattered little to Thomas Russell and he had no intention of informing. More psychological means of procuring information are suggested in Wickham's dispatch to London: 'His (Russell's) temper of mind and natural character are such that nothing would be so likely to take such a step as kindness to his relatives when you have it in your power to do them mischief'. These were ominous words for Margaret and John Russell! On the day after her brother's arrest, Margaret's lodgings in Wood Street were raided by police. Dismay at the arrest and chagrin at ignorance of his return to Ireland are evident in her unfinished, perhaps interrupted, letter to John: 'Our unfortunate brother who I find has been in the country was last night I understand arrested and is at present in the Castle.'[7]

Nor was John Russell spared government's suspicious regard. Correspondence from Dublin Castle to Whitehall stressed the importance of examining his papers. The authorities knew that he had visited Paris during the autumn of 1802. Now, almost a year later, he was an Ensign in the reserve army. This position rendered him even more vulnerable to reprisal on foot of his brother's activities. Perhaps fortunately for himself, he had just written an alarmed reply to Margaret's ingenuous query: 'You asked about our friends in France – pray mention no such matter again – because had your letter fallen into bad hands, I might have been taken up tho' innocent – as friends in France might mean Bonaparte and God knows I would not wish to see him here.' Inevitably, John Russell was questioned in London. Yet, no further action was taken against him although attempts were made to trick his prisoner-brother into incriminating him.[8]

At Kilmainham Jail

From Dublin Castle, Russell was taken, not to Newgate, but to Kilmainham. Due to the malevolent activities of its medical superintendent, Edward Trevor, the prison had become 'a place of fright and fear, for prisoners and prison staff alike'. Trevor, a shadowy figure whose treatment of Anne Devlin evidences something near to sadism, exercised a sway that produced casualties of mind and body. In both Kilmainham and Newgate there was a paradoxical mixture of lenience and severity. A fairly liberal regime of visits permitted access of wives and friends. Yet, at the whim of 'Dr' Trevor or George Dunn, the chief gaoler, savage cruelties were visited on inmates. This arbitrary power is reflected in the obsequiously composed 'memorials' which unfortunate prisoners were forced to make in pursuance of basic necessities of life.

At Kilmainham, Russell joined Emmet, Quigley and other leaders of the insurrection. Almost immediately, steps were taken positively to identify him as a returned state prisoner and insurrectionary leader in the north. James Witherspoon, his host at Knockbracken, was brought to Kilmainham to connect Russell with activities in County Down. Despite extreme pressure, Witherspoon gave no more than non-committal responses to every question. Once more, Russell's confidence in the 'men of no property' was justified. Two soldiers, brought from Fort George to identify their former prisoner, were presumably less discreet than Witherspoon.[9]

A deluge of congratulation reached Dublin Castle from loyalists hostile to everything of which Russell was a symbol. The egregious Chicester Skeffington, whose blatant self-advertisement rendered him obnoxious even to the Castle, argued for Belfast as the place where Russell was most likely to receive a capital sentence. James McGucken, posing as a republican while sedulously informing Dublin Castle, suggested that Russell be hanged at Belfast. Matthew Forde, High Sheriff for Down, recommended trial at Downpatrick as an effective deterrent to all who sympathised with insurrection. The decision to send Russell to Downpatrick was taken by the viceroy, Hardwicke, for tactical reasons. Hardwicke informed the Home Office that he had set up a special commission for Antrim and Down in order 'to clear the gaols in these counties'. The presidents of the special courts would be Baron George and Mr Justice Osborne. On 24 September, the viceroy informed Whitehall that he would send Russell to Downpatrick: 'Considering the magnitude of his treasons lately committed, and how great an object it is to show how successfully they were exposed and defeated, and the strong desire expressed by several gentlemen of the North to have him tried where the example of his execution would have the greatest effect, I have preferred sending him to the North to proceeding against him as an exiled traitor.' Clearly, officialdom assumed he would be convicted of high treason and executed. Hardwicke was advised that sufficient evidence to hang Russell had been extracted from prisoners then in jail in Downpatrick.[10]

Spies at Kilmainham

Since interrogation was patently fruitless, the authorities tried indirect means of eliciting information from Russell. Not for the first time, Leonard McNally debased his legal profession by trawling at the Castle's behest. For that very reason, his report must be taken to reflect the Castle's interests. In tone, it is self-serving and ingratiating. The official line peddled by govern-ment was that 1798 and 1803 arose from the hostility of Catholics towards Protestants. According to McNally, Russell 'attempted to deny this but admitted the murders committed at Scullabogue ... which he defended by saying that they were goaded to those excesses by the ravishings, house burnings, tor-tures, etc, etc.'. Even McNally's bias could not fully hide Russell's views as the barrister reported on 'the necessity of ren-dering the lower orders of the people ... more comfortable, which if done it would be impossible for any set of men to urge them to rise'. Russell also mentioned three manifest injustices which occupied him for many years: tithes, taxes and landlords' oppression of their tenants. Tithes for the established clergy (Anglican) were unjust alike to Catholics and Presbyterians. If the established clergy were to be supported it should be from treasury funds, rather than from people who were not members of the Anglican church. The exaggerated benefices claimed by the established clergy 'could well be dispensed with'.[11]

In regard to oppression by landlords McNally thought it pru-dent simply to relay the view that leases should be granted in perpetuity. Absent are Russell's strictures on men of property and his stated opinion of aristocrats as a fungus in the body politic. On the legislative union of England and Ireland the re-port was equally anodyne: the old conflict of oppressor and op-pressed should be replaced by a sisterly relation of benevolence. For his trouble, McNally had reaped scant reward. He had re-ceived no information other than that already committed to print by Russell. The Castle officials learned nothing about Emmet's rising or about French movements beyond what they already knew. It is possible that Russell mistrusted Leonard McNally: it is certain he would not endorse the government line on the rising of 1803.

After Russell's arrest, the London home of James O'Farrell was raided by police. O'Farrell had been an active United Irishman during the 1790s and was detained after the rising of 1798. Around 1800 he went to London where he attained some prosperity as an accountant in the trading house of Gordon and Murphy at Moorefields. When his name was discovered among Russell's papers, either at Margaret's lodgings or at John's home in London, he was questioned by the English authorities. Eventually, he was brought to Dublin, not as a prisoner but maintained in the city at government expense. Perhaps by inducement, perhaps by threat, he was persuaded to report on conversations with Thomas Russell and to give an assessment of John Russell's political involvement. These reports were carefully sifted by Wickham and sent for perusal by the British Home Office. Although O'Farrell was a far more honourable character than McNally, his extended memoir tends to flaunt a political orthodoxy and to stigmatise the hardihood of Emmet's followers. On 24 October, more than six weeks after Russell's arrest, Wickham minuted O'Farrell's deposition to London. The memoir presents yet another, albeit indirect, account of Russell's state of mind in March 1803 and the precarious situation of the Irish exiles in Paris at that time.[12]

O'Farrell's memoir confirms Irish disillusion about Napoleon and his entourage. Russell had given several instances of 'the corruption and tyranny of the French government'. The foreign minister, Talleyrand, had obstructed every attempt to assist Ireland: 'Were it not for his treachery the other expeditions against Ireland would have succeeded and the Irish freed.' Russell believed Talleyrand 'sold every expedition that was ever planned against Ireland to the English government – except that under General Humbert'. As to Napoleon, Russell believed he would not help Ireland. His designs were on England: Ireland was only a means to further ends. According to James O'Farrell, Russell avowed that 'if he was an Englishman he would lose a hundred lives in resisting Napoleon'. The only French officials to be trusted were General Humbert and a few Jacobin generals, 'warmly attached to the Irish'.

There was also 'the London brother', John Russell, who may have little grasped his jeopardy. In effect, O'Farrell shielded him as 'the most harmless and credulous man on earth'. However, there were items of information which he had brought from the Rue Colombier. For example: Thomas Russell was much in the company of French generals whose republican leanings had earned disfavour of the First Consul. Again, in their plans for a rising, the Irish in Paris understood that Livingston, the American minister, would provide funds to buy 30,000 stand of arms. Other items of information disclose the exiles' uncertain grasp of Napoleon's realpolitik – some anticipated that Bernadotte, one of Napoleon's chief marshals, 'would be appointed General-issimo to the army in Ireland'.

Despite all this, Thomas Russell may have believed that an impending war between England and France was the opportunity for Emmet's rising. This is the tenor of a letter to John Russell which, although dated from Paris, seems to have been written in London on 25 March 1803. The letter details an exchange at the Tuileries between Napoleon and Lord Whitworth (the British minister) on 13 March. The First Consul threatened immediate war unless Britain evacuated Malta. 'Malta or War', Napoleon is reported to have said. With none-too-clear logic, Russell advised his brother: '… I consider the war (if it takes place, as I must say I am confident it will) of such a nature that I sincerely wish you may not be in the Army.' Perhaps this enigmatic reference can be linked to another, equally enigmatic, reported by James O'Farrell: 'He (Russell) said the Republicans of France expected to recover their liberty thro' the medium of Ireland.' Unfortunately for Emmet and Russell, the expectations of these republicans did not mirror the pretensions of France's imperial-leaning Consul.[13]

James O'Farrell knew how to bend with the prevailing wind. His account of how he dismissed further revolution in Ireland both helped himself and diverted government interest from John Russell:

> I shewed how impossible it was for a few men in Paris to know the actual state of their own country who had been so long separated from it in Fort George and who were never visited by any others but desperate men like themselves, and finally if they expected to find the sentiments of '96 and '97 in the people of Ireland, they would be happily deceived.[14]

Loyal Friends in Belfast

In Belfast there were more than gentry and informers. A month after Russell's arrest Martha McTier urged her brother to use every influence he could that Russell be deported rather than executed. Despite the undoubted efficacy of Drennan's pen it is doubtful if he had purchase with Dublin Castle. Nor was Drennan in close sympathy with Russell's latest project. Martha McTier had not forgotten her house-guest and much-admired confidant! Other Belfast friends were also eager to help. In particular, Mary Ann McCracken closely followed Russell's movements in the weeks after his arrest. She may have visited him in Kilmainham and, during the same trip to Dublin, may have provided Margaret Russell with finance as well as psychological support. She certainly instructed her business agent in Dublin, James Orr, to procure £200 for Russell's use. This gesture has been interpreted as an attempt to organise the escape of the man she both loved and admired. Margaret Russell, who was allowed to visit her brother more than once, is said to have passed £100 to him. Due to a combination of circumstances (whether rapacity or sense of duty on a warder's part remains unclear) a scheme of rescue was thwarted. The *Belfast Newsletter* later alleged that 'Before he left Kilmainham … it appeared that he (Russell) had entertained hopes of making an escape, with this design he endeavoured to ingratiate himself with the turnkey and actually gave the man £100 and a hint of a further sum. His keeper had too much integrity however to be deluded by bribery and … communicated the circumstance immediately to the Jailer.'[15]

A political testament

Margaret Russell's determined loyalty is noteworthy during the several periods of her brother's imprisonment. While he was in Fort George she had performed several difficult tasks for him. Now she visited him repeatedly in the grim confines of Kilmainham and perhaps collaborated in the scheme for his rescue. On Sunday, 2 October, she went to the prison for a religious service conducted by the Reverend Foster Archer. Archer had been of help to Russell during his years in Newgate and, it will be remembered, was a correspondent of Dr Cupples, the nervous Lisburn rector. There is the possibility that he and Russell may have known each other outside the troubled circumstances of prison. A humane man, he had shown himself ready, where necessary, to identify abuses within the prison system. Nonetheless, as Inspector of Prisons he was sufficiently part of that system to file a report on the service at Kilmainham prison chapel. Couched in quasi-official language, the memoir is a valuable indication of Russell's state of mind in the closing weeks of his life. Its veracity is all the more likely since it avoids the orthodoxies of the memoirs fashioned by McNally, O'Farrell and, later, Trevor.[16]

Foster Archer remarked on the 'apparently great devotion' with which Russell took the sacrament. After the service, Russell again approached the altar-table to make a declaration of his state of conscience. Archer, who seems to have been a somewhat staid man, remarked on Russell's demeanour as with joined hands and upturned eyes he made this declaration. According to Archer's report, the short confession seemed to have been studied for the purpose of delivery in the chapel. Despite the clergyman's discomfiture, he claimed in his report to give a 'nearly verbatim' account of Russell's declaration:

> In the awful Presence of God and at this Holy Table I ac-
> knowledge myself to have been guilty of many Immoral
> Acts, many Impieties and negligence of Sacred Duties, but as
> to Political Opinions and Political Actions I have ever been
> led by what Reason, the Result of deep Meditation and
> laboured Reflection have shown me to be Right. I never in-
> tended by what I have politically done any other than the
> Advantage of my Fellow Creatures and even the Happiness
> of my Adversaries. Whether the Lord shall be pleased to ex-
> tend my life for forty years or to cut my thread of Existence in
> an hour, I shall not cease from the work I have began nor give
> it up but with life itself.

In style, the declaration is sufficiently close to Russell's intense self-analysis to suggest that Archer's summary is accurate. Its religious overtones are found in the extended covering-letter to his narrative from Fort George. The clergyman's further reaction is significant: he wrote of the 'cant of Enthusiasts' used by Russell about civil and religious matters. Thus, Russell spoke of 'the kingdom of Jesus, the fulfilling of the Prophecies relating to the bringing home of the Jews which he said was now commenc-ing'. For the student of Russell's political stances it is interesting that he believed ' the French Arms were instruments God would use for that that Nation (as the Romans had done before on Christ's appearance in the Flesh finished the conquest of the Civilised World) would in like manner subdue the whole earth ...'. This tendency to interpret politico-historical events in the frame of Christian scripture casts light on some of Russell's apparently foolish initiatives. His confidence that unjust governments were coming to an end may explain his perseverance against all odds in Antrim and Down. Likewise, his optimism that small resources could attain a God-given purpose may explain his haphazard precedures during the attempted rising.[17]

Two other references in Archer's report are of biographical interest. The clergyman detailed a specialised discussion of biblical Greek in regard to 'the end of the age'. Clearly, Russell was still preoccupied by texts with millenarian overtones. Subsequent generations of biblical exegetes would bear out his linguistic arguments, if not his specific interpretation. It also emerged that Russell had practised his religion while in Paris – he had received comunion in the Jansenist church in Paris during Christmas 1802.[18]

By 2 October, Russell had known of the decision to send him to Downpatrick. In somewhat leaden fashion Archer mentioned Dr Cupples of Lisburn as one who would assist him 'in his last moments … if the event of his trial should be unpropitious'. Later in the week, Russell interviewed the medical superintendent, 'Dr' Edward Trevor. As a result of that meeting he composed a memorandum for the Castle authorities on the requisites for a just and peaceful Ireland. Given his appalling record in treatment of prisoners, it can be assumed that Trevor's intervention was yet another attempt to harvest information for the authorities and to ingratiate himself at the Castle. With that reserve, the memorandum and a covering letter by Trevor himself can be examined for indications about the circumstances and thoughts of Thomas Russell during his final days at Kilmainham.

With self-serving intent, Trevor emphasised the satisfactory conditions under which Russell was held. Doubtless, it suited official interests to record that Russell felt beholden to chief secretary Wickham for the treatment 'he has received during his confinement at Kilmainham'. According to 'Dr' Trevor, the prisoner's only complaint was 'how he was exposed to view in the Jail'. Trevor insinuated that he himself was Russell's guarantee he would 'not be roughly treated by Sheriffs or Constables going to Downpatrick and (at Downpatrick) he would receive the same attention as he had done in Kilmainham for which he was thankful to Mr Wickham'. The would-be humanitarian recorded that Russell had asked him to accept documents for his sister 'in case any fatality attended him' at Downpatrick. With this rider, Trevor conveyed Russell's injunction to government for 'lenient and merciful measures' to those defeated in Emmet's uprising. From a missive later sent to Dublin Castle Trevor's real purpose emerges. It was to gain information about John Russell. The stratagem failed: on 18 October, Trevor again wrote: '(Russell) has not as yet mentioned a word relative to his brother, and I have thought it best not to speak to him on it lest he might suppose I was pressing for any other object than the real one you intend towards his brother.'[19]

CHAPTER FOURTEEN

Downpatrick

In the view of Dublin Castle, it was better to try Thomas Russell at Downpatrick. The administration hoped thereby to intimidate whatever remnants of 'disaffection' still remained either in Antrim or Down. In addition, the possibility remained of a further trial in Dublin on head of the Emigration Act of 1798 which had banished Russell by name from the country. Thus, on 12 October, he was taken under heavy guard to Downpatrick. Here he was committed for trial and placed in the town jail. Dr Trevor, still masquerading as protector, had travelled with the cavalcade. In the jail, Russell was lodged separately from the other prisoners in rooms provided by the prison's keeper. Writing to Dublin Castle to confirm arrival, Trevor reported the absence of the High Sheriff, Matthew Forde. Trevor's remark that he would not visit Russell until an official letter was transmitted to the Sheriff heightens the suspicion that Dublin Castle still hoped to elicit information from Russell by duplicity. Somewhat unctuously, Trevor reported irregularities at the jail and proposed to notify the Attorney-General of them. According to Trevor, 'access to Mr Russell is by no means difficult'.[1]

By 14 October a commission of Oyer and Terminer had been inaugurated under Baron George and Mr Justice Osborne. The commission was designed by government 'to clear the jails of Antrim and Down'. In effect, its means proved to be transportation, imprisonment or execution. Addressing the commission, Baron George vaunted the changed circumstances in the north: people once 'disaffected' were so no longer. The judge's remarks carry some ring of truth – careful propaganda about the sectarian nature of 1798 and the promise held out by the Act of Union had changed the temper of the day. So, too, had memory of repression from 1796 to 1798. Yet among those scheduled for trial by the commission in Down or Antrim were several whose views had not changed since the 1790s. Most remarkable is James Witherspoon, the Presbyterian weaver of Knockbracken, who had sheltered Russell and Hope the previous July. Neither inducement nor threat could make him testify against Russell. Similarly, John Witherspoon (son of James) and Fergus McCartan (Loughinisland) remained silent. Michael Corry, the Downpatrick shoemaker who had turned out on the night of 23 July, maintained his refusal to turn King's evidence despite the offer of pardon on a capital charge. Perhaps one of the most poignant entries on a list of those charged with High Treason refers to young Rogers, the fourteen-year-old Carnmoney boy: 'This boy was taken in the act of distributing Russell's proclamation in Carnmoney. He is a hardened boy refusing absolutely to give an account from whom he received them.'[2]

Writing to Frank McCracken, Russell argued that government had already decided on his death. In that case he wished to make his death 'as useful to the cause that I live for and your brother and so many have died (for)'. Although he had refused to mount a defence, now he agreed to do so in the hope that cross-examination of crown witnesses might assist others charged before the commission. A prominent Dublin barrister named Henry Joy, cousin of the McCrackens, was engaged to lead for Russell. He would be assisted by an attorney named Bell. James Ramsey, a young Belfast lawyer, also showed remarkable courage in entering on this apparently hopeless task. Otherwise, the happenings of the week preceeding the trial remain unclear. Russell's letter to the McCrackens indicates that they had very quickly moved to help him. The letter, accepting the services of counsel, is suggestive of high morale and shows no sign of fear. After an attempt to dissuade the McCrackens from coming to the prison ('which would be fruitless and could only serve to draw suspicion on you and your family'), Russell gave notice that he would speak at the trial about his own political and religious convictions. Even at this stage he considered the failure of Emmet's projected insurrection to be surprising and confessed that 'with some of the reasons I am still unacquainted'. Above all, Russell's unflinching resolve is expressed: 'I have no wish to die … but had I a thousand lives I would willingly risk or lose them in the Cause and be assured Liberty will in the midst of these storms be established.' The lengthy missive concludes with a commendation of Margaret Russell to the

McCrackens. This trust was carried out faithfully. In particular, Mary Ann McCracken would be an assiduously faithful protector of Margaret until she died at 'The Retreat', Drumcondra, Dublin in 1834. It is typical of Russell to end on a profoundly religious note: 'Politically I have done nothing but what I glory in, morally I acknowledge myself a grievous sinner. I trust for pardon and mercy thro' my saviour as I do most sincerely forgive all who are about to take my life.'[3]

Mary Ann McCracken, practical and ever-sensitive to Russell's fortunes, resolved to go to Downpatrick. Already she had arranged a safe house for him near Belfast and, after his arrest, had provided money to arrange his escape. Now, she endeavoured to dissuade at least one witness for the crown from testifying and procured an indication from another that he would refuse to give evidence. It is instructive to read the cool estimation by Mary Ann McCracken and Ellen Rabb of these potential witnesses and of their ability to withstand official pressure. Unfortunately, Mary Ann's intention to visit Downpatrick came to the notice of Charles Teeling, a fastidious man who had suffered much in 1798. Teeling listed the disadvantages of going to Downpatrick – incrimination of her elderly parents, the possibility of retribution, and what she brusquely termed 'other absurdities'. To her lasting regret, Mary Ann was dissuaded on account of her mother's upset. Nevertheless, she was prepared 'to defy all prohibitions ... if it be possible to do any good by going'.

Her letters disclose intense mental turmoil in the days before Thomas Russell's trial. She wrote more than once to her confidante Eliza Templeton, the sister of John Templeton. In the first of these letters Mary Ann remarks that she had 'scarcely slept last night contriving plans and schemes but all to no purpose'. Hardly to no purpose. She succeeded in getting one man, MacCullagh, to refuse testimony for Russell's prosecution. And she arranged for Thomas McHugh, an employee of Frank McCracken, to visit Downpatrick jail to investigate what might be done for him. Two letters to Russell from this remarkable woman are extant. On 15 October she explained what had prevented her from coming to the prison: 'the well meant tho' ill judged officiousness of a friend'. Nonetheless, she emphasised her eagerness to do whatever Russell might suggest: 'It would be to us a source of continued regret and self-reproach were we to suffer ourselves to be deterred from doing anything which would either essentially serve you or even contribute in the smallest degree to your satisfaction'. With the letter Mary Ann enclosed what she termed 'a small supply' of money. It is clear that despite their new reading of the political situation, many of Russell's other Belfast friends did not prove disloyal to him. Martha McTier could inform her sister-in-law that 'He experienced he had real friends there, who, even at the last, were of use and comfort to him, and, in spite of former denunciations, subscriptions were readily offered to obtain all that was possible.' No one, however, was more solicitious than the McCracken sisters and Eliza Templeton.[4]

In the days before the trial, crown officials interviewed Russell. It was reported in Belfast that 'he asked for all his friends, was cheerful and easy, even to gaiety, talked of the news of the day, the politics of Europe ... and on some point said he supposed they would have his head off before that'. Edward Trevor sinuously pressed his offices on the prisoner. Even at this late stage, Trevor's design was to procure information helpful to government. The plan was thwarted by Russell who limited himself to a memorandum on reform for transmission to government. In the memoir which eventually reached London, he urged political, fiscal and religious change. As an ex-magistrate he argued that the magistracy should be reshaped. He called for a full-time, salaried magistracy purged of bigotry and favouritism. He instanced the bias of existing magistrates who were no more than place-hunters. All too frequently, the people's only recourse for justice was to humane officers of the British army. The defence barrister, Henry Joy, had also visited him and, as he had promised, informed him of Mary Ann McCracken's solicitude on his behalf.[5]

Trial at Downpatrick

On 20 October Thomas Russell appeared in court, not as magistrate, but as a prisoner on charge of High Treason. In the background, as he well knew, was his breach of the Emigration Act of 1798 by which he was specifically banished from Ireland. The presiding judge was Baron George while the prosecution was led by the Attorney-General, Standish O'Grady. Among the jury were as many as six men who had earlier professed United Irish views. Attornies Joy and Bell had the difficult task of Russell's defence.

The strategies available to the defence were limited. Russell would not permit defence witnesses to be called on the ground that they would be imperilled thereby. Nor could he provide an alibi. Hence, the main defence strategy was cross-examination of witnesses for the crown. Of necessity, Henry Joy's opening was tenuous. He challenged the court's jurisdiction in that there had been no overt act of rebellion in County Down. The Attorney-General had little dificulty in proving that a number of people had gathered near Downpatrick on the night of 23 July. Standish O'Grady also cited the meeting at Anadorn where Russell was present. The proclamation of Emmet's rising at the dolmen near Loughinisland was not mentioned. Another submission by Henry Joy was that the act under which Russell was indicted was inoperative being an English statute from before the Act of Union. This, too, was over-ruled by the judge.

Witnesses from Dublin, including Major Sirr and some army officers, proved that an insurrection had taken place there with plans for subsidiary uprisings in Belfast and Downpatrick. Accounts of the meetings at Loughinisland and Anadorn drew a comprehensive picture of Russell's involvement there. William Cosby (a yeoman from Saintfield), Henry Smith (Anadorn) as well as James Fitzpatrick, Patrick Lynch and Fr McCartan (all of Loughinisland) gave their evidence, in Lynch's case very reluctantly. In the absence of counter-testimony it accumulated to a formidable case against the prisoner. In Russell's view, the Attorney-General attempted to turn tragedy into farce by an unworthy gibe at the prisoner's dress. By late evening the prosecution appeared unbreakable. When Baron George charged the jury the interval of consideration was short. A verdict of guilty was returned.[6]

If a trial is drama then the cast at Downpatrick presented a tragedy. The prisoner was composed and dignified. The judge was courteous if stern. Some of the jury may have thought of an earlier time when their opinions differed little from the prisoner in the dock. The witnesses were powerless men caught up in a scene not of their making. Baron George, according to custom, invited Russell to speak before sentence. Henry Joy had advised him against making the address he had originally composed. Thus, Russell's speech had to be written in the unquiet circumstances of the trial itself. Nevertheless, it was a creditable exam-

ple of sincerity, conviction and restrained style. Russell commenced in his habitually gracious way by thanking the judge for
his patience, the prosecution lawyers for their 'humane attention' and his own attornies for the skill they had employed on
his behalf. His address recapitulated the political and religious
vision which had animated him since first he entered on the
United Irish programme. According to the *Belfast Newsletter* he
repeatedly asserted that he looked back with pleasure to his
political career of the previous thirteen years. He asked that he
might be 'the only one that would fall' and insisted that the
other prisoners had been induced 'to join in a business which
did not originate with themselves'. Doubtless, it was a poignant
moment when he referred to those members of the jury whose
earlier ideals had influenced him when first he came to Belfast as
a member of the garrison in the town.

The address from the dock showed Russell's rock-like certitude
on political matters and his self-deprecation on what he termed
his own personal sinfulness. Reports of the trial indicate that at
first the sympathy of the court for him was evident. This sympathy
altered when he proposed changes in the state's treatment of the
poor. To cite the *Belfast Newsletter*, 'he expatiated in favour of
ameliorating the condition of the lower class'. Here was an
emphasis which was now unfashionable given the reactionary
climate of the time. The visionary strand so evident in Russell's
jottings emerges as he argued that 'the saviour of the world will
show his sign to mankind and the boundaries of the kingdoms
will be pointed out'. For many of his auditors this was an evidence of 'enthusiasm', not to say derangement. At the conclusion
of a speech lasting nearly half an hour, Russell asked for three
days' grace to finish a script on which he was engaged. As well,
he asked that his body be given to his friends for burial with his
parents at Kilmainham's Royal Hospital.[7]

That Russell's extraordinary personality exercised influence on
the court is not simply a piety of nationalist tradition. Sources
less friendly to his cause also remarked on his dignified behaviour. From Dublin Castle William Wickham observed to
London's Home Office that he had 'behaved with firmness and
propriety'. Martha McTier reported on the favourable impression created by this unusual prisoner: 'The officers who guarded
him, the man who took him, even Sirr, Osborne, the judge, etc,
etc, never tire of his praise.' Writing to Dr Drennan, Martha

McTier tells of how a certain Mr Cole repeated in Belfast Russell's speech 'word for word' and 'never, never, could forget the appearance, manner and voice of the man who uttered it'. Not unreasonably from a judicial point of view, the presiding judge lectured on the 'incalculable miseries' which now hung over Russell and his colleagues. Allowing that the prisoner was once 'a worthy and deservedly esteemed member of the community', the judge regretted that 'a gentleman of education could so pervert his understanding as to implicate poor ignorant men in acts of rebellion'. To the charge from the bench that he had asserted what he knew to be false, viz. that French troops had landed at Ballywalter, Russell was now precluded from replying.

As capital sentence was pronounced the judge recommended that Russell should use the short time left to him 'in making his peace with God and in endeavouring to atone for the miseries his crimes and infatuated conduct (had) brought ... on not a few members of (the) community'. No stipulation was made about the deferral of execution asked for in the speech from the dock. After the judge's address, Russell listened to his sentence 'with the greatest composure, bowed respectfully to the court and then retired in the custody of the Sheriff'.[8]

Execution

On return to the jail Russell was informed that stay of execution would not be granted. Behind the request was not a plan of escape or rescue. Nor was the literary work he had in mind a political testament. Strangely perhaps, it was a commentary on Francis Dobbs' exotic publication applying biblical prophecies to the Irish political scene. Russell's prospects, therefore, were grim since execution was normally carried out in a matter of hours after sentence. The captain of the guard, Captain Gordon, seems to have extended basic courtesies to Russell during these last hours. They conversed desultorily and later Gordon recalled the 'affectionate, grateful and religious' letter which Russell mandated to his sister. It was Mary Ann McCracken who ensured that the letter was forwarded to Margaret in Dublin. R. M. Young in his *Historical Pieces of Old Belfast* claims that among Russell's papers was a note inscribed 'The Nation will support my sister'. Ever attentive to detail, Martha McTier remarked that he had twice dreamed of Eliza Goddard while at Downpatrick.

It is part of the Russell enigma that he was reputedly a distant cousin of the Sheriff, Matthew Forde. And so he was also a cousin of the Reverend Arthur Forde, chaplain at Downpatrick jail, a brother of the Sheriff. As with the Reverend Foster Archer, Russell engaged in theological argument with the Reverend Forde and bequeathed his own Greek bible to the chaplain. On the morning of execution (21 October) Thomas Russell was twice given the eucharist. He had received another letter from Mary Ann McCracken promising to care for Margaret and any other friend he might name. As well, Mary Ann requested the memento of a lock of his hair. It fell to the deputy sheriff, Fulton, to summon Russell to execution about noon. He did so with some humanity and was treated in the same fashion by Russell. On the way to the makeshift scaffold at the front of the prison, 'he bowed to some gentlemen he passed and gave them his good wishes, directed the hangman in his office and put the rope around his neck himself'.[9]

Florence Wilson effectively recreates the perspective of the Co Down farmer within the crowd and with whom this study commenced:

> By Downptrick gaol I was bound to fare
> on a day I'll remember, feth;
> for when I came to the prison square
> the people were waitin' in hundreds there
> an' you wouldn't hear stir nor breath!
> For the sodgers were standing, grim an' tall.
> round a scaffold built there fornent the wall,
> an' a man stepped out for death!
>
> An' I know'd the set, an' I know'd the walk
> an' the sound of his strange up-country talk.

These lines recreate the tradition that Russell briefly addressed the crowd assembled behind the soldiers. In terms at once religious and political he is represented as speaking of both forgiveness and hope that 'the wrong would cease and the right prevail'.

So ended the life of one of the most colourful personalities in Irish political history. In the manner of the time he was beheaded after death and his body was taken into the jail. Martha McTier informs us that he was placed in 'a thick heavy oak coffin' already prepared in the prison yard. Martha hoped 'some old friends might with just propriety be ordered to carry this coffin to his sister'. It was not to be. Mary Ann McCracken saw to Russell's burial in the nearby cemetery of the parish church. Later, she commissioned the simple memorial over the resting place of 'The Man From God-Knows-Where'. It is starkly inscribed: 'The Grave of Russell'. The Belfast community which had once adopted Russell found itself deeply affected by his death. John Templeton resigned from the Belfast Literary Society to avoid Dr McDonnell who had subscribed to the reward for his capture. It took twenty years before Templeton and McDonnell spoke again and then through the good offices of the one who had loved Russell most deeply, Mary Ann McCracken. That tragedy is expressed in the *Epitaph on the Living* sent by William Drennan to his sister some weeks after Russell's death:

Stop, passenger awhile attend;
If business will allow.
Here lives a man who sold a friend
And lately lost a cow.

Here lives the man who could subscribe
to hang that friend at last;
whom future history will describe
the Brutus of Belfast.

Let this man live and mind his trade
but in unbounded space
should he e'er chance on Russell's shade
O let him hide his face.

CHAPTER FIFTEEN

Who Was 'The Man from God knows where' ?

I

Thomas Russell's place in the Irish republican canon is an honoured one. Several factors underline his importance: his foundational role in the United Irishmen; his influence on Tone; his continued association with Belfast republicanism; his work among people of no property; his perseverence in the quest for social justice and political independence. Then, there is the air of mystery about him so well captured by Florence Wilson's appellation 'The Man From God-Knows-Where'. Russell's particular significance is inseparable from the extraordinary phenomenon of the 1790s in Ireland: a middle-class, largely Protestant, republicanism which was separatist in thrust, inclusive in aspiration and with an explicit philosophy of human rights. For all the diversity within its ranks, it represented another version of the continental Enlightenment. Its primary commitment was to a secular, plural Ireland where the churches would be disestablished and the rights of citizens extended to the whole 'nation'. Despite his own attachment to 'revealed religion', Russell belongs to that movement as one who 'stood by its cradle and went with it to its grave'.[1]

The social project envisaged by Tone, Russell, McCracken and Hope, might have succeeded if the United Irish leadership had met with more fortunate circumstances and had shown more determination. In time of crisis the leadership was not up to its task. Yet, favourable circumstances are created rather than given by hazard. And the bite of repression shattered the resolve of many leaders, forcing them into disarray. Some, like Robert Simms, retired from active politics. Others welcomed the Act of Union pushed through by Castlereagh and Pitt. Thereafter, they became respectable burghers who reprobated the lack of pragmatism shown by Russell. For many reasons, the movement initiated by Tone and Russell foundered in the aftermath of 1798 to remain only a memory of what might have been. That movement held out for a brief moment the promise of 'a national but pluralist dispensation'. Such a dispensation was unfortunately not realised but its generous possibility motivated the finest minds in subsequent generations.

A nostalgic assessment of the 1790s would do little justice to people such as Russell, Tone, McCracken and Hope. They were more than dreamers or noble failures. The events of 1798 marked Irish society even in the throes of defeat. The United Irishmen achieved a certain triumph even in failure. The memory of those who died (in the main, people of no property and no subsequent eminence in either balladry or oral tradition) inspired further resistance to injustice. Likewise, though the ideal of union – a 'cordial union of all Irishmen' – was quickly shattered, its relevance endures more than two hundred years later. Pitt's Act of Union was never in the programme of Tone or Russell. It was an altogether different measure, inimical to their aspirations. Nor did Pitt, Castlereagh and Cornwallis intend that enactment for republican purposes. Indeed, in one frame of reference it can be argued that 1798 and 1803 served the longer purposes of Whitehall. Yet, a consequence of the Act of Union and, indirectly, of the United Irish movement, was the displacement of the venal politicians of College Green. No longer did they hold undisputed sway. The Act of Union signalled the beginning of the end for an Ascendancy which Russell came to detest even more than English rule. In the decades after 1801, measures called for by Russell and Tone occurred progressively through sustained political pressure: Catholic emancipation, removal of disabilities placed on Dissenters, abolition of tithes, disestablishment of the Anglican church, initial steps towards solving 'the land question', the consolidation of the rule of law rather than the despotism of petty squires. Despite their apparent victory in 1798 and the consolidation of their personal fortunes in 1801, the hitherto unlimited power of the Protestant ascendancy was curbed. That, at least, would have rejoiced the heart of Thomas Russell and Theobald Wolfe Tone.

II

Thomas Russell represents more than an outstanding individual

who had quit the ascendancy to espouse a popular cause. On
such a reading he would be no more than a personable hero or
an outsider whose mystique proved fatal for himself and his followers. Despite his legendary personal charm, he is primarily to
be understood in the context of the United Irish Society and
everything it represented. As did Tone, Drennan and Hamilton
Rowan, Russell moved from enthusiasm for Grattan's Whig programme towards a more radical understanding of religious toleration and parliamentary reform. Religious emancipation and
legislative reform were the original aims of the United Irishmen.
Against that background one has to place their initial programme of 'forwarding a brotherhood of affection, a community
of rights, and an union of power among Irishmen of every religious persuasion'. Subsequent historical work has disclosed both
the nobility and the fragility of the United Irish endeavour.[2]

Russell's early posting to Belfast introduced him to the radicalism of Samuel Neilson, William Sinclair and, later, Henry Joy
McCracken. From Belfast, one disenfranchised group reached
out towards another. The Dissenters' economic power and their
developed civic culture outstripped the less homogeneous or-
ganisations of the Catholics. In some cases, their radicalism went
beyond anything Catholic leaders might sanction in the early
1790s. Yet, with the idea of a common programme of reform, the
'Establishment nightmare' was becoming a reality. The programme of union was a delicate task, fraught with risk from
clerical hostility and a prevalent mistrust, sedulously fostered
by government. In attempting to further the 'brotherhood of affection ... and union of power among Irishmen of every religious
persuasion', few were more active than Russell. Due to a combination of circumstances – his surrender of army commission and
magistracy, his librarianship in Belfast, his extended field trips –
he was in a singular position to spread the idea that governmental
injustice could effectively be opposed. The *modus operandi* of the
United Irishmen was, originally, to raise such consciousness
among the dispossessed and others desirous of political change.
The circumstance of war with France at once rendered the task
more hazardous and yet confirmed that the old order could be
unseated. In spreading a gospel of change, Russell appears to
have been outstanding, although the contribution of McCracken,
Neilson, Hope and Putnam McCabe should not be overlooked.
It remains part of 'the Russell enigma' that his personal magnet-

ism conferred on him a prominence not only among United Irishmen but even in the eyes of government. Perhaps there is an element of genuine puzzlement in his own comment that Dublin Castle's Thomas Pelham had expressed 'very exaggerated notions of my talents and influence'.[3]

Thomas Russell linked political independence to religious freedom, just taxation, relief of poverty and fair administration of law. Certainly there is a dash of utopianism in his journal entries during mid-1793. In July of that year he believed that governments would wither and 'little more than society would remain'. Adopting Thomas Paine's distinction between government and society, Russell argued that in proportion as government became more 'simple', society would improve. Having less to do with human laws, people would be more inclined to respect divine ones. The journal at this point details a prevalent contradiction: men committed murder or robbery without compunction if a king or minister desired it. In such circumstances, murder was not termed murder while robbery was deemed 'lawful plunder'. The root of this aberration was obvious: since the rich made the laws, the vices of the rich – 'adultery, gaming dueling (sic), luxury' – were considered honourable. Hence, Russell argued that 'Property must be alter'd in some measure' (entry for 9 July 1973).

Although he has left no political testament other than his pamphlet of 1796, it is clear that he had moved farther to the left than the Dublin United Irishmen might sanction. This *Letter to the Irish People* is imbued with anger against social injustice and loud in its call for change. It is stronger in denunciation of widespread abuse than in the provision of specific alternatives. Given the circumstances of the time, such general canvas is the most that could be expected. It is no depreciation of his pamphlet to suggest that Russell was fortunate to be spared that test of political power – its exercise. His 'triumph of failure' is to be remembered as one who died 'that the Wrong might cease and the Right prevail'. Along with Hope and McCracken he became an exemplar of the demand for religious toleration and social justice.

III

Despite his origins in the County Cork and his long association with Dublin, Russell is to be seen as a man of the north. Belfast

was his spiritual home in regard to political thought and aspiration. The United Irish Society was founded there and, for a while
at least, in Belfast was most thoroughly organised. In Dublin, its
leaders were more closely aligned to the Whig opposition from
which many of them came. The Catholic Committee had its own
concerns even when its more assertive leadership worked
alongside United Irishmen. Cumulatively, these factors may
have retarded the impetus of the United Irishmen in Dublin. The
character of the northern society was different although it, too,
changed during the 1790s. In the north, Presbyterian resentment
of aristocratic predominance entrained hostility to Dublin Castle
and College Green. Coupled with this, although by no means
identically, was the political and cultural assertiveness of Belfast
merchant families. They noticed the alignment of French republicanism with their own interests, particularly in the early 1790s.
Dismay at revolutionary excesses in France was balanced by desire for free trade, personal rights and equality before the law.
Such a programme seemed a valid application of the French
motto *liberté, fraternité, égalité*.

Although Brendan Clifford's assessment of the particular affinity
between Russell and Belfast may be questionable, yet his account of Belfast politics is perceptive.[4] In the Belfast of the 1790s
there was deep attachment to Enlightenment values, in particular to Paine's account of 'the Rights of Man'. (It took Mary Ann
McCracken systematically to extend this as far as the equality of
man and woman). No matter how worthy, such radicalism was
untested by the exercise of political power. It was, again to cite
Clifford, a general or transcendental radicalism which came
under pressure, first in 1796 and then in the disarray of 1798.
After 1801, middle-class interests seemed better served in the
'new order' created by the Act of Union. As to the religious grievances of Dissenters, these were in part addressed by the *regium
donum* to Presbyterian clergy. Gradually, the radical clergymen
of the 1790s, exemplified by James Porter, William Steele
Dickson and Sinclair Kelbourne, were outflanked in the theological dissensions preoccupying Dissenters in the early nineteenth
century. In regard to the Catholic leadership, it reverted to displaying its own loyalty. The charter of Maynooth College, the
counter-revolutionary discipline subsequently imposed on
diocesan Catholic clergy, ensured that a sullen compliance was
exacted from the rank and file of the people.

IV

It is at once the achievement and the tragedy of Russell to have retained an ideal clarified in the Belfast of the 1790s and strengthened by the sacrifice of so many of his friends in 1798. Why did Russell's vision, focused in the Belfast of the 1790s, remain unchanged? To explain this by attachment to 'the cause' would be mere tautology. There is the factor of loyalty to intimate friends such as Tone, McCracken and, probably, Emmet. Again, prolonged imprisonment in Ireland and Scotland had isolated him from changes which had occurred in the political temper of people he knew best. Yet, John Templeton more than once had warned him of new divisions and new enthusiasms running counter to the idealism of the 1790s. Hence, it is insufficient to 'explain' his perseverance as the desperation of one who, having suffered much, could not properly estimate the cost of further resistance. A process analogous to that which changed Wolfe Tone from a successful publicist of the Whig party to a dedicated revolutionary, can be predicated of Russell.

Thomas Russell was at first enamoured of Grattan's oppposition party – too much so for Tone's liking. Yet gradually he went from one degree of radicalism to another. It is, perhaps, surprising that one who twice held an officership in the King's army nonetheless should become enthusiastic for French intervention in Ireland. Yet, that was the case even though, for reasons as much religious as political, he later became disillusioned with the French government. Long years of imprisonment were for him a time of reading, reflection and observation of events in Ireland, although such observation was through the prism of his friends' experiences. He left Newgate and Fort George more committed than ever to the cause of Irish freedom, the cause of the people of no property – no matter whether they were Catholics or Protestants. Even more, despite the warnings of Templeton, he was convinced that success would only be achieved through armed force. The grip of a corrupt oligarchy could not be loosened in any other way. The flaw in his thinking was to suppose, as he wrote to Templeton, that the 'cordial union of Irishmen' persisted and that 1798 had shown who were the friends and who the enemies of the people.

It is pointless to ask what he might have become had he persevered in the army or the magistracy – or, for that matter, what might have emerged if the scheme outlined by himself and Tone for the Sandwich Islands had been accepted. The more relevant fact is that he turned his back on an Ascendancy to which he had access but within which he did not rest easily. In passing, it is noteworthy that Lord Cornwallis shared his contempt for Irish gentry and ultra-loyalists. Their rabidly anti-democratic views and sectarian arrogance evoked the anger of both rebel and viceroy. Whatever about Cornwallis, it is certain that Russell could never be comfortable among the squires and the magistrates.

Thus, he persevered in his singular move towards the dispossessed, in particular towards the Catholics. Distinct from the United Irish leadership in Dublin, distinct from Tone and the middle-class Catholic leaders, he moved through and sympathised with the small tenant farmers, the weavers and other working people. He was virtually unique among the radicals for his *entrée* to the richest and poorest circles. The journal records visits to the mansion of Thomas Wogan Browne at Castle Browne as well as to the cottages of weavers and tenant farmers. At the commencement of this study it was noted that Russell's 'strange up-country talk' probably reflected his Anglo-Irish upbringing. Nevertheless, the small farmers of Antrim and Down, the displaced working-men of the Mudler's Club, accepted him as a friend and confidant. Russell understoood that a revolution was worthless if it did not address the problems of the poorer groups. This sympathy cost him dearly. To cite his own journal, he had beggared himself for the good of his country.[5]

V

It is clear that Russell shared the current enthusiasm for new scientific and cultural ideas. Despite a sketchy formal education, his reading went across the spectrum of literary, historical, scientific and political studies. With his Belfast friends he shared an enthusiasm for the post-enlightenment expansion of knowledge, except its religious scepticism. Nor was this confined to his tenure as librarian in Belfast. It continued into his imprisonment, despite unsettled conditions. Nonetheless, he differed from some of his friends by an enduring sympathy with the old Gaelic order. Whereas, Tone was impatient with the harpers' festival at Belfast in July 1792 – 'strum, strum and be damned', he told his diary – Russell was interested both in the Irish language and the Gaelic order. The battle of Aughrim in 1691 was seen by him as the regrettable defeat of that order. Here, notably, he differed from Robert Simms who saw 'the Glorious Revolution' as a vindication of the rights of individual conscience. Here, too, he differed from William Drennan and from Samuel Neilson. Again, he disagreed with many of his colleagues who were freethinkers or Deists. Russell, on the contrary, had a vivid biblical faith and strong belief in revealed religion. On that account, he came to reject Napoleonic law which he saw as atheistic and inhumane. Despite his religious bent he could not accept the establishment of one religious tradition at the expense of another. So, he maintained opposition both to tithes and to Anglican establishment in a country where the majority were either Catholics or Presbyterian dissenters. Perhaps Thomas Moore's words most tellingly express the nuance of that ancient quarrel in regard to an establishment where:

... armed at once with prayer-books and with whips,
blood on their hands, and Scripture on their lips,
tyrants by creed, and torturers by text,
make this life hell, in honour of the next![6]

VI

Part of the Russell enigma is his own extraordinary personality. As with Tone, there is a danger of idealising him. It would detract from historical veracity to overlook what he himself recognised and endeavoured to overcome. Undeniably, the years 1793-4 were low points for his morale. His brother's death, personal poverty, worry about his sister at Drumsluice, political uncertainty in Belfast and Dublin, all can be linked to a dalliance with drink and, at times, prostitutes. On more than one occasion he minuted these shortcomings. For all his sensitivity, Russell had found it difficult to move from the solitary life of the army barrack to the gentler arts of domestic converse. John Gray's realistic judgement cannot be neglected: 'In one noticeable area, his relations with women, he was unable to make the transition, with guilt-ridden one-night stands contrasting starkly with the hopeless failure of his idealised love for Eliza Goddard ...'.[7] Although Tone and Robert Simms rebuked him in a fondness for drink, there is no suggestion that this led Russell into unwise political judgement or to endangering others. It did, however, add to his feelings of guilt.

Otherwise, he had an unusual ability to captivate people of all kinds. Thomas Pelham's high estimation of his personal character was doubtless sincere, although it did not help his release. After his execution, the normally reliable Martha McTier observed how even his political enemies spoke well of him: 'The officers who guarded him, the man who took him, even Sirr, Osborne, the judge, etc, etc, never tire of his praise'. Mrs McTier further remarked that he was 'an agreeable, improving, fascinating visitor in my family for two years ... during that time I never heard a sentence or word from him that did not do him honour as a religious, moral man, a polite finished gentleman (where he chose) and an entertaining, improving companion'. All his collaborators retained their high regard for him, perhaps with the exception of Dr McDonnell, even when their paths diverged. It is a good sign of Russell that people of modest social importance also paid tribute to him – James Hope's praise has already been noted, as have the fulsome words of Mary Dalton, one-time prisoner at Newgate.[8]

Russell's familial and romantic attachments gave him considerable difficulty. Grief over the death of Ambrose took him to the verge of nervous collapse. His father's death entrained not only grief but also a sense of duty to Margaret which was so heavy as to be almost pathological. In imprisonment and in freedom, he worried about her dependence and impoverishment. Appeals to his friends on her behalf tried their patience almost beyond endurance. Margaret was a loving sister, deeply loyal to her much-admired brother. More than once she undertook difficult missions for him while he was interned at Fort George. It is a paradox that although Russell's concern for her lasted even to the day of his death yet, so far as can be established, he did not contact her on his return to Ireland. The exigencies of his secret mission will not have permitted frequent or open access to her in Dublin. Coupled with her earlier complaint that she knew little of his movements, this elusiveness indicates that he subtracted himself from her nervous oversight when he deemed it necessary.

From his earliest days in Belfast Russell was received with cordiality by the McCrackens of Rosemary Lane. Between him and Henry Joy McCracken was a particular sympathy in mind and ideal. The two men were destined to enter subsequent tradition as popular heroes enshrouded by an aura of gallantry and courage. Yet, McCracken's sister, Mary Ann, has not received her deserved place in Irish historiography. An enthusiast for womens' rights, even among the United Irishmen, she was generations ahead of her time in her practical feminism. During the 1790s she, too, was a critical observer of governmental repression. From 1796 she was of eminently practical support to the Kilmainham and Newgate prisoners. Unusually for her day, she managed an extensive textile business with great success. She deployed her considerable wealth in educational and social projects to offset prevalent injustices affecting women and children. To the end of her life – she died in 1866, aged 96 – she opposed slavery in America and the British colonies. It was she who evidenced that Russell would take no foods produced by slave labour even when this meant abstinence from sugar products.

Between these remarkable people there existed respect and friendship. Mary Ann McCracken's later descriptions of Thomas Russell hint at more than 'platonic' interest. More than forty years after his death, she spoke of his appearance: 'His mouth was the most beautiful, particularly when he smiled, I ever saw; and so perfectly truthful, as if so truthful himself he never suspected deceit in others.' It was she who sent Russell a moving account of her brother's death on the morrow of his execution. It is fanciful to speculate on Russell's deeper feelings for this outstanding woman. His letters remain chivalrous and courteous – but no more. A certain formality is suggested by Mary Ann's later remembrance of his tendency to swear and her diffidence, because of 'the stateliness of his manner', to rebuke him. Yet, their similarity of views, their constancy in adversity, their mutual trust in the last days of Russell's life remain a striking feature of their noble friendship.

An element of instability in Russell's life was his relationship with Eliza Goddard. The association was a major source of unhappiness for him, especially at times when his morale was lowest. Was it unrequited love? A figment of his imagination? Why was he so tentative in approach to this mysterious young woman? There were times when their relationship brought intense happiness to Russell: he wrote in 1794 of the exquisite joys of their early love. Eliza Goddard's father, a place-hunter and a bully, was fiercely hostile to Russell. Greed and political animosity motivated John Goddard's opposition to any friendship between Eliza and Russell. Nevertheless, confusion on Russell's part was also a factor in the unhappy outcome of their romance. On one occasion, he asked Martha McTier to be an intermediary for him – a role she briskly declined.

From the early 1790s, every possibility of domestic happiness for Russell was impeded by his unremitting infatuation. On one occasion it seemed as if he would marry another woman, but even then his motivation was unclear. One takes the impression that no one ever affected him so deeply as did Eliza who, to the end of his life, exercised the charm of the unattainable. Matilda Tone intimated on one occasion that Russell's tempestuous feeling would never allow him to be happy with any woman other than Eliza Goddard. It would be unrealistic to suggest that Eliza was in some way blameworthy. One or two of Russell's journal entries show that his fastidiousness about 'gravity' may have been oppressive for a woman barely over twenty years of age. The main significance of this troubled friendship is the turmoil which made Thomas Russell an emotional refugee even in Belfast where he felt most at home.

Despite his gallantry and that impressive mien which so capti-vated Theobald and Matilda Tone, Russell suffered from an habitual self-doubt. This is clear in his memorandum on his thir-tieth birthday as well as in journal entries. It is noteworthy that to the day of his death he distinguished his moral failings from his political stances. The dichotomy is strangely absolute. On the first he is hesitant and guilt-laden. On the second, he entertains no doubt. A sense of personal unworthiness about drink and re-lations with women recurs throughout the journal. Inevitably, this raises question of his emotional preparedness for the com-mitment of marriage. Again, his particular concern with mar-riage conventions – bitterly hostile to the Napoleonic provision of divorce, favourable to the strict laws of the Gracehill settle-ment – has a certain irony given his own unhappy experiences.

VII

Why did Russell so consistently pit himself against overwhelm-ing odds? How could a man versed in military ways have acted as he did in July 1803? It is insufficient to cast him as the perennial rebel, the indomitable outsider. Russell's idealism did not lack a tempering realism. He noted, for example, that regular British troops were thinly spread across the country. In addition, he believed that the militias could be suborned if they witnessed initial successes of the projected rising. The knock-on effect of capturing Dublin, Downpatrick and, perhaps, Belfast was potentially great. Again, Russell was convinced of the earlier United Irish line that once popular attention was fixed on a political objective, the people's demand could not be resisted for long. It is clear that his understanding of the political context was the same as that expressed by his *Letter to the Irish People* in 1796. The prevalent injustice arose from political-economic imperialism underpinned by Anglican church-establishment. In Russell's view, the ills of such establishment cried out for remedy: rectors who were all too frequently bigoted magistrates, tithes and church taxes, disenfranchisement of Dissenters and Catholics. This least bigoted of men diagnosed in Defender activities a reaction to Orange depredation in the north of Ireland. He recognised what government persistently denied, viz. that Orange activity (unchecked in Armagh, Fermanagh, Down and Antrim) was at the root of discontent and agrarian 'outrages'. With the more radical United Irishmen, he saw Orangeism among the main threats to a just and peaceful Ireland. Nevertheless, he persisted in the hope that Orangemen could be persuaded of the benefit of union in the whole people's interest.

VIII

A complication in assessing Thomas Russell is his penchant for religious enthusiasm. Already, his religious belief set him off from some of his colleagues in the United Irishmen and from most of the French revolutionists. His belief in the doctrines of Christianity impelled him to consider writing against Paine and Godwin whose Enlightenment tenets denied many of these doctrines. Yet, the religious strand of Russell's character went beyond the purely intellectual. An awareness of moral failure with overtones of morbid guilt seemed to haunt him at certain junctures of his life. His recurrent confession of moral failure in regard to intemperance, disordered sexuality and irreverence in speech has already been noted. Nevertheless, he retained an ability sharply to distinguish moral fault from political radicalism. In regard to morals he may have been excessively self-punitive: in regard to politics he entertained no doubt on the rectitude of his cause.

Despite these patterns of religious scruple, Russell had no difficulty in opposing the hierarchies of both Anglican and Roman
Catholic churches. The opposition was implicit rather than explicit. In both churches, the leadership had repeatedly con-
demned opposition to the ruling civil power. According to the
bishops' utterances, people like Russell were virtually outlawed
from good ecclesiastical standing. This did not induce in him
any trace of conscientious scruple. Part of the reason for this insouciance was that his religious bent was scriptural rather than
institutional. To an extraordinary degree, Russell was conver-
sant with the bible and with minutiae of scriptural interpretation. The Reverend Foster Archer had noticed his application of
technical religious arguments to specific political instances.
Again, in the course of his prison narrative, written in December
1800, Russell propounds a view of world history which is biblical rather than political. Here, a strain of religious prophetism
leads him to suggest that, the 'old age' having come to an end, a
'new age' of divine justice would now be instituted.

The phenomenon of religious fundamentalism is too complicated
for it to be predicated of Russell in any simple way. Its rock-like
certitudes are based on little evidence other than a literal interpretation of key-texts. It is notoriously resistant to other evidences while relying on arcane signs and portents. Thomas
Russell's personal dispositions were not coherent with religious
fanaticism, sectarianism or triviality. Yet, he was imbued with a
sense of divine providence and convinced of a universal battle
between good and evil. His surviving papers contain extensive
notations of biblical texts associated with apocalyptic predic-
tions. Foster Archer's report of the Kilmainham meeting at the
prison chapel in October 1803 pointedly refers to the prophecies
which exercised Russell's mind. Again, Russell's association
with Francis Dobbs from 1798 (and, perhaps, earlier) raises the
question of how far he had travelled the millenarian avenue. If
Alexander Marsden's note from Dublin Castle has any credibility,
it was on Dobbs's arguments about the incidence of a 'new age'
of virtue, justice and harmony that Russell proposed to write in
the hours before his execution. Attending to these admittedly
sketchy indications, one has to entertain John Gray's suggestion
that Thomas Russell became influenced by 'millenarian vision'.
In Gray's view, Russell sought to overcome 'through political
salvation and religious redemption, the disabilities of a life he

despised'. An hypothesis of this kind might explain his persistence in his desperate attempt to rouse people in County Down during those fateful days of late July, 1803.[9]

It should be noted that in late eighteenth-century Ireland the influence of millenarian prophecies was strong among both Dissenters and Catholics. By 1800, Francis Dobbs had brought the *genre* to a fine point in his arguments against the Act of Union. Russell's association with Dobbs is instructive in attempting to understand his acceptance of this mode of thought. Yet, as Nancy Curtin has shown, the use of millenarian arguments was relatively widespread among the United Irishmen and, indeed, in Defender and Orange communications. Such argument was employed both as a propaganda device and, sometimes, as a 'validating charter' for radically innovative policies. The manipulative possibilities were considerable. Samuel Neilson is reputed to have inserted millenarian arguments in the *Northern Star* 'to please his country readers'. On the other hand, the Reverend Steele Dickson, the Reverend Ledlie Birch and Russell himself sincerely believed not only that God was on their side but that 'the course of divinely ordained history assured victory to the opponents of the administration'. Such belief motivated their resistance against overwhelming odds even though it did not augur well for the specific application of political principles in a democratic society to which they undoubtedly aspired.[10]

IX

In attempting to understand a figure like Russell one has to consider a problem which applies in an Ireland of many generations after his death. Are those only to be honoured who 'succeeded'? And what is 'success'? History, it is said, sheds few tears for losers. Yet, such a stance says more about historians than about those they study. Historical revisionism in Ireland shows a residual hostility to figures like Thomas Russell. People such as he, Tone, Emmet and Pearse, are either dismissed as 'dreamers' or otherwise diminished. Yet, the persistent memory of Russell in popular tradition challenges the bias of much academic writing. On one criterion – the tenet that success betokens merit – Thomas Russell was a failure. In the context of Castlereagh or of the lesser politicians who governed Irish society during the

1790s, he was a 'dreamer', lacking in 'realism', a naïve enthusiast. On another, perhaps more durable, criterion, Russell's failure remained to motivate other generations of Irishmen and women. There were those, like Florence Wilson's farmer outside Downpatrick jail, who said:

> *'Please God'* to his dying hope
> and *'amen'* to his dying prayer.

Thomas Russell and his colleagues fostered a tradition which aspired to universal values of justice, tolerance and imprescriptible rights. In his background – a Protestant, an army officer, a 'gentleman' in the narrow sense coined by the ascendancy – Russell does not fit neatly into the later mould of Irish republican separatism. Yet, even in these very differences, Russell and the Belfast republicans of the 1790s pose an ineluctible question to Irish and British people who live so many generations after them. The questions have to do with political courage, creative imagination and an ability to enter the world of the 'other', especially the dispossessed and the excluded.

R. R. Madden, a sympathetic biographer, suggests that Russell 'was not a man calculated to guide and control and direct the affairs of a national movement to a successful issue'. (*Lives*, 111, 11, p 281). The enigmatic Dr McDonnell whose own 'prudence' led him to subscribe to a reward for Russell's capture thought he was 'diffuse, easily taken with novelties, and soon generalised' (ibid. 280). It worried McDonnell that Russell 'dwelt much on religious politics, particularly the obscure parts of Scripture'. If all political utopias are dreams, then Russell was a dreamer. He was one of those individuals who challenge oppressive societies in the name of reform and, even, revolution. Thomas Russell and his colleagues of the 1790s can be seen thus. They challenged the existing order and tried to outline a more tolerable alternative. That is utopian vision at its best. For a while, it seemed that their vision could be achieved through a broadly-based people's movement. In the short term, their defeat was a tragedy, especially for Catholics and Presbyterians. Sectarian divisions were once again fostered by those who feared a union of Irish people.

In Russell's own case, utopian outlook was tinged with religious enthusiasm. It can be argued that such an amalgam of religion and politics led to faulty judgements on his part. Yet, if such an argument is to be credible, it must take account of the historical uncertainties about Emmet's rising which still persist. It is certain that Russell was uniquely positioned where three orders, hitherto mutually hostile, met and interacted. His imaginative sensibiliities evoked an abiding sympathy for the old Gaelic order. His adoption by Dissenter radicals in Belfast fired him with democratic republican motivations. And his niche within the Anglican ascendancy, for all its tenuousness, placed him in the company of Grattan, Curran and other advanced Whigs. His enthusiasm for millenarian symbols should not be a pretext for overlooking his unusual political and cultural generosity. Through him one can glimpse a time when Protestants, Catholics and Dissenters tried to understand each other. In the 1790s, some people endeavoured through a just, tolerant and humane political order to set aside ancient quarrels and endemic injustice.

Thereafter, 'the Russell enigma' must be allowed to stand: the restlessness; the personal charm; the driven quest for a new Ireland. His perseverance in an unprofitable demand for social equity challenges selfishness and complacency even today. It is possible that his tendency to conflate politics and religion would have rendered him unsuited to 'the art of the possible'. Since he never did exercise political power that must remain an untested hypothesis. It is hoped that these chapters may at least depict Russell's extraordinary dedication to a cause which obsessed him. The temptation to present him purely as 'hero' is to be resisted. It is more important to learn from his achievements as well as his shortcomings. For all the strands of Russell's life which remain unexplained, his noble vision of political virtue, of an Ireland both just and free, can still inspire an inclusive politics for the country. In her *History of the United Irishmen*, Rosamund Jacob makes the somewhat large claim: 'Before 1791 there were in the country only the British colonists and the enslaved Irish; after that year parties took a new dimension – those who stood for privilege and foreign government, and those both of Irish and British stock, who stood for an Irish nation, democratic and independent.'[11] Despite its broad sweep, Jacob's assertion comes close to describing 'the man called Russell'.

Afterwards

James Hope left Dublin's Coombe area. He returned to the north and worked for many years as a weaver. He never lost his radical democratic views. Similarly, he retained a critical view of the abuse of religion to underpin social injustice. He and Rose Hope named their three sons after Henry Joy McCracken, Thomas Russell and Robert Emmet. 'Jemmy' Hope was able to assist R. R. Madden in the compilation of the *Lives and Times of the United Irishmen*. 'The Weaver of Templepatrick' died in 1853 and is buried at Mallusk, Co Antrim. Mary Ann McCracken and Israel Milliken saw to the erection of his headstone.

Margaret Russell's situation did not improve. Her little school, situated over a 'dram-shop', did not prosper. In 1825 she petitioned the Viceroy for the return of her brother's papers and some money which had been impounded by the prison authorities at Kilmainham. Thomas Russell's Belfast friends kept up their contacts with her. Eliza Templeton wrote frequently. Dr McDonnell sent advice and some money. Once again, it was Mary Ann McCracken who was most generous. Mary Ann got her a place at 'The Retreat' at Drumcondra, Dublin. Margaret Russell died at this house in 1834, aged eighty two. She bequeathed her brother's papers to Miss McCracken.

John Templeton, one of Russell's sincerest friends, lived until 1825. He continued his scientific work and maintained his interest in Dublin's Botanic Gardens. Just before his death he was reconciled with Dr McDonnell through the intermediacy of Mary Ann McCracken. While he read the political context in 1803 differently from Russell, he did not relinquish his views on the necessity for an equitable social order.

Eliza Templeton survived her brother by many years. Even in

1859 she was able to visit Mary Ann McCracken and, doubtless, will also have helped Dr Madden in preserving the memory of the great figures of the 1 790s.

William Hamilton, barrister and soldier, was eventually arrested by the Castle authorities. He spent some years in prison until his release by the Fox administration. He went to South America where he joined the armies of Simon Bolivar. He died there after distinguished service in Bolivar's anti-colonial endeavours.

Mary Ann McCracken, the bravest and most generous of all, has been neglected by Irish historians. More recently, Mary McNeill's fine work has paid due tribute to her courage, her intelligence and her feminism *avant la lettre*. Mary Ann reared her brother's little daughter, carried on an extensive business in muslin and opposed slavery until the day of her death. Even in her eighties she handed out anti-slavery literature at Belfast docks. In Belfast she never ceased to work for the poor, especially poor women. She died, aged ninety six, on 26 July 1866. To her we owe in large part that the spirit of the 1790s was not forgotten. It was she who had every right to say: 'This world affords no enjoyment equal to that of promoting the happiness of others'. That, too, could be the epitaph of Thomas Russell.

Sometime in the 1840s two army officers, Captain J. Russell and Captain J. Hamilton, visited Thomas Russell's simple grave at Downpatrick. Both men were nephews of 'The Man fom God knows where'.

Notes

Introduction to Footnotes

Russell's Journal is to be found at four locations. Three of these are in the Rebellion Papers at the National Archives in Dublin. For clarity I refer to these in the traditional numeration (SPO/15/6/3, SP0 620/20/33 and SPO 620/21/23). The fourth is in the Sirr Papers at Trinity College, Dublin (Ms 868/1). C.J. Woods has done invaluable work by making these available in his meticulous edition and collation, published in 1991 as *Journals and Memoirs of Thomas Russell.*

Other papers of Russell (letters and manuscripts as well as letters to him) are in collection at TCD (Sirr Papers, Mss 868/1 and 868/2). Also at TCD are the Madden Papers where several letters from and to Russell are found (chiefly Ms 873). As well, in these Madden papers is the material provided Dr Madden by Mary Ann McCracken in preparation of his *Lives of the United Irishmen.*

The fortunate circumstances by which this material has been preserved for subsequent historians are well expounded by Dr Woods in his introduction to *Journals and Memoirs of Thomas Russell.*

Principal Manuscript Sources are as follows:
Drennan Letters. Public Record Office N. Ireland (PRONI).
Frazer Manuscripts. National Archives, Dublin. (Nat. Arch.).
Madden Papers. Trinity College, Dublin. (Ms 873).
Pratt (Camden) Papers. Kent Archives (Maidstone) (Ms U 840).
Sirr Papers. Trinity College, Dublin. (Mss 868 and 869).
Rebellion Papers. National Archives, Dublin (SPO 620/1-67).
State of the Country Papers. National Archives, Dublin.
Public Record Office (Kew). Home Office (HO 100/114/113-23; 100/31 210 and 227; 100/33/91-93).

Royal Irish Academy. Ms 23 K 53 (Burrowes).
ibid. Ms 24 K 48 (A. H. Rowan).
Tone Manuscripts. Trinity College, Dublin(Mss 2041-50).
Westmorland Letters. National Library of Ireland, (394).

Contemporary Newspapers:
Belfast Newsletter; Dublin Evening Post; Northern Star; Walker's Journal.

Chapter One

1. For early years, cf. Madden, *Lives,* iii, ii, pp 137-45; MacGiolla Easbaig, *Tomás Ruiséil,* pp 17-25; An Bráthair Peadair, *Inniú,* 30.10.1953; Dunlop, *Nat. Dict. Biography,* pp 473-5.
2. cf. C.J. Woods, *Journals and Memoirs of Thomas Russell,* pp 15-16. Hereafter referred to as *Journals.* References to Russell's journal will throughout this study give the relevant context in Dr Woods's book. Once again, I express my indebtedness to Dr Woods for this fine work which makes Russell's thought so easily available.
3. John Gray, 'Millenarian Vision', *Linen Hall Review,* Spring 1989, pp 5-6.
4. cf. Russell's journal entries throughout 1793, especially his memoir on the death of John Russell, 16 and 21 August 1793, SPO 620/15/16/3, cf. Woods, *Journals,* pp 96-107.
5. My thanks to J.J. Kavanagh (Drumahane) for his gracious introduction during November 1994 to the place of Russell's birth.
6. Journal entry post 10 March 1793, S.P.O., 620/21/23, cf.Woods, *Journals,* p 149; also Nathaniel Burton, *History of the Royal Hospital,* p 223.
7. Journal entry for June 1792, SP0 620/15/16/3, cf. Woods, *Journals,* pp 62-3.
8. cf. Mac Giolla Easbaig, *Tomás Ruiséil,* p 19.
9. Letter from India (10.2.1784) in TCD Ms. 868/1/262; re application to Lord Wellesley cf. J.W. Hammond in *Irish Press,* 15.12.1955.
10. TCD Ms. 868/1/262.
11. Journal entry after March 1794, SP0 620/21/23, cf. Woods, *Journals,* pp 147-9.
12. cf. Madden, *op. cit.,* pp 145-6; Mac Giolla Easbaig, *op. cit.,* pp 223; Dunlop, p 473, Col ii.
13. Mac Giolla Easbaig, *op. cit.,* pp 22-3.
14. C.J. Woods dates this meeting 3rd July (*Journals,* pp 16-7). Yet, cf. Marianne Elliott, *Wolfe Tone,* pp 94 et seq.

15. T. Wolfe Tone, *Life,* i, pp 34-5; TCD Ms. 2046/26-26v.

16. cf. 'Fugitive Pieces by Wm. Tone (and others)' in Tone (Dickason) Mss. (TCD). cf. also Elliott, *Wolfe Tone,* pp 98 and 433.

17. Mac Giolla Easbaig, *op. cit.,* p 28; Elliott, *Wolfe Tone,* pp 99 et seq.

18. Nancy Curtin, *The United Irishmen,* p 6.

Chapter Two

1. cf. Elliott, *Wolfe Tone,* pp 94-101; TCD Ms. 2046, 26-26v.

2. cf. Elliott, *Wolfe Tone,* pp 134-137.

3. cf. McNeill, *The Life and Times of Mary Ann McCracken,* pp 43-53. Hereafter, *Mary Ann McCracken.*

4. cf. Elliott, *Wolfe Tone,* pp 119 et seq.

5. Clifford, B., *Thomas Russell and Belfast,* p 7.

6. cf. McNeill, *Mary Ann McCracken,* p 72; Drennan Letters, letter 1062, (9th Oct 1803).

7. Journal entries through April 1791, TCD Ms 868/1/40-43v, Woods, *Journals,* pp 49-52.

8. Entry for Feb-March 1791 (probably notes of a lecture delivered in Dublin), SP0 620/15/6/3, cf. Woods, *Journals,* pp 44-6.

9. Entry for 10 April 1791, SP0 620/15/6/3, cf. Woods, *Journals,* p47.

10. Entry, probably for March 1791, SPO 620/15/6/3, cf. Woods, *Journals,* p 39.

11. Smyth, Jim, *The Men of No Property,* pp 19-20.

12. Entry, c. March, 1791, SPO 620/15/6/3, cf. Woods, *Journals,* p 43.

13. Entry c. Feb 1791, SP0 620/15/6/3, cf. Woods, *Journals,* p 37.

14. Entry mid-Feb 1791, SP0 620/15/6/3, cf. Woods, *Journals,* pp 35-6.

15. Entry July 1791, SP0 620/15/6/3, cf. Woods, *Journals,* pp 57-8.

16. Entry for 21 April 1 791, TCD Ms 868/1 / ff 40-3v, cf. Woods, *Journals,* pp 50-1.

17. Entry for 2 March 1791, SP0 620/15/6/3, cf. Woods, *Journals,* p 40.

18. Madden, Morgan and Mac Giolla Easbaig offer inconclusive arguments for this dramatic change in Rusell's life.

19. PRO(E), H.0. 100/31/210 and 227.

20. Elliott, *Wolfe Tone,* pp 123-124.

21. *ibid.,* p 125.

22. PRO(E), H.0. 100/33/91-93.

23. *ibid.*, 100/33/91 .

24. Rowan, A. Hamilton, *Autobiography*, pp 153-155.

25. Elliott, *Wolfe Tone*, pp 121-133.

26. *ibid.*, p 126.

27. *ibid.*, pp 16 et seq.

28. Entries for July and Aug 1791, SP0 620/15/6/3, cf. Woods, *Journals*, pp 57-8 and 61.

Chapter Three

1. Elliott, *Wolfe Tone*, p 138.

2. For a lively account of this visit to Belfast, cf. Elliott, *op. cit.*, pp l37-47.

3. *ibid.*, pp 139-141.

4. M. McNeill, *The Life and Times of Mary Ann McCracken*, p 75. Russell and Tone shared a convention whereby P.P. (parish clerk) referred to Russell and 'Mr Hulton' was a code-word for Tone.

5. Tone, *Life*, Vol l. pp 41-51; Elliott, *Wolfe Tone*, p 143.

6. TCD Ms. 873/669; Tone, *Life*, Vol 1, p 36; Elliott, *Wolfe Tone*, p 143.

7. N. Curtin, *The United Irishmen*, p 9; PRO(E) 100/34/41-2.

8. *Drennan Letters*, letters 311 -18; also Elliott, *Wolfe Tone*, p 160.

9. Lord Cloncurry (V. Lawless), *Personal Recollections*, pp 32-3.

10. H. Landreth, *The Pursuit of Robert Emmet*, p 21. This refers to a letter from Westmorland to chief secretary Hobart sometime in 1791-2. Cf. C.J. Woods, 'The Place of Tomas Russell in the United Irish Movement' in Gough and Dickson, *Ireland and the French Revolution*, p 97, n 6.

11. Dublin: *National Journal;* Belfast: *Northern Star.* Cf. N. Curtin, *The United Irishmen*, p 212-13 for an account of the Dublin paper's deficiencies.

12. S. Mac Giolla Easbaig, *Tomás Ruiséil*, p 54.

13. For Robert Simms's admonition cf. TCD Ms 868/2/307-8 and TCD Ms 868/2/262-3.

14. Wm. Drennan more than once adverted to the niggardly response by the Catholic Committee to Russell's efforts on behalf of Catholic claims.

15. For Jones Armstrong's letters, cf. TCD Mss 868/2/172 and 868/1 /204

16. Journal entry for June 1792. SP0 620/15/6/3, cf. Woods, *Journals*, pp 62-3.

17. S. Mac Giolla Easbaig assumes the 'G' letter to be from Russell's pen. Certainly, the letter expresses Russell's own views and in many ways reproduces his literary style. Yet, as distinct from the later 'E' letter, there is no external proof that the 'G' letter is Russell's.

Chapter Four

1. Elliott, *Wolfe Tone*, pp 172 et seq.
2. Journal for 16 and 21 August 1793, SP0/620/15/6/3, cf. Woods, *Journals*, pp 96-107.
3. *ibid.*, Woods, p 101.
4. *ibid.*, Woods, p 1 04.
5. *ibid.*, Woods, p 106.
6. *ibid.*, Woods, p 107.
7. Re Catholic Convention, cf. Daire Keogh, *The French Disease: The Catholic Church and Radicalism in Ireland 1790-1800*, esp. pp 123-8.
8. Journal as above. Woods, pp 98-9.
9. 'Duties of Christian Citizens'. Dr Troy issued this pastoral in February 1793. It was well received by Dublin Castle. Cf. D. Keogh, *The French Disease*, pp 62 et seq.
10. cf. Russell's *Letter To the Irish People* (SP0 620/27/3).
11. Journal entry for late April-early May 1793, SP0 620/20/33, cf. Woods, *Journals*, p 74.
12. Journal entry for 20 March 1793, SP0 620/20/33, cf. Woods, *Journals*, p 66.
13. TCD Ms 868/2/34.
14. Journal entry for 21-24 March 1793, SP0 620/20/33, cf. Woods, *Journals*, pp 66-8.
15. Journal entry for 3 April 1793, TCD Ms 868/1/ff 100-100v, cf. Woods, *Journals*, p 70.
16. Journal entry for 4 April 1793, SP0 620/20/33,. cf. Woods, *Journals*, p 72.
17. Journal entry for 20 March 1793, SP0 620/20/33, cf. Woods. *Journals*, p 65.
18. Journal entry for 16-24 April 1793, SP0 620/20/33, cf. Woods, *Journals*, p 72. Later, Wm Drennan prompted Martha McTier to ask the committee's generosity to Russell.
19. Journal entry for 24 April 1793, SP0 620/20/33, cf. Woods, *Journals*, p 73.
20. Journal entry for 7 May 1793, SP0 620/20/33, cf. Woods, *Journals*, p 74.

21. Journal entry for early May 1793, SP0 620/20/33, cf. Woods, *Journals*, p 75.
22. Journal entry for 10 May 1793, SP0 620/20/33, cf. Woods, *Journals*, p 76.
23. Journal for 7 May 1793, SP0 620/20/33, cf. Woods, *Journals*, p 74.
24. Journal for mid-May 1793, SP0 620/20/33, cf. Woods, *Journals*, p 76.

Chapter Five

1. Re book clubs, parish meetings and freemason resolutions, cf. Brendan Clifford. *Thomas Russell and Belfast;* Jim Smyth, *The Men of No Property* and Kevin Whelan, 'The United Irishmen, the Enlightenment and Popular Culture' in Dickson, Keogh and Whelan, *The United Irishmen*, pp 269-296.
2. Journal entry for 19 May 1793, SP0 620/20/33, cf. Woods, *Journals*, p 77; *Drennan Letters*, p 166, letter 443 (circa July 1793); Clifford, *Thomas Russell and Belfast*, p 42.
3. Journal for mid July 1793, SP0 620/20/33, Woods, *Journals*, p 80.
4. K. Whelan, *art. cit.*, pp 280-1.
5. Journal for mid July 1793, SP0 620/20/33, Woods, *Journals*, p 81.
6. Journal for mid July 1793, SP0 620/20/33, Woods, *Journals*, p 82-3.
7. Journal for mid July 1793, SP0 620/20/33, Woods, *Journals*, p 88.
8. R. R. Madden, *Antrim and Down in '98*, p 108. Also M. McNeill, *Mary Ann McCracken*, p 94.
9. Alongside the compliance by the Whig opposition with government there was also a certain diminution in the ardour of Whiggish elements among the Dublin United Irishmen.
10. Journal entry 2 Sept 1793 SP0 620/21/23, Woods, *Journals*, p 121; also post-27 Sept 1793, SP0 620/21/23, Woods, *Journals*, p 124.
11. Journal for 8-9 Sept 1793, SP0 620/21/23, Woods, *Journals*, p 127. Also entry for 19 and 20 Oct 1793, SP0 620/21/23, Woods, *Journals*, p 1 33.
12. Entry for 2 Sept 1793, SP0 620/21/23, Woods, *Journals*, pp 109-121 .
13. Entry for 2 Sept 1793, SP0 620/21/23, Woods, *Journals*, p 112.
14. Entry for 4 Sept 1793, Woods, *Journals*, p 119.
15. Entry for 9 Sept 1793, SP0 620/21/23, Woods, *Journals*, p 123.
16. Entry for Aug-Sept 1793, SP0 620/21/23, Woods, *Journals*, pp 158-160.

17. Defence of *Northern Star*, cf. entry for 19 and 20 Oct 1793, SP0/21/23, Woods, *Journals*, pp 132-3.

18. Entry for 13 and 14 Nov. 1793, SP0 620/21/23, Woods, *Journals*, p 134.

19. Entry for 14 Nov 1793, SP0 620/21/23, Woods, *Journals*, p 135.

20. M. McTier, *Drennan Letters*, p 175, letter 449.

21. Madden, *Lives*, iii,ii, p 397.

22. Entry for early Dec 1793, SP0 620/21/23, Woods, *Journals*, p 138.

23. Entry for mid Dec 1793, SP0 620/21/23, Woods, *Journals*, p 140.

24. Entry mid-December 1793, SP0 620/21/23, Woods, *Journals*, p 139.

Chapter Six

1. John Anderson, *History of the Belfast Library*, p 91.

2. Anderson, *op. cit.*, p 13.

3. Journal entries for 17 and 18 Jan 1794, SP0 620/21/23, cf.also Woods, *Journals*, pp 140-1. Also entry for 13 or 14 Feb, 1794, SP0/620/21/23, Woods, *Journals*, p 146.

4. C. J. Woods, 'The Place of Thomas Russell in the United Irish Movement', in Gough and Dickson, *Ireland and the French Revolution*, p 89.

5. cf. Mac Giolla Easbaig, *Tomás Ruiséil*, p 85.

6. R. R. Madden, *Antrim and Down in '98*, p 306; T. J. Campbell, *Fifty Years of Ulster*, p 287.

7. Journal entries for 19 and 20 Jan 1794, also for 29 Jan, SP0/620/21/23, Woods, *Journals*, pp 141-2 and 144.

8. Journal entries for 19 and 20 Jan 1794, SP0 620/21/23, Woods, *Journals*, pp 141-2.

9. Journal entry re 22-24 Jan 1794, SP0 620/21/23, Woods, *Journals*, p 143.

10. Journal entry *eo. loco .*, cf. Woods, *Journals*, p 144.

11. Journal entry for I Feb 1794, *eo. loco.*, Woods, *Journals*, p 144.

12. TCD Mss 868/2/32 and 868/1/ ff. 15-20v; journal entry for 29 Jan 1794 re his niece's marriage to Wm. Hamilton, SPO 620/21/23, cf. Woods, *Journals*, p 144.

13. TCD Ms 868/1/ff.15-20 and 868/2/159. Also journal entry for 4 Nov 1794, TCD Ms 868/1/ff 15-20, Woods, *Journals*, p 174.

14. TCD Mss 868/1/184 and 868/1/146 et seq. Also TCD Ms 868/1/206.

15. Journal entry post 10 March 1794 (SPO 620/21/23 pp 81-88) details Russell's grief. Cf. Woods, *Journals,* pp 147-152. Cf. also MacGiolla Easbaig, *op. cit.,* p 90.

16. Margaret wrote on 29 March. cf. TCD Ms 868/2/32. For Tone's letter, cf. TCD Ms 868/2/229.

17. Journal entry for 30 June 1794, SPO 620/21/23 pp 88-9, Woods, *Journal,* p 156.

18. A particularly troubled entry for 9 June 1794 shows the extent of Russell's desperation, TCD Ms 868/1/ff 184-5v, cf. Woods, *Journals,* p 151 .

19. *Drennan Letters,* 13-9-1794, letter 526. Cf. TCD Mss 873/655/6, 868/2/116 and 121.

20. TCD Ms 868/2/55.

21. Journal entry for 24 Sept 1794, SPO 620/21/23, Woods, *Journal,* p 159.

22. Re Jacobin Club at Belfast, cf. Nancy Curtin, *The United Irishmen,* pp 139-40. Reference to younger, more violent, men is made in Russell's journal entry for 3 to 9 Nov 1794, TCD Ms 868/1/ff15-2Ov, Woods, *Journals,* p 173.

23. Re Gracehill community it is interesting that Russell minutely observed this Christian group and admired its way of life. His detailed journal entry is found at SPO 620/21/23, and TCD Ms 868/1/ff 21-3v, 52-3. Cf. Woods, *Journals,* pp 163-70.

24. Journal entry for 3 Nov 1794, TCD Ms 868/1/ff 15-20v, Woods, *Journals,* pp 171 et seq.

25. *ibid.,* cf. Woods, *Journals,* p 173.

26. *eo. loco.,* also *Drennan Papers,* PRO(NI) T 765 C, no 540,562.

Chapter Seven

1. Wm. Johnston to John Lees, *Pratt Papers* (Archives Office, Maidstone, Kent), A.O. U 840. 0146/3. Re Jacobin Club, *ibid.,* U 840 0147/4/2. Re Martha McTier's remark, cf. Wm. Drennan Letters, PRO(NI) T765/548.

2. Journal entry for 13-14 March 1794, TCD Ms 868/1/Foll 317v317. Woods, *Journals,* pp 184-5.

3. Re McNeven's query, TCD Ms 868/1/2. Nancy Curtin dates the meeting which approved the new United Irish constitution at 10 May 1795. Cf. Curtin, *The United Irishmen,* pp 90-116, for a valuable analysis of the organisational structure of the United Irish movement during the mid-1790s. Cf. also Curtin's article 'The Transformation of the Society of United Irishmen into a mass-based revolutionary organisation, 1794-6', in *Irish Historical Studies* , xxiv, no 96 (Nov.1985), pp 463-492.

4. M. McNeill, *Mary Ann McCracken*, pp 104 et seq.

5. McNeill, *op. cit.*, p 102, from Hayden and Moonan, *A Short History of the Irish People*, p 425.

6. McNeill, *op. cit.*, p 103.

7. Johnston's report, cf. *Pratt Papers,* U 140, 0 146/3 (May 1795).

8. Mac Giolla Easbaig, *Tomás Ruiséil,* p 102; Madden, *Lives,* iii, ii, p 180.

9. Report of John Smith (Bird), SP0 620/27/1; also Nancy Curtin's, 'The Transformation of the Society of United Irishmen', *Irish Historical Studies,* xxiv, no 96, p 472 et seq.

10. SPO 620/22/28.

11. Frazer Mss 2,15 (Nat. Archives).

12. For discussion of this, cf. Elliott, *Wolfe Tone,* pp 256 et seq.

13. For Tone's stay at Belfast, cf. Elliott, *Wolfe Tone,* pp 258 et seq. For Rowland O'Connor's information, cf. *Pratt Papers,* A0 Maidstone, Kent, U 840, 0 147/4/1. For Mgt. Russell's reaction and Thomas Russell's own comments on Tone's visit. cf. TCD Ms 868/2/65 and TCD Ms 873/330. For Tone's later comment, cf. facsimile of hotel bill in Elliott, *Wolfe Tone,* after p 308.

14. Elliott, *op. cit.*, pp 258-9.

15. Re Defenders, cf. Marianne Elliott, 'The Defenders in Ulster', in Dickson, Keogh and Whelan, *The United Irishmen. Republicanism, Radicalism and Rebellion*, pp 222-33. Also Thomas Bartlett, 'Defenders and Defenderism in 1795' in *Irish Historical Studies* (May 1985), pp 373-394.

16. For Camden's exchange of letters with the Duke of Portland, cf. SPO 620/22/19 and PRO(E) H0 100/57/265-6. Re N. Alexander's comment, cf. SP0 620/26/36. Cf. Nancy Curtin, 'The Transformation of the Society of United Irishmen', *Irish Historical Studies,* xxiv, no 96, pp 478-9.

17. Samuel McSkimmin, *Annals of Ulster,* pp 33-4.

18. PRO(E) H0 100/87/5-7. Also Elliott, *Wolfe Tone,* p 231.

19. Dickson, *Revolt in the North,* p 117.

20. K. Whelan, 'The United Irishmen, The Enlightenment and Popular Culture', in Dickson, Keogh and Whelan, *The United Irishmen. Republicanism, Radicalism and Rebellion*, p 285. Louis Cullen, 'The Internal Politics of the United Irishmen', in Dickson, Keogh and Whelan, *op. cit.*, 178-9.

21. A. McNevin to Dublin Castle (27 June 1796), SPO 620/23/197. Cf. also Russell's letter in *Dublin Evening Post*, 22 Dec 1796.

22. John Smith to Dublin Castle in late 1796, cf. SPO 620/27/1.

23. N. Curtin, 'The United Irish Organisation in Ulster: 1795-8', Dickson, Keogh and Whelan, *op. cit.*, pp 214-5 24. cf. *Drennan Letters*, p 222, letter 544. 25 TCD Ms 868/2/72 for Mgt's admonition. Cf. TCD Ms 868/2/76 for her letter of Jan 1796. For other remarks on Russell's elusiveness, cf. TCD Ms 868/2/243 and 868/1/164.

26. TCD Ms 868/2/72.

27. Russell was in the habit of meeting every call from Margaret with money remittances. Here and there in his correspondence are hints of deeper indebtedness the cause of which remains unclear. Cf. for example a letter from John E. Cairns of Dungannon who, it would seem, was a creditor of Russell's.

28. TCD Ms 868/2/176 (Margaret Tone) and also TCD Ms 868/2/174 (Peter Tone's letter of thanks).

29. TCD Ms 868/1/193.

30. SPO 620/27/3.

Chapter Eight

1. Re Castlereagh, cf. M. McNeill, *Mary Ann McCracken*, pp 108 et seq. Re arrests, cf. *Northern Star*, 12-19 Sept.1796, *Freeman's Journal*, 20 Sept 1796. Also *Drennan Letters*, p 240, letter 629 for Martha McTier's reaction.

2. *Freeman's Journal*, 20 Sept 1796; *Drennan Letters*, p 241, letter 630.

3. C. Teeling, *History of the Irish Rebellion*, p 23.

4. Frazer Mss 2.40 (Nat. Archives).

5. S. Mac Giolla Easbaig, *Tomás Ruiséil*, p 118; re Wolfe's instruction, cf. SPO 620/25/1 30.

6. Application by the Simms brothers, cf. SPO 620/1/2/1. Re McCracken's complaint, cf. McNeill, *Mary Ann McCracken*, p 151 and, re the Rev. Gamble, *ibid.*, p 147. Re Thomas Russell's generous remark cf. TCD Ms 873/655/4v.

7. TCD Ms 868/2/112 and TCD Ms 868/2/88.

8. TCD 868/2/248.

9 . *Evening Post*, 22.12.1796.

10. From the foundation of the Orange order attacks on Catholics had increased both in frequency and viciousness.

11. SPO 620/54/14; Dickson, *Revolt in the North*, p 206.

12. Wm. Sampson, *Memoirs of William Sampson*, p 367.

13. On Dr Mitchell, cf. TCD Ms 868/2/270. Re Mary Ann McCracken's remarks, cf. McNeill, *Mary Ann McCracken*, pp 154-5; re Neilson's illness, cf. SPO 620/53/81.

14. SPO 620/1 6/3.
15. SPO 620/1 6/3.
16. TCD Ms 873/655.
17. TCD Ms 868/1/125; SPO 620/16/3.
18. TCD Ms 868/1/35 and 868/2/288.
19. TCD Ms 868/1/ff. 2-4. (re self examination Nov 21st 1797).

Chapter Nine

1. Marianne Elliott, *Wolfe Tone,* pp 324-333.
2. Re Tone's remark, cf. TCD Ms 2049/204. Also, Dickson, *Revolt in the North,* p 104 et seq. Cf. also Lecky, *History,* Vol 4, pp 265-274.
3 M. McNeill, *Mary Ann McCracken,* p 142.
4. Dickson, *Revolt in the North,* p 114.
5. McNeill, *op. cit.,* p 142.
6. *ibid.,* p 150; also SPO 620/54/14.
7. SPO 620/53/ 204 and 205 for grocery accounts to Russell; TCD Ms 868/2/292 for Simms letter.
8. TCD Mss 868/2/309-10,281 and 292.
9. TCD Ms 868/2/307. 'General Clarke' probably is Daniel Cullinane, a Co Tipperary 'scarlet pimpernel'. Other aliases were 'Lordonnier', 'Fr Murphy', 'Thorington'. Cf. H. Landreth, *The Pursuit of Robert Emmet,* p 154.
10. TCD Ms 868/2/241 (Smith); TCD Ms 868/2/302 (Templeton); reply from Russell TCD Ms 873/634.
11. TCD Ms 873/634.
1 2. TCD Mss 868/2/306, 313, 315.
13. TCD Ms 868/2/229 and 868/2/277 (R.Simms); TCD Ms 868/2/258 (W.Simms) and TCD Ms 868/2/311.
14. TCD Ms 868/2/1 29.
15. TCD Ms 868/2/100 (Mgt Russell) and TCD Ms 868/2/245 (Osborne).
16. Narrative of Dec.1800, TCD Ms 873/655/7.
17. *Drennan Letters,* p 266, letter 692.
18. SPO 620/7/74/5 (McNally's information).
19. SPO 620/1 6/3.
20. Mary Ann McCracken's letter at SPO 620/16/3.
21. Dickson, *Antrim and Down in '98,* p 80.
22. TCD Ms 873/855/1-13 for narrative.
23. Prisoners' document is at SPO 620/39/321. Also Elliott, *Wolfe Tone,* p 384.

24. Cornwallis Correspondence, Vol 2, pp 357, 337,372.

25. *ibid.*, pp 375 and 379-81.

26. *ibid.*, p 390.

27. *ibid.*, pp 403 and 376.

28. Madden refers to a document seeking French assistance, cf. *Lives,* iii, ii, p 18 5 . For Cornwallis's postponement of emigration cf. SP0/620/52/218.

29. For Tone's remark. cf. TCD Tone (Dickason) Mss (Aug-Sept 1798), also Elliott, *Wolfe Tone,* p 384.

30. SP0 620/16/3

31. TCD Ms 868/1/29.

32. TCD Ms 868/1/168 and 266; TCD Ms 868/2/102.

33. TCD Ms 868/2/279.

34. TCD Ms 868/1/124 and SPO 620/15/2/15.

Chapter Ten

1. TCD Ms 868/2/125. SP0 620/7/74/2 (re McNally's information).

2. SP0 620/7/74/2 and 3.

3. TCD Ms 868/1/272 (letter to Mgt.). For the journey to Fort George, cf. Wm. Steele Dickson, *The Confinement and Exile of William Steele Dickson,* pp 102-82, Mac Giolla Easbaig, *Tomás Ruiséil,* pp 136-148.

4. TCD Ms 868/1/281 and TCD Ms 868/1/270.

5. SP0 620/16/3 (to E. Cooke); prisoners wrote from Newgate on 21 May 1 799.

6. TCD Mss 868/1/275 and 868/1/279.

7. TCD Mss 868/1/285 and 7; TCD Ms 868/1/283.

8. TCD Ms 868/1/295.

9. Mac Giolla Easbaig, *Tomás Ruiséil,* pp 142-44.

10. cf. *Memoir of T.A. Emmet and R. Emmet,* Vol 1, p 319; also Elliott, *Partners in Revolution,* p 325.

11. *Viceroy's Postbag,* p 258.

12. For covering note and narrative, cf. TCD Ms 873/655/1-13.

13. TCD Ms 868/1/291; also 868/1/297 and 868/1/301.

14. R. R. Madden, *Lives,* iii, ii, p 200. Also Drennan's letter for 16 June, 1802.

15. TCD Ms 868/1/631.

16. TCD Ms 868/1/299.

Chapter Eleven

1. C.J. Woods, 'The Place of Thomas Russell in the United Irish Movement', Gough and Dickson, *Ireland in the French Revolution*, p 94.

2. SP0 620/12/140; TCD Ms 868/1/305.

3. TCD Ms 868/1/307(to Mgt Russell); SPO 620/12/145 (re James O'Farrell); SP0 620/11/130 (Simms brothers).

4. H. Landreth, *The Pursuit of Robert Emmet*, pp 115-23; *Memoir of T.A. Emmet and R. Emmet*, (hereafter, *Memoir*),Vol 1, p 305; Ml. Quigley's information SPO 620/13/177.

5. Dublin Castle's reaction cf. *Viceroy's Postbag*, pp 274 and 402; *Memoir*, Vol 1, p 53; Landreth, *The Pursuit of Robert Emmet*, p 116.

6. *Memoir*, Vol 1. pp 53 et seq.; Madden, *Lives*, iii, ii, pp 208 et seq.; Elliott, *Partners in Revolution*, pp 305-12; *Memoirs of Miles Byrne*, Vol. 1, passim.

7. Mrs Rabb's letter, cf. TCD Ms 873/627; *Drennan Letters*, p 324.

8. Elliott, *Partners in Revolution*, p 308.

9. Russell to Mary Ann Hamilton, TCD Ms 873/643.

10. Landreth, *The Pursuit of Robert Emmet*, pp 175-182; Mac Giolla Easbaig, *Tomás Ruiséil*, pp 162-172.

11. TCD Ms 873/680; also TCD Mss 873/656 and 873/627.

Chapter Twelve

1. Baron George's summing up will be dealt with later in this text.

2. For list of Antrim and Down prisoners (30.11.1803), cf. SP0 620/1 2/1 42.

3. *Viceroy's Postbag*, p 417 for McClelland's remarks.

4. Landreth, *The Pursuit of Robert Emmet*, p 231.

5. cf. SP0 620/64/1 54.

6. Report of Russell's trial (re Anadorn), *Belfast Newsletter*, 25 Oct 1803.

7. *eo. loco.*

8. Re Loughinisland, *Belfast Newsletter*, 25 Oct 1803.

9. Dickson, *Revolt in the North*, p 207; Landreth, *The Pursuit of Robert Emmet*, pp 231.

10. cf. the argument of Landreth, *The Pursuit of Robert Emmet*, pp 388-412. It should be noted that Landreth's thesis has been questioned to some degree by Leon O'Broin's subsequent work, *The Unfortunate Mr Emmet*, published in 1958 .

11. cf. SP0 620/64/154; SPO 620/64/95; SPO 620/67/89; SP0 620/64/1 28.

12. *Drennan Letters*, (M. McTier to W. Drennan), letter 1062.

13. re Fr McCartan, cf. Dickson, *Revolt in the North*, p 208; re Rev Thomas Beatty, cf. SP0 620/11/130.

14. TCD Ms 873/627.

15. *Drennan Letters*, p 329, letter 1057 and SP0 620/11/158.

16. TCD Ms 873/627.

17. *eo. loco.*

18. R.R. Madden, *Lives*, iii, ii, pp 217 et seq. Also TCD Ms 869/-7/Folio 118; Landreth, *The Pursuit of Robert Emmet*, pp 308-11.

Chapter Thirteen

1. Cf. examination of Daniel Muley at Dublin Castle for what follows, SP0/620/11 /138/1 4. Also, Mary Muley, TCD Ms 869/5/ ff. 101 -2.

2. SP0 620/11 /138/14.

3. SP0 620/67/93.

4. Mac Giolla Easbaig, *Tomás Ruiséil*, pp 189-200 for account of arrest. Re Mrs. Rabb's comment, cf. TCD Ms 873/627.

5. H. Landreth, *The Pursuit of Robert Emmet*, pp 308-11; *Memoir of Thomas Addis Emmet and Robert Emmet*, Vol 2, p 237.

6. Re dispute, cf. *Frazer Manuscripts*, Vol 2, 131 (National Archives). Also, W. Cox, *Remarks By One of the People To Whom John Swift Emerson Has Appealed*, SP0 620/50/93. Re Russell's spirited remark, cf. Landreth, *The Pursuit ...*, p 311.

7. PR0 (E) HO 100/114/113v re dispatch to London by Wickham. For Margaret's poignant letter, cf. SP0 620/12/154.

8. For John Russell's well-founded alarm, cf. SP0 620/12/154.

9. cf. *Documents Relating To Ireland 1795-1803*. Account of secret service money granted for five days' diet of two men brought from Fort George to identify Russell. The amount was £3. 0. 1.

10. *Viceroy's Postbag*, p 423. Also Mac Giolla Easbaig, *Tomás Ruiséil*, pp 190-1.

11. *Viceroy's Postbag*, pp 421-423; PRO(E) H0 100/114/119-20; PRO(E) H0 100/114/121-4.

12. especially PRO(E) H0 100/114/121-4.

13. PRO(E) H0 100/114/113 and 117.

14. PRO(E) H0 100/114/124.

15. cf. *Drennan Letters*, p 330, letter 1062; also McNeill, *MaryAnn McCracken*, p 21 5; *Belfast Newsletter*, 28-10-1803.

16. SP0 620/50/21.
17. *ibid.*
18. *ibid.*
19. *Viceroy's Postbag,* p 424; also PRO(E) H0 100/114/121.

Chapter Fourteen

1. SPO 620/1 2/1 49.
2. SP0 620/12/142 for this list.
3. Letter to Frank McCracken, TCD Ms 873/642. cf. M.McNeill, Mary Ann McCracken, pp 214-26.
4. McNeill, *op. cit.,* p 220 et seq.
5. Russell's manuscript is not available. For its substance, cf. *Viceroy's Postbag,* pp 423-26.
6. For an account of the trial, cf. TCD Ms 873/626 (James Cleland); *Dublin Evening Post,* 25-10-1803; *Belfast Newsletter,* 25-10-1803.
7. *Dublin Evening Post,* 22-10-1803.
8. *ibid.* For Russell's speech from the dock, cf. TCD Ms 873/700 and notes in his hand TCD Ms 873/686
9. R.M. Young, *Historical Pieces of Old Belfast,* p190; M. McTier, *Drennan Letters,* letters 1064-68, pp 330-333.

Chapter Fifteen

1. C.J. Woods, 'The Place of Thomas Russell in the United Irish Movement', in Gough and Dickson, *Ireland and the French Revolution,* p 82.
2. Cf. Nancy Curtin, *The United Irishmen. Popular Politics in Ulster and Dublin 1791-1798* (Clarendon, Oxford), 1994; Dickson, Keogh and Whelan, *The United Irishmen. Republicanism, Radicalism and Rebellion,* (Lilliput, Dublin), 1993. The citation in text is from *Rep. Comm. Sec.* (Lords), 1798, appendix dcccxxxviii.
3. TCD Ms 873/85 5/7.
4. Brendan Clifford has argued thus in his *Belfast and the French Revolution* (Belfast 1989).
5. Journal entry for 19-5-1793, SP0 620/20/33, Woods, *Journals,* p.77; also for Jan 22 1794, SPO 620/21/23, Woods, *Journals,* pp 143-4.
6. Thomas Moore's satire 'Intolerance'. In *The Poetical Works of Thomas Moore* (Yardley and Hanscomb, London), n.d.g., p 176.
7. John Gray, *The Linen Hall Review,* Spring 1992, Vol 9, no 1, p28.

8. M. McTier, *Drennan Letters,* letter 1065a, to Mrs S. Drennan. Re Mary Dalton, cf. TCD Ms. 868/2/288.

9 John Gray, 'Millenial Vision. Thomas Russell Reassessed', *The Linen Hall Review,* Vol 6, no 1, Sept 1981, p 6.

10. For analysis of religious millenarianism in northern politics, cf. Nancy Curtin, *The United Irishmen,* pp 174-201.

11. Rosamund Jacob, *The Rise of the United Irishmen1791-1794,* p66.

Bibliography

Anderson, John, *History of the Belfast Library and Society for Promoting Knowledge, commonly known as the Linen Hall Library*, Belfast, 1888.

Beckett, J. C., *Protestant Dissent in Ireland. 1687-1780* (Studies in Irish History), Faber, 1948.

Bigger, F. J., *Four Shots From County Down*, Belfast, 1918.

Burton, N., *A History of the Royal Hospital, Kilmainham*, Dublin, 1843.

Butler, Hubert, *The sub-prefect should have held his tongue and other essays*, (ed. R. F. Foster), Allen Lane (with the Lilliput Press), London, 1990.

Byrne, Miles, *Memoirs of Miles Byrne* (2 Vols.), ed. S. Gwynn, Dublin, 1907.

Byrne, Miles, *Notes of An Irish Exile of 1798*, Maunsel, Dublin, no date.

Campbell, Flann, *The Dissenting Voice. Protestant Democracy in Ulster from Plantation to Partition*, Blackstaff Press, Belfast, 1991.

Campbell, T. J., *Fifty Years of Ulster*, Belfast, 1941.

Castlereagh, Viscount, *Memoirs and Correspondence of Viscount Castlereagh*, (12 Vols.), ed. C. Vane, London, 1848.

Charlemont, Lord, *Charlemont Correspondence* (2 Vols.), ed. J. Gilbert, Dublin, 1894.

Clifford, Brendan, *Thomas Russell and Belfast*, Athol Books, Belfast, 1988.

Clifford, Brendan, *Belfast in the French Revolution*, Historical Aid Educational Society, Belfast, 1989.

Cloncurry, Valentine, *Personal Reflections of The Life and Times of Valentine Lawless, Lord Cloncurry*, Dublin, 1849.

Colchester, Charles, *Diary and Correspondence of Charles Abbot, Lord Colchester*, (3 Vols.), Murray, London, 1811.

Corish, P. J. (ed.), *Radicals, Rebels and Establishments*, (Historical Studies XV), Appletree Press, Belfast, 1985.

Cornwallis, Charles, *Correspondence of Charles, First Marquis Cornwallis* , (3 Vols.), ed. Charles Ross, Murray, London, 1859.

Cox, Watty, *Remarks By One of The People To Whom John Swift Emerson Has Appealed*, J. Shea, Dublin, 1804.

Cronin, Sean, *A Man of the People – Jimmy Hope*, Scéim na gCeardcumann, Drogheda, 1964.

Curtin, Nancy, *The United Irishmen. Popular Politics in Dublin and Ulster, 1791-1798*, Clarendon Press, Oxford, 1994.

Daly, John Bowles (ed.), *Madden R. R.: Ireland in '98*, 1888. (A selection of texts from Madden's work).

Dickson, Charles, *Life of Ml. Dwyer*, Browne and Nolan, Dublin, 1944.

Dickson, Charles, *Revolt in the North: Antrim and Down in 1798*, Clonmore and Reynolds, Dublin, 1960.

Dickson, D., Keogh, D. and Whelan, K. (eds.), *The United Irishmen. Republicanism, Radicalism and Rebellion*, Lilliput, Dublin, 1993.

Dickson, Wm. Steele, *The Confinement and Exile of W. S. Dickson*, 2nd ed., Stockdale, Abbey St, Dublin, 1812.

Dobbs, Francis, *Memoirs of Francis Dobbs*, Dublin, 1800.

Drennan, William, *The Drennan Letters 1776-1819*, ed. D. A. Chart, Belfast, 1931.

Elliott, Marianne, *Partners in Revolution. The United Irishmen and France*, Yale University Press, New Haven and London, 1982.

Elliott, Marianne, *Wolfe Tone: Prophet of Irish Independence*, Yale University Press, New Haven and London, 1989.

Emmet, T.A., *Memoir of Thomas Addis and Robert Emmet. With their Ancestors and Immediate Family.* (2 Vols.), The Emmet Press, New York, 1915.

Fortescue, J. W., *A History of the British Army* (3 Vols.), London, 1911.

Foster, R. F., *Modern Ireland 1600-1972*, Allen Lane, London, 1988.

Gilbert, J. T., *A History of the City of Dublin*, James Duffy, Dublin, 1861.

Gilbert, J.T., *Documents Relating to Ireland 1795-1804*, Dublin, 1893, (re-printed by Irish University Press, 1970).

Gough, H. and Dickson, D. (eds.), *Ireland and the French Revolution*, Irish Academic Press, Dublin, 1990.

Jacob, Rosemary, *The Rise of the United Irishmen*, Harrap, London, 1937.

Joy, Henry, *Historical Collections Relative to the Town of Belfast. From the Earliest Period to the Union with Great Britain*, Berwick, Belfast, 1817.

Killen, John, *A History of the Linen Hall Library 1788-1988*, Linen Hall Library, Belfast, 1990.

Landreth, Helen, *The Pursuit of Robert Emmet*, Browne and Nolan, Dublin, 1949.

Lecky, W. F. H., *A History of Ireland in the 18th Century*, (5 Vols.), London, 1892.

Madden, R. R., *The United Irishmen: Their Lives and Times*, (3 Vols.), J. O'Neill, no date.

Madden, R. R., *The Lives and Times of the United Irishmen*, (3rd ed, especially volume 2), Dublin, 1846.

Madden, R. R., *Antrim and Down in 1798*, Glasgow, 1888.

Madden, R. R., *Literary Remains of the United Irishmen*, Dublin, 1887.

Medland, W. M. and Weobly, Chas., *A Collection of Remarkable and Interesting Trials*, (2 Vols.), London, 1804.

MacAnBheatha, Proinsias, *Jemmy Hope: An Chéad Sóisialaí Éireannach*, Foilseacháin Náisiúnta Teo, Cathair na Mart, 1985.

Mac Giolla Easbaig, S. N., *Tomás Ruiséil*, Cló Móráin, Baile Átha Cliaith, 1957.

McCaughey, Terence P., *Memory and Redemption: Church, Politics and Prophetic Theology in Ireland*, Gill and MacMillan, Dublin, 1993.

McDermot, Frank, *Theobald Wolfe Tone and His Times: A Biographical Study*, MacMillan, London, 1939.

McNeill, Mary, *The Life and Times of Mary Ann McCracken 1770-1866. A Belfast Panorama*, Alan Figgis and Co, 1960. Republished by Blackstaff Press, 1988.

McNeven, William James, *Pieces of Irish History*, New York, 1807.

McSkimmin, S., *Annals of Ulster*, James Cleland, Belfast, 1906

Ó Broin, Leon, *The Unfortunate Mr Emmet*, Clonmore and Reynolds, Dublin, 1958.

Owen, D. J., *History of Belfast*, W. and G. Baird, Belfast and London, 1921.

Ryan, Frieda, *A History of Kilmainham Gaol*, Mercier Press, Dublin and Cork, 1988.

Sampson, Wm., *Memoirs of William Sampson*, Leeburg, Virginia, 1817.

Smyth, Jim, *The Men of No Property*, Gill and MacMillan, Dublin, 1992.

Stewart, A. T. Q., *Narrow Ground. Aspects of Ulster 1609-1969*, Faber and Faber, 1977. A revised edition: Aldershot Gregg Revivals, 1993.

Teeling, C.H., *History of the Irish Rebellion and Sequel*, Irish University Press, 1972.

Tone, W., *Life of Theobald Wolfe Tone*, (2 Vols.), Washington, 1826.

Walsh, John Edward, *Ireland Sixty Years Ago*, McGlashan, Dublin, 1847.

Wilson, Florence M., *The Flight of the Earls and Other Poems*, Dublin, 1918.

Woods, C. J. (ed.), *Journals and Memoirs of Thomas Russell*, Irish Academic Press in association with The Linen Hall Library, Dublin and Belfast, 1991.

Young, R. M., *Historical Notices of Old Belfast*, Belfast, 1896.

Articles

Curtin, Nancy, 'The Transformation of the Society of United Irishmen into a mass-based revolutionary Organisation 1794-1796' in *Irish Historical Studies* (XXIV), no 96 (Nov. 1985), pp 463-492.

Dunlop, Robert, entry 'Thomas Russell' in *Dictionary of National Biography*, Vol XVII, 1909.

Elliott, Marianne, 'The Origins and Transformation of Early Irish Republicanism' in *International Review of Social History* XXIII (1978), pp 405-428.

Gray, John, 'Millenial Vision: Thomas Russell Reassessed' in *Linen Hall Review*, Vol 6, no 1 (Spring 1989), pp 5-9.

Gray, John, 'Review of C. J. Woods' in *Linen Hall Review*, Vol 9, no 1, (Spring 1992), pp 8-9.

Kavanagh, J. J., 'Thomas Russell – The Man from God-Knows-Where' in *The Mallow Field Club Journal*, 1985, (no 3), pp 55-62.

Killen, John, 'John Templeton – the Gilbert White of Ireland and the Friend of Everyman' in *Linen Hall Review*, Vol 9, no 3/4, (Winter 1992), pp 4-8.

Morgan, James, 'Sketch of the Life of Thomas Russell' in *Ulster Magazine* (1), 1830, pp 39-60.

McDowell, R. B., 'Proceedings of the Dublin Society of United Irishmen' in *Analecta Hibernica* (17), 1949, pp 83-143.

Peadar, an Bráthair, 'God Knows Where – Sin Dromach Sheain' in *Inniú*, 30-10-1953.

Woods, C. J., 'The Place of Thomas Russell in the United Irish Movement' in *Ireland and the French Revolution* (eds. Gough, H. and Dickson, D.), Dublin, 1990, pp 83-96.

Appendix

Florence Wilson's ballad imaginatively recalls the outline features of Thomas Russell's activity from 1795 to 1803 .

The opening verses depict Russell's work in Co Down during winter of 1795 when reconstruction of the United Irish movement was under way. F. J. Bigger, in his *Four Shots From County Down*, assumes that Andy Lemon's tavern was the Buck's Head at Loughinisland. It should be noted that in 1803 the proprietor was James Fitzpatrick.

Later verses depict 'the time of the Hurry' when in 1798 people 'quet from mindin' the farms' to fight under McCracken and Munro. 'Young Warwick' is the Reverend Archibald Warwick of Kircubbin who was executed along with the Reverend James Porter of Greyabbey. Both were Presbyterian clergymen.

As the ballad moves to a close it re-echoes the supposition that French help was under way in 1803 – 'Boney had promised help to a man in Dublin town'. A hint of the debacle in July-August 1803 is given in the lines:

> But no French ships sailed into Cloughey Bay
> and we heard the black news on a harvest day
> that the cause was lost again.

The dramatic final verses connect Russell's last words to the impression he made on his listeners during his visit to their townland on that 'night of snow' in winter 1795.

The Man From God knows where

Into our townlan' on a night of snow
rode a man from God knows where;
None of us bade him stay or go,
nor deemed him friend, nor damned him foe,
but we stabled his big roan mare;
for in our townlan' we're decent folk,
and if he didn't speak, why none of us spoke,
and we sat till the fire burned low.

We're a civil sort in our wee place
so we made the circle wide
round Andy Lemon's cheerful blaze,
and wished the man his length of days
and a good end to his ride.
He smiled in under his slouchy hat,
says he: 'There's a bit of a joke in that,
for we ride different ways.'

The whiles we smoked we watched him stare
from his seat fornenst the glow.
I nudged Joe Moore: 'You wouldn't dare
to ask him who he's for meeting there,
and how far he has got to go?'
And Joe wouldn't dare, nor Wully Scott,
And he took no drink – neither cold nor hot,
this man from God knows where.

It was closing time, and late forbye,
when us ones braved the air.
I never saw worse (may I live or die)
than the sleet that night, an' I says, says I:
'You'll find he's for stopping there.'
But at screek o'day, through the gable pane,
I watched him spur in the peltin' rain,
an' I juked from his rovin' eye.

Two winters more, then the Trouble year,
when the best that a man could feel
was the pike that he kept in hidin's near,
till the blood o' hate an' the blood o' fear
would be redder nor rust on the steel.

Us ones quiet from mindin' the farms
Let them take what we gave wi' the weight o' our arms
from Saintfield to Kilkeel.

In the time o' the Hurry, we had no lead –
we all of us fought with the rest –
an' if e'er a one shook like a tremblin' reed,
none of us gave neither hint nor heed,
nor ever even'd we'd guessed.
We men of the North had a word to say,
an' we said it then, in our own dour way,
an' we spoke as we thought was best.

All Ulster over, the weemin cried
for the stan'in' crops on the lan'.
Many's the sweetheart and many's the bride
would liefer ha' gone to where he died,
and ha' mourned her lone by her man.
But us ones weathered the thick of it
and we used to dander along and sit
in Andy's, side by side.

What with discourse goin' to and fro,
the night would be wearin' thin,
yet never so late when we rose to go
but someone would say: 'do ye min' thon' snow,
an' the man who came wanderin' in?'
and we be to fall to the talk again,
if by any chance he was one o' them –
The man who went like the win'.

Well 'twas gettin' on past the heat o' the year
when I rode to Newtown fair;
I sold as I could (the dealers were near
only three pounds eight for the Innish steer,
an' nothin' at all for the mare!)
I met M'Kee in the throng o' the street,
says he: 'The grass has grown under our feet
since they hanged young Warwick here.'

And he told me that Boney had promised help
to a man in Dublin town.
Says he: 'If you've laid the pike on the shelf,
you'd better go home hot-fut by yourself,
an' once more take it down.'
So by Comber road I trotted the grey
and never cut corn until Killyleagh
stood plain on the risin' groun'.

For a wheen o' days we sat waitin' the word
to rise and go at it like men,
but no French ships sailed into Cloughey Bay
and we heard the black news on a harvest day
that the cause was lost again;
and Joey and me, and Wully Boy Scott,
we agreed to ourselves we'd as lief as not
ha' been found in the thick o' the slain.

By Downpatrick goal I was bound to fare
on a day I'll remember, feth;
for when I came to the prison square
the people were waitin' in hundreds there
an' you wouldn't hear stir nor breath!
For the sodgers were standing, grim an' tall,
round a scaffold built there fornent the wall,
an' a man stepped out for death!

I was brave an' near to the edge of the throng,
yet I knowed the face again,
an' I knowed the set, and I knowed the walk
an' the sound of his strange up-country talk,
for he spoke out right an' plain.
Then he bowed his head to the swinging rope,
whiles I said 'Please God' to his dying hope
and 'Amen' to his dying prayer
that the wrong would cease and the right prevail,
for the man that they hanged at Downpatrick gaol
was the Man from God knows where!

Index